# Revolutionary
# Organization

# Revolutionary Organization

**Institution–Building Within
The People's Liberation Armed Forces**

Paul Berman
Yale University

**Lexington Books**
D.C. Heath and Company
Lexington, Massachusetts
Toronto          London

Library of Congress Cataloging in Publication Data

Berman, Paul.
    Revolutionary organization.

    1. Lúc lúóng võ trang nhân dân giai phóng miên Nam Viêt Nam.
2. Vietnamese Conflict, 1961–
I. Title.
DS557.A6B416                          301.29'597                    73–1564
ISBN 0–669–85456–5

Published simultaneously in Canada.

Printed in the United States of America.

International Standard Book Number: 0–669–85456–5

Library of Congress Catalog Card Number: 73–1564

To my mother Edith

# Contents

## List of Figures

# List of Tables

# Preface

American withdrawal from the rice paddies and battlefields of Vietnam signaled not peace for Vietnamese but merely a new phase of their tragic war. As time passes, Americans inevitably will shift their attention elsewhere. Perhaps then the Indochina War will be viewed in a perspective transcending United States involvement and international power struggles. Dispassionate history will record this war as a revolution, a revolution by which Vietnam confronted its fate in a modern world.

My exposure to some of the realities of the Second Indochina War began in 1965 when I examined intensive interviews, conducted by the Rand Corporation with former members of the National Liberation Front of South Vietnam—the so-called Viet Cong. This testimony of Vietnamese peasants convinced me that many significant aspects of the revolution resided not in the killing and in the clash of armies. Rather it lay in profound changes occurring in people's lives. Within the revolutionary organization of the NLF, bonds of authority, self-interest, and belief in a new order were being developed that foreshadow the emergence of a modern nation. This book represents my attempt to understand how these processes of institutional development work.

The central research question can be stated simply: why do peasants obey a new authority? This question is obviously not unique to the Vietnamese War. Thus, the findings and conceptualizations of various social science disciplines dealing with related inquiries can be called upon to seek an answer. Any "answer" is bound to be complex, however, for it requires an analysis of relationships between the characteristics of the new authority and the cognitions and motivations of peasants. Moreover, unless distinctive features of the culture in which the revolutionary organization was embedded are taken into account, analysis will be meaningless. Accordingly, this study explicitly treats critical aspects of the Vietnamese village culture as they affected the cognitions and motivations of individuals and, consequently, the nature of the revolutionary organization.

Vietnamese village society is complex, subtle, and extraordinarily fascinating. The analysis palely reflects its richness and variety. Throughout the study, I focused on salient, commonly-held traits of Vietnamese peasants, particularly those features that contrast with Western and modernized man. This emphasis is appropriate, I believe, for salient characteristics are often the most basic and, consequently, the most likely to affect the development of new institutions. Whatever value my simplications about Vietnamese culture may have derives from the generous assistance of many Vietnamese scholars, both native and American. Rather than risk causing embarrassment to them due to my interpretations, I shall let my debt of gratitude rest in the work itself and not identify them individually.

Many friends and scholars provided pivotal analytical advice and criticism over the years. In the formative period of this study, my colleagues at the Rand Corporation and the Massachusetts Institute of Technology offered sound comments on how, and how not, to proceed. At the Rand Corporation, Harvey Averch, Frank Denton, Alexander George, Nathan Leites, James Schlessinger, and Gus Shubert pushed me in the direction I ultimately took. Frank Denton's early help and friendship amounted more to collaboration than advice. William Kaufmann, Ithiel de Sola Pool, and Lucian Pye of M.I.T. contributed time and patience as well as insights reflected throughout the study. Colleagues at Yale University discussed, read, rediscussed, and reread various drafts of this book. Peter Busch, William Foltz, J. Richard Hackman, Gerald Kramer, Charles E. Lindblom, John Low-Beer, Bruce Russett, and Bradford Westerfield encouraged me and prevented my attempts to apply the wisdom of diverse disciplines to the Vietnamese revolutionary organization from going far astray. John T. McAlister, Jr., Samuel Popkin, and James C. Scott commented penetratingly, often painfully so, on complete drafts and offered wise counsel that greatly influenced the final product. This listing expresses my gratitude for all the direct and indirect contributions of these scholars without assigning to them any of this work's numerous failings whose responsibility rests with the author.

My appreciation to Jacqueline, my wife, stems less from her tireless typing than her devotion during difficult times. My children, Stephen and Christine, have grown up during the Vietnamese War. May it be that when they are old enough to understand this book, the Vietnamese people will have found peace.

# 1

## Revolution and Institutionalization

The struggle in Vietnam was always more than a military battle over which faction would rule. From its origins in anticolonial activities and open warfare after World War II, and more particularly, in the renewed warfare of the Second Indochina War that constitutes the historical frame of this study, the antagonists fought over the nature of Vietnamese society. The Communists sought a transformation of the traditional Vietnamese way of life into a new political, economic, and social order and they did so by means that clearly mark the war as a revolution.

This war's revolutionary basis is often dismissed because of limited conceptions of revolution heavily influenced by the French and Russian experiences. The collapse of the old regime and the violence and struggle for power among new groups characterize these "great" Western revolutions. Accordingly, academic analysis has been directed towards explaining the "causes" of revolution in terms of the conditions of social, political, and economic unrest and disintegration under the old order; or towards examining the leaders of the emergent groups and recreating their struggle; or towards charting the "anatomy" of the revolution from its beginning"—the date of the fall of the *ancien régime*—to its "end" in the restoration of order.[1] But the course of the Second Indochina War flowed in markedly different channels. Rather than a dramatic, spontaneous collapse of the old regime, the Communists followed a deliberate strategy to gain control; rather than a clear beginning, the origins of the war lay muted and deep in social changes and political forces that developed prior to the Resistance Movement which ended French colonial rule and established the "two" Vietnams; rather than a brief period of violence and elite struggle, conflict took the form of protracted guerrilla warfare. Yet, notwithstanding these contrasts, the Vietnamese Revolution held the promise of accomplishing that which fundamentally distinguishes the French and Russian revolutions from other acts of violence and upheaval: the creation of a new political order.

The rise of a new order, not simply the fall of the old, made the great revolutions successful and memorable. The French and Russian revolutions—and one could add such non-Western revolutions as the Chinese Communist, Mexican, and Cuban revolutions—resulted in sweeping fundamental change. This change constituted more than the displacement of political leaders and policies; it affected all levels and aspects of society—social structure, norms and values, patterns of economic and political activity, and the way individuals thought of others, of their society, of nature, and of themselves. Nor was change temporary.

1

These revolutions eventually institutionalized their newly founded orders. In politics, old patterns of authority gave way to new stable political relationships; old beliefs of what was right and proper in the political sphere were replaced by new concepts of legitimacy.

Regardless of its causes, its beginnings, or its anatomy, successful revolution engenders dual transformations of society—namely, the violent destruction of the existing ways of life and the development of new and enduring institutions.[2] Precisely these revolutionary processes were at work in the prolonged war waged in Vietnam.

The traditional political order of Vietnamese society coexisted at two levels.[3] At the base were villages. Each village was self-contained, highly integrated culturally, socially, and economically, highly independent from other villages, and largely self-governing. The traditional Vietnamese dynastic state with its mandarin bureaucracy served as a political superstructure connecting and coordinating the otherwise autonomous villages for such purposes as public works, religious functions, and military functions. The village, rather than particular individuals, had collective obligations to the state. In collecting taxes, raising *corvées*, or gathering soldiers, the state dealt with a Council of Notables representing the village as a whole. There was, as McAlister and Mus suggest, a "skillful division of labor. The state—from the military, judicial, and religious point of view—was centralized and authoritarian. No village could have defied it with impunity. But because of the distribution of administrative duties between it and the villages, especially in economic matters, the state weighed lightly."[4] In short, peasants, firmly rooted in their village life, were loosely linked by means of an administrative structure to a weak but nonetheless centralized political system that could sporadically and in limited ways mobilize their energies. The institutional bonds holding this system together stemmed from two, closely related sources: common interests and a common belief in a Confucian tradition that prescribed and held such an order to be legitimate.

French colonial rule, particularly in the period between the world wars, eroded the traditional political order, threw the nation "off balance."[5] In addition to solidifying regional separations and creating an urban, Westernized elite which was itself frustrated and remote from the countryside, French rule had major impacts upon both the political superstructure and the villages. The moral ties of legitimacy linking peasant and village to the state were largely severed. Though the colonial administration penetrated into village life (particularly by means of a regularized recording of individual births and deaths within the villages and increased French control over the Council of Notables in financial matters),[6] French reforms simultaneously eroded the traditional leadership and internal cohesion of the village. In the Mekong Delta, this deterioration took a particularly perverse form with the establishment of wealthy landowners and a tenancy system that, in some areas, replaced many of the customary village functions and relationships.

The Japanese occupation of World War II dealt a final blow to the authority

of French colonial rule and paved the way for the August 1945 proclamation by
Ho Chi Minh, leader of the Viet Minh, of the founding of the Democratic Republic of Vietnam. Of course, this claim was rejected by the French and, indeed, by
large segments of the Vietnamese population, particularly in the South. In the
war that followed, a major ideological appeal of the Viet Minh was national
salvation from foreign imperialists. Yet, this War of Resistance (from 1947-1954)
was more than an anticolonial struggle. It was the beginnings of a revolution. Not
only were the Communists seeking to oust the French and to gain control, they
were replacing the declining traditional order with new patterns of authority.

The Viet Minh's strategy of revolution, adopted (though modified) from the
Chinese Communists, was based upon the building of a revolutionary organization. Rather than a small, exclusive Party, the Viet Minh mobilized the masses
of peasants so that they participated in the Resistance. This participation took
the form of membership in a revolutionary organization composed of the Party,
the military, and a network of civilian associations within villages. By means of
"parallel hierarchies" (territorial and vertical) of command and control, members—whether peasants, soldiers, Party members, or leaders—were integrated into
a centralized political structure.[7] This central authority began to supplant the
traditional political superstructure with its loose links to autonomous villages.
More significantly, where the Viet Minh were successful, they displaced the
Vietnamese society at its base: the village. Unlike the great Western revolutions
where central state power was destroyed and reconstituted as a prelude to the
development of lasting social, political, and economic changes, the Viet Minh
revolution proceeded locally and piecemeal. Since their opponents' forces
controlled the urban centers, the Communists concentrated on gaining control
over villages and local areas where the true power in this decentralized order
had always existed. Step by step, they consolidated their influence over more
and more local areas. At each step, the network of organizations provided new
opportunities for peasants to participate in a changed social order; by so doing,
new patterns of authority were instituted that linked village and villager into the
centralized political order. In short, the Communist revolutionary strategy was a
strategy of organization building, one that employed the revolutionary organization as both a means and an end for, in Samuel Huntington's words, "mating
the mobilization of new groups into politics to the creation and institutionalization of new political organization."[8]

The Viet Minh expansion of territorial control was more successful in the
North than the South of Vietnam. Though guerrilla forces in the South were
sporadically effective, areas fully under Viet Minh control were limited to the
narrow central portion of Vietnam and to such regions of the Mekong Delta as
the Ca Mau peninsula and the territory surrounding the Plain of Reeds. The
Geneva Accords of 1954 which ended the war—at least, temporarily—recognized
a division of the country, one solidified in the "Two Vietnams." From the
standpoint of the Communists, the revolution had not been completed.

The next half dozen years saw the resettlement of population across the demilitarized zone (including the regroupment north of approximately eighty thousand Viet Minh), the failure of general elections to be held in July 1956, the establishment of the Republic of Viet Nam under the leadership of Ngo Dinh Diem, and the virtual elimination of domestic competitors to the Saigon regime. Though the Republic of Vietnam controlled urban areas and, with the help of U.S. aid, maintained a substantial military force, it was little more than an "attenuated French colonial regime."[9] The Saigon government's attempts to establish itself in the countryside did not evoke widespread support among the peasants; rather than institutionalizing new patterns of authority, Saigon's intervention into village life was often either ineffective or further exacerbated the erosion of the traditional village cohesion that had been in decline throughout the twentieth century. In short, when the Communists decided in the late 1950s to resume the revolution in an overt form, they had two essential tasks: to defeat a Vietnamese opponent who had military might but not legitimacy in the countryside and to establish their own authority among a peasantry not yet emerged from its traditional isolation and ways of life.

The appeals and tactics of the National Liberation Front differed from the earlier Viet Minh because the situation had changed: the South was highly fractionated, its economic and social conditions were distinct from the North, and the NLF's opponents no longer represented a colonial regime.[10] But the basic revolutionary strategy was similar. Building upon the remnants of the foundation established during the Resistance, the NLF began mobilizing peasants by engaging them in a network of civilian and military organizations.[11] As before, the civilian organizations consisted of a variety of socioeconomic associations at the village level and of an administrative-political hierarchy that both operated within the village and linked the village leadership to a highly centralized authority. In some "liberated" areas, the Front became the de facto government. By the end of 1968, the NLF's civilian membership numbered approximately 300,000, of whom about 40,000 were full-time members of the administrative-political bureaucracy often referred to as the "infrastructure."[12] The military component of the Front, the People's Liberation Armed Forces (PLAF), consisted of a Main Force army numbering about 60,000 troops at the end of 1968 and Regional or Local guerrilla forces of approximately 180,000 peasants. In short, the Communists again employed a piecemeal, locally-oriented organizational process to mobilize a sizable portion of the peasantry.

Only by ignoring the lessons of the First Indochina War could this mobilization be viewed in strictly military terms as simply a means for conscripting an army and providing a logistic and intelligence base. It did this, of course, and rather effectively. But its significance went beyond the military for, as John McAlister aptly puts it, such mobilization "effects a revolution even as it lays the basis for more sustained military efforts."[13] Peasants recruited into the revolutionary organization became more than soldiers in a temporary fighting force; they potentially became subjects integrated into a new institution founding the basis for a nation-state.

Understanding such institutional development requires analyses of how and why the revolutionary organization works. Some studies have intensively examined the revolutionary organization by focusing on the formal structure and doctrine of the organization—its hierarchical command, control, and communications system, its emphasis on strict obedience, its declared ideology, its manipulative techniques. Ironically, these descriptions—explicit, concrete, and by-and-large accurate—often block a deeper understanding of the dynamics of the revolutionary organization. The essence of the revolutionary organization lies not only in its formal structure but in its mass base within cultures whose traditional patterns of social, political, and economic intercourse revolve around village life and whose psychological dynamics militate against transvillage concerns. To develop an extensive membership, the revolutionary organization must overcome villagers' predispositions, introduce new roles and social patterns, shift traditional loyalties, and induce people to risk their lives. Unless peasants adapt to these roles, integrate into the social patterns, accept new patterns of authority, and tolerate the stresses inherent in rapid and violent change, the organization will be unable to maintain itself and the revolution will fail. That is, the revolutionary organization must create enduring institutional bonds. This book attempts to understand how, why, and under what conditions new institutions can be developed by examining the revolutionary organization of the People's Liberation Armed Forces of the NLF.

Perhaps the dominant view of the success of the PLAF is expressed by Douglas Pike in his influential book *Viet Cong*, which insists that the strength of the PLAF lay in its organizational structure and techniques *rather* than in revolutionary ideology:

> Americans and others often assumed that the NLF army members were fanatics. Because they performed well in combat, it was argued, they were highly motivated, which meant dedication to an ideological cause. Thus the search was for the essence of this belief. It proved elusive, largely because it did not exist. The best of the military units . . . were highly effective because they were composed of professionals . . . What impelled them was not ideology so much as professional competence, much like the United States Marines or the French Foreign Legionnaire . . . The strength of the NLF was the result of careful organization building, not the product of some unique spirit or élan. [14]

This position denies ideological convictions and ignores the revolutionary context—empirical positions this study challenges—but, does it answer the question of *why* the NLF was able to build a strong organization?

Pike's analysis reduces to a description—a reasonably accurate one—of the formal structure, principles, and techniques of the organization. Where in this "explanation" are the complex dynamics of human motivation which bind any organization together? One is left with two impressions: on the one hand, of professional soldiers à la the French Foreign Legionnaire who fight as mercenaries devoid of political sentiments or, on the other hand, of naive peasants entrapped by a coercive, alien organization.[15] Could an organization so composed maintain its mass base? Could it withstand extreme adversity without providing its members significant social-psychological compensations, without satisfying their basic needs, drives, and values, without establishing in their minds a feeling that their activities were right and proper? It could not. In the American army, the average soldier's effectiveness derives from his personal, rather than political, motivations and from his identifications with his primary group; yet the American soldier also believes himself to be part of an organization that serves proper ends in a stable society he values and considers legitimate.[16] Surely, peasants coping with a highly uncertain social situation and a vacuum of state power do not *automatically* accord legitimacy to a revolutionary organization. The PLAF had to establish its authority, had to develop motivations that served its ends, had to institutionalize new patterns of peasant behavior. To explain the source of the PLAF's organizational strength, we must understand the processes of institutionalization tying peasants to the revolutionary organization.

Institutionalization by a revolutionary organization consists of three tasks. First of all, peasants must be *mobilized* to become members; secondly, they must be *integrated* into the new organization in such a way that they comply with its demands; thirdly, the organization must *maintain* itself against the disintegrative stresses of sustained warfare. This study examines how these tasks were accomplished by the PLAF. That is, we will explain why and to what extent the PLAF succeeded in building and maintaining a revolutionary organization.

Part I views revolutionary mobilization as an organization-building process occurring in its particular cultural context. In the social science literature on political development and modernization, mobilization has come to mean that broad process of social change defined by Karl Deutsch as one "in which major clusters of old social, economic, and psychological commitments are eroded or broken and people become available for new patterns of socialization and behavior."[17] We will see that the recruitment of peasants into the PLAF was more than induction into an army: it was, in the cultural and historical context, truly a process of mobilization implying both an "uprooting or breaking away from old settings, habits, and commitments" and the indoctrination of "new patterns of group membership, organization, and commitment."[18]

Mobilization will be analyzed by examining how and why peasants responded to Front recruitment activities. We will show that "joining" was not just an act but a process that began with the peasant's initial exposure to NLF recruitment and ended with his *acceptance of membership*. Chapter 3 lays the foundation by postulating core personality characteristics of Vietnamese

peasants derived from a reasonably common village culture. These basic traits
establish the broad dimensions of receptivity of Vietnamese to Front recruitment. Chapter 4 describes the recruitment activities and examines why, and to
what extent, these activities were successful, given psychocultural predispositions,
in mobilizing peasants. The Front's recruitment activities employed a flexible,
pragmatic mixture of coercion (armed propaganda teams, village pressure,
entrapment, threats, forced induction, etc.) and persuasion (ideological and
nationalistic appeals, rewards of status, satisfactions of excitement, etc.). It will
be argued that the Front's success depended upon offering peasants opportunities to achieve rewards (notably of social advancement) and convincing them—*by
means appropriate* to the culture—that their concerns with security were best
served in the revolutionary organization.

Part II examines how peasants were integrated into the PLAF. Integration,
as used here, denotes the process whereby individuals are coordinated and controlled for a unified purpose. This conception is more specialized than some
definitions in the literature on political development.[19] Nonetheless, its
implicit organizational character is appropriate because the revolutionary organization serves as an embryonic social and political order; hence, integration into
this organization is analogous to integration of a citizen into a common political
process.

Chapter 2 (which details our approach for analyzing institutionalization as
an organizational process) argues that the way individuals become integrated
into organizational life can be described and explained for any formal organization, and most particularly for a revolutionary army, by the way and the extent
to which the organization attempts to obtain compliance from its members, on
the one hand, and how and why individuals adapt, on the other hand. That is,
the analysis will focus on the individual, on why he complies with authority, on
how he becomes embedded within the structure of the organization, and on what
institutional bonds develop.

A striking organizational characteristic of the Front was the type of
compliance it sought and the techniques used to achieve compliance. The PLAF
sought total revolutionaries—members who complied voluntarily because of their
absolute commitment to the organization. Such commitment, whose ideal norms
are described in Chapter 5, is often thought to be at the heart of the revolutionary organization. Yet, as Chapter 4 shows, new recruits were not committed
revolutionaries when they entered the Front: they had to be molded, their
"consciousness had to be raised." To do so, the PLAF employed overt political
and ideological indoctrination. But more importantly, as Chapter 6 describes,
the entire organizational structure and processes—from its hierarchical authority
and information system to its prescribed group social structure, from its rewards
to its sanctions, from its interpenetrating political and military command apparatus to its confession and self-confession sessions—socialized the recruit so that
he would become committed.

To what extent did the PLAF create committed revolutionaries? We will argue that some soldiers became committed. Yet, we also will show that commitment failed to materialize for most soldiers. Since integration was not realized solely on the basis of commitment, then why did soldiers who were not totally committed comply with Front demands? What patterns of authority were established and to what extent did the PLAF control, channel, and integrate such soldiers into a viable organization? Chapter 8 treats these questions.

Part III examines maintenance. Revolutions inevitably generate stress: stress from without in the form of opposing forces and the dangers and deprivations of fighting them and stress from within due to the strains inherent in people adapting to a new order. Unless the compliance with authority, the developing feelings of loyalty and identification, the evolving institutional bonds are capable of withstanding these pressures, the organization cannot maintain itself and the revolution cannot be successful.

How resistant was the PLAF to stresses of a protracted war? How cohesive were the bonds linking the peasant to the organization? How vulnerable was the authority structure to disintegration? Could the satisfactions, rewards, needs fulfilled by membership outweigh the dangers and uncertainties of seemingly endless combat? Chapter 9 deals with these questions of maintenance.

Samuel Huntington has forcefully argued that the development of a traditional society into a nation-state requires the creation of political institutions capable of governing.[20] The Communist revolutionary strategy in Vietnam offers an organizational model for accomplishing such political development. The significance of this model rests not only in its potential for overthrowing regimes that, in any event, lack popular support and cannot, or will not, foster changes that must come. The promise it holds is that of organizing society on a new basis; one that integrates individuals into a national order, that produces effective central authority, that promotes legitimacy. The institutional bonds established within the revolutionary organization prefigure this promised order. And though the processes by which these links develop may be telescoped and exaggerated by the revolutionary context, they illustrate how institutionalization can occur. By analyzing these processes as they occurred within the People's Liberation Armed Forces, we hope to illuminate both this revolutionary model and the profound changes in people's lives necessary to institutional development.

# 2 A Microstructural Approach

To be successful and complete, a revolution must become institutionalized—i.e., establish regularized patterns of behavior including most particularly new patterns of authority. In the Vietnamese Communist strategy, the revolutionary organization is a vehicle for institutionalization for insofar as institutional bonds develop within the revolutionary organization tself, peasants become integrated into a nascent political order. To study such institutionalization, one could examine those major historical and social forces that profoundly affect the course of nation-building. Without denying the value of analyzing such "macro" processes, this study pursues a different tact. We focus on the individual and how he becomes integrated into the structure of the revolutionary organization. We call this analysis of institutionalization in the PLAF a "microstructural approach" to emphasize our dual concern with the individual and the organization.

A microstructural approach concentrates on describing how and explaining why individuals who make choices, seek goals, possess motivations, and perceive alternatives adapt to an organization which, by means of its structure, norms, and processes, attempts to control and coordinate its members.[1] The revolutionary organization is similar to any formal organization—be it corporation, army, or government—in that it must control its members in pursuit of its goals. Since the PLAF was an army, a Communist organization, and a peasant movement, it differed from a prototypical formal organization in various unique ways. Since revolution involves rapid change, extreme stress, and a challenge to the traditional order, questions of coercion, ideology, establishing authority, and legitimacy play more prominent roles in the revolutionary organization than in a stable organization embedded in a stable society. Nonetheless, with due adjustments for the special character of the revolutionary organization, we believe that institutionalization within the PLAF is best studied by approaching it as one would analyze any organization.

The following section outlines the analytical framework that guides and structures the analysis. Thereafter, this chapter indicates various restrictions on the scope of the inquiry. The last section discusses the nature of our data, raises critical methodological concerns, and indicates the various means for coping with data problems employed throughout the study.

9

**Analytical Approach**

*Purposive Behavior and Compliance*

Our approach rests on several premises drawn from the literature of organization theory, political science, psychology, and sociology.[2] First of all, individual behavior within organizations can be usefully viewed as purposive.[3] That is, people seek goals and make choices within the constraints of their environmental situation. A purposive act entails a decision wherein the individual processes information from his environment to arrive at a choice. The cognitions and motivations that determine the way the individual processes information will be referred to as his psychological state. Understanding purposive behavior thus requires knowledge of both the environment impinging upon the individual and his psychological state. Though peasants act purposively in the same sense as Western, modern men do, they often are pictured as slaves to their environment, as irrational beings unable to act in their own self-interest. By systematically analyzing *both* environmental forces and the psychological state of Vietnamese peasants involved in the PLAF, we hope to avoid such unfortunate ethnocentrism.

As an initial step in analyzing the psychological component of purposive behavior, Chapter 3 offers a partial model of commonly-held Vietnamese peasant personality characteristics. Such a model assumes (a) that all individuals develop relatively stable personality traits, which we call a personality structure, and (b) that Vietnamese peasants have, in several critical aspects, similar personality structures, i.e., one can analytically formulate a *modal Vietnamese peasant personality*.[4] The justification for the second assumption will receive extended comment in Chapter 3. Rather than attempting to capture personality—especially Vietnamese personality—in its full complexity, this study focuses only on aspects that are crucial for explaining behavior in an organizational context. Chapter 3 argues that Vietnamese peasants may be characterized as to the way they typically structure information impinging upon them; we shall call this trait their *orientation towards action*. Moreover, we shall postulate key values, needs, drives, and primary beliefs held by peasants that weighed heavily in their evaluation of alternatives as members of the PLAF. Furthermore, we shall hypothesize that Vietnamese peasants typically approached interpersonal relationships and authority relationships in ways which profoundly affected their organizational behavior (a point to be developed further below). These hypothesized aspects of Vietnamese peasant personality were characteristic of peasants before they entered the Front. Knowing these *prior* characteristics is essential if we are to analyze critical dynamics of the revolutionary organization—viz., the ways in which peasants changed after entering the Front and the ways the Front had to accommodate deeply ingrained characteristics of the Vietnamese peasantry.[a] Part II, particularly chapters 7 and 8, deal with these questions.

---

[a]From a methodological standpoint, we are trying to avoid circularity. Using the available literature, we describe a general modal personality of Vietnamese peasants. This de-

Since people act purposively, an organization can influence the behavior of its members in either, usually both, of two ways: (a) by controlling the environment impinging upon the individual or (b) by socialization. Socialization affects the individual's psychological state (in a variety of ways) and thus indirectly influences the choice he makes on any single act. Virtually all formal organizations attempt to shape their members, though how deliberately and intensively varies. As the introduction noted, a striking characteristic of the PLAF was the extent to which it deliberately sought to socialize peasants into becoming committed revolutionaries; chapters 5 and 6 describe the Front's socialization mechanisms. Such techniques did not necessarily have their desired effects; chapters 7 and 8 examine their effectiveness in the PLAF.

In addition to the indirect effects of socialization, the organization can influence the individual directly by its control of the immediate environment impinging upon him. As will be shown, the PLAF attempted not only to monopolize the information coming to the individual about external events such as the progress of the war, success in combat, and the like, but also sought to control fully the milieu of its members. Perhaps the most significant direct influence on any single act is communication to the individual of the behavior the organization *expects* of him; we call this (implicit or explicit) communication a *demand*. "Demand" denotes the whole range of expected behavior ranging from highly specific orders to routine activities to general norms prescribing how one ought to behave and, indeed, believe.[5]

The importance of demands for analyzing organizational behavior is obvious: they establish a situation to which the member must respond. He may respond in a variety of ways, of course. Insofar as an individual acts in accord with a demand made by the organization, we say he complies and call the behavior an act of *compliance*.[6] A premise fundamental to understanding how formal organizations operate is that demands are regularized in organizations and, moreover, that the responses of individuals to such demands become routinized. Therefore, we assume that a regularized *pattern* of demand-response behavior develops for each individual. Such characteristic organizational behavior will be called a pattern of adaptation; insofar as a pattern of adaptation consists predominantly of compliant behavior, it will be called a pattern of compliance. *Institutionalization* is the process whereby these patterns of behavior develop; an institution itself can be thought of as the set of these regularized patterns of demand-response behaviors.[7] How an organization attempts to obtain compliance, on the one hand, and how individuals accordingly adapt, on the other

scription serves as a foundation for the analysis of characteristics of peasant members of the PLAF. The data for the latter analysis are interviews with former PLAF members. If these data also were used to derive modal personality traits, then we would be unable to determine if such traits were characteristic (a) of peasants *before* they entered the Front or (b) of *only* those peasants who entered the Front. Therefore, we could neither analyze socialization effects nor the effect of cultural patterns on the PLAF. Consequently, the issue of preselection to develop the revolutionary organization versus socialization could not be examined.

hand, are dual, core features of institutionalization. Therefore, this study will describe and characterize the patterns of adaptation—particularly of compliance—in the PLAF and explain why soldiers adapted in the way they did.


### Authority

We deliberately, though arbitrarily of course, chose the term compliance to refer to the influence relationship wherein an individual acts in accord with an organizational demand. To avoid confusion, our meaning of compliance vis-à-vis such other concepts as "authority" requires clarification.

A demand communicates the desires of the organization; it may induce compliance and it may do so automatically, without further consideration by the individual. Not all demands are obeyed, of course, nor are all those which are followed obeyed automatically. But at times people do follow commands simply because they are commands. We shall call this type of compliance relationship one of *authority* (or, alternatively, we say that compliance is due to authority or that the demander exercises authority over the complier).[8]

The sense of authority, as used here, posits that the individual simply accepts a demand as the premise for his behavior and acts accordingly. Authority does not characterize all compliance—nor all influence—relationships. Before discussing the nature of authority further, it may be helpful to contrast authority with two other modes of obtaining compliance—viz., agreement and self-interest.

An individual may comply because he believes that following the demand will lead to a desirable outcome in terms of goals other than his own self-interest. That is, he *agrees* with the efficacy, wisdom, appropriateness, correctness, etc., of a demand for the attainment of some purpose, but ignores the consequences of complying or not upon himself. In thus complying, the individual accepts the perceived purpose of the demander and suspends consideration about his interests (which may or may not be in conflict); an authority relationship, in contrast, implies a complete suspension of all such considerations. Compliance due to agreement was an important source of institutional influence over the individual in the PLAF. The Front wanted its members to believe in the "correctness" of their actions. Indeed, it will be shown that the PLAF's use of persuasion, "education" (i.e., socialization) and control of the informational environment were effective in obtaining compliance because peasants (or, at least, some peasants) became convinced of the correctness of their activities.

Whether or not a person evaluates his response in terms of ends other than his own self-interest, he may act from concern with the effects of his behavior upon *himself*. Thus, one may comply because of sanctions—i.e., incentives or disincentives, rewards or penalties, gratifications or deprivations—that the individual anticipates will follow from his act of compliance or noncompliance. Since the type of rewards and penalties important to people depend upon their personality

structure, Chapter 3 describes social sanctions and mechanisms of imposing
sanctions (e.g., loss-of-face) that might be particularly important to Vietnamese
peasants. Chapter 6 describes the system of sanctions used in the PLAF, and
chapters 7 and 8 examine the effect of sanctions on establishing compliance and
integration in the PLAF.


### Generalized Acceptance of Authority

Compliance due to authority characterizes a relationship wherein evaluation
of consequences, whether in one's own interests or in another's, does not take
place. This willingness to follow automatically a single demand presupposes
a more generalized acceptance of authority. That is, a pattern of compliance (or
of adaptation) usually includes a set of demands that the individual regularly
accepts as his decisional premises; we refer to these demands, following Barnard
and Simon, as the individual's *area of acceptance of authority*.[9] The connotation of an area of acceptance is that a member acquiesces, on a prior basis, to
certain "rules of obedience," certain prescribed norms of behavior, certain
jobs and activities that predispose him towards following authority if the demand
is within his acceptable range.[10] For a demand outside of the area of acceptance, the organization needs to use persuasion or sanctions or both and, in any
event, may or may not succeed in obtaining compliance. In short, authority
may be both *generally accepted* and *generally limited*.

Generalized acceptance of authority is fundamental in an organization
because it establishes a stable set of *expectations* of obedience. Institutionalization and coordination of disparate individuals rely on such stable expectations.
For these reasons, this study focuses on a pattern of behavior, rather than on
a single act. In particular, we are concerned with analyzing an individual's area of
acceptance and explaining why he accepts (a limited set of) rules of obedience.

People may accept authority in a generalized sense for a large variety of
reasons, and several reasons are likely to operate in combination for any empirical reality. Thus, we will find that such elements as coercion, status rewards,
membership in the Party, concerns with security, identification with the primary
group, with cadre, and with the organization itself, nationalistic sentiments, and
beliefs in revolutionary goals and ideology affected the development of authority
in the PLAF.

Another aspect central to the acceptance of authority (and to institutionalization) is the consonance of the organizational structure, processes, and norms
with the customs, mores, and beliefs about authority implicit in the culture. The
organizational literature often assumes yet rarely analyzes—at least in "micro"
terms—the consonance of the organization with the culture in which it is
embedded.[11] Such an assumption may be appropriate in a stable society. But
in a revolution, where change is the byword, consonance cannot be assumed.

Thus, we take as important empirical concerns: (a) the extent to which the
PLAF was consonant with the culture and (b) the ways cultural predispositions
constrain organizational dynamics even within a revolutionary organization.
Our microstructural approach for dealing with the notion of consonance and its
effect on the acceptance of authority rests on the assumption that a component
of the individual's basic personality is a set of primary beliefs and motivations
relating to obedience; we call this an *orientation towards (accepting) authority*.
Moreover, we assume that an orientation towards authority is culturally induced;
in particular, Chapter 3 hypothesizes various aspects of the orientation towards
authority characteristic of Vietnamese peasants.

An orientation towards authority includes such implicit psychocultural
sentiments as how likely individuals are to accept rules of obedience and the conditions that foster or inhibit acceptance. More particularly, cultures prescribe
moral notions of how authority relations ought to be structured and when people
ought to obey. Thus, an individual may believe he ought to accept authority, in
a generalized sense, because the institution itself conforms to "his own moral
principles, his own sense of what is right and proper in the political sphere."[12]
We call this belief a feeling of *legitimacy* towards the institution (or that the
individual accepts a set of authority relationships as legitimate or that the individual accords legitimacy to the institution).

It is beyond the scope of this chapter to explore the concept of legitimacy
or even to justify the above definition in comparison to other conceptions in the
literature.[13] However, since legitimacy will be examined for the PLAF, it is
appropriate to note some special aspects of this definition. Legitimacy, in the
conception used here, is not a necessary condition for the acceptance of authority, but one of a large possible number of reasons for obedience. Thus, even
though the Front evidently established authority, we take as proper subjects of
empirical analysis whether, to what extent, and why legitimacy was accorded
to the NLF by its members. Moreover, even when legitimacy exists, we consider
it a *moral predisposition* to obey, rather than a sufficient condition; hence, the
analysis will examine the role played by feelings of legitimacy in the initial
acceptance of membership in the Front (Chapter 4 on mobilization), in establishing patterns of compliance (Chapter 8 on adaptation and integration), and in
the continued acceptance of membership in the Front under conditions of
stress (Chapter 9 on maintenance).

### Integration

Any organization with a division of labor, particularly a mass-based
revolutionary organization, must coordinate the activities of its members to
achieve its ends. We use the term *integration* to denote the process whereby
members' behaviors are coordinated to achieve a unified purpose.

Integration requires a command and communications structure that decides on means and ends, that divides organizational activities into individual tasks, that gathers and disseminates both external and internal information. Organizations obviously differ in the nature of their command and communications structures. Such structural aspects as the degree of hierarchy, the centralization of command, the pervasiveness of monitoring, and the like profoundly affect integration. Accordingly, Chapter 6 describes structural features of the PLAF— e.g., its parallel, interpenetrating Party and military hierarchies, its "democratic centralism," its three man cell, and its informant system. But the problem of developing an integrated organization is more than one of devising a bureaucratic structure: it involves the way members relate to the structure.

If all members had unlimited areas of acceptance of authority, then the study of integration would be reduced to examining who commands whom. However, few members can be expected to accept authority so totally, even in a revolutionary organization that emphasizes complete commitment and obedience to the organization. Indeed, it is likely that individuals will differ in the extent to which they accept authority (and, more generally, in the degree to which they develop compliant behavior). Therefore, integration depends upon matching the behavior expected of each individual (i.e., the demands) to those demands with which he would comply. That is, ceteris paribus, the more that members are assigned to roles (activities, tasks, jobs, responsibilities) that they can be motivated (and are able) to do, the more integration. We will see that the PLAF's criteria for selecting Party members and promoting soldiers to cadre positions attempted such matching.

Even were an organization able to allocate people to roles in an optimum way, authority needs to be buttressed by other organizational influences (if high levels of coordination are to be achieved). Modern organizational analyses have shown that the informal social system—particularly the primary group within which the individual lives his day-to-day existence—exerts direct and profound influence on individual behavior. Chapter 8 examines quite closely the extent to which identification with the primary group and its cadre developed in the PLAF. However, whether primary group influence reinforces compliance (e.g., by isolating individuals who do not act in accord with demands), or blocks compliance (e.g., by the individual's approval from the group being contingent upon his following group norms that are in conflict with organizational demands) depends upon the way the informal social system is embedded into the formal structure.

The primary group can be embedded into the formal structure in several ways. One powerful way occurs when group norms correspond to organizational norms; we will show that the PLAF attempted to promote the development of group norms to attain such a correspondence. Another related means can be provided by a two-step link: the primary group follows its leader who is linked directly to the command structure and who himself may have a larger area of acceptance than those below him. We refer to these indirect links of the individual to the command structure as *structural integration* to distinguish it from the more direct bonds to the organization reflected in acceptance of authority— e.g., in feelings of legitimacy.

Thus, integration depends upon the formal command and communications structure, upon compliance, upon the allocation of members with different willingness to accept authority to appropriate roles, and upon the way the informal social system is embedded into the formal structure. Chapter 8 describes and evaluates integration in the PLAF.

### Mobilization

Though our main concerns revolve around institutionalization, we cannot avoid analyzing the prerequisite task of a revolutionary organization seeking a mass membership: mobilization. In the narrowest sense of the word, "mobilization" is recruitment (or induction) into the organization. It is not obvious that one needs to know how, or indeed why, a person joined an organization to understand his behavior once a member. But a peasant joining a revolution is another matter. He is, in effect, making a "decision to participate" in an embryonic political order.[14] Two aspects of the revolutionary organization make this participation decision particularly significant. First of all, becoming a member of the PLAF involved a process consisting of three phases: (a) initial exposure or entry into the Front, (b) persuasion to accept membership, and (c) acceptance of membership. Acceptance of membership implied a generalized acceptance of Front authority. Secondly, by becoming a member, the peasant was removed from his village environment and became subject to intensive socialization within the organization. Thus, the how's and why's of the decision to participate form a necessary prelude to examining the ways in which peasants adapted to Front life.

Mobilization will be analyzed in microstructural terms by examining how and why Vietnamese peasants responded to Front recruitment activities. This focus on the individual inevitably fails to capture the macro-flow of events and shifts in social forces that affect the revolution's ability to attract supporters. Thus, the analysis will be directed towards the process of recruitment-acceptance and not towards evaluating "macro" conditions in Vietnamese society.

### Maintenance

If an organization is to endure, it must be capable of withstanding stress. Insofar as the organization can prevent the decay of its integration and its patterns of compliance, the institution *maintains* itself (or the organization maintains its institution or institutionalization is maintained).[15]

Maintenance of a revolutionary organization poses special difficulties since a revolution intrinsically causes stress. In addition to the problems of combat and the deprivations of prolonged warfare, peasants face the internal pressures of adapting to the changed ways of life that form the essence of revolution. Analyzing the organization under these extreme conditions provides a means of assessing the depth of the loyalty, the legitimacy, the "reservoir of diffuse support" engendered by the revolutionary organization.[16] With this purpose in mind, Part III analyzes maintenance primarily in terms of two crucial considerations: the cohesiveness of institutional bonds and the durability of structural integration.

Maintenance of the organization requires that people stay in the organization (or, at least, that not all members leave). A measure of the strength of the bonds tying the individual to the institution is the force and conditions needed to break these bonds and, therefore, cause him to leave. We call this measure *cohesion*. Cohesion, as used here, is thus the probability of a member continuing his participation in the organization.[17]

Cohesion is a particular act of compliance. They are not synonymous, however. A pattern of compliance signifies a regularized demand-response set for an individual and, as such, it constitutes a psychological predisposition for any specific action. In other words, individuals are likely to be inclined towards cohesion in a way that reflects their adaptation. Yet, when pressures of war— intensified demands from the organization as well as increased deprivations and deaths—mount, the satisfactions, rewards, and needs fulfilled by membership are put to their ultimate test. The soldier continually weighs, consciously or subconsciously, these cohesive and disintegrative forces; the result—in a conceptual sense—is a decision to stay or leave. Chapter 9 estimates the extent to which various patterns of compliance induced cohesion in the PLAF; this is done taking into account stresses from combat and from intrinsic organizational pressures. By so doing, we will be testing the strength (and limits) of the institutional bonds developed by the revolutionary organization.

### Limitations on Scope

To realize an objective as ambitious as understanding the developmental dynamics of a revolutionary organization in a culture as little researched as the Vietnamese forces us to limit the scope of this study. This section briefly indicates concerns about the Vietnamese War that cannot be dealt with here though they are important for understanding the substance of this revolutionary conflict.

Vietnam is a society in flux. Neither the Second Indochina War nor its predecessor, the Viet Minh anticolonial war, began the vast processes of social change engulfing Vietnam. These wars exacerbated the disintegration of traditional Vietnamese society that followed from French colonialism. Clearly profound historical and social forces set the stage for the revolutionary conflict. But it is beyond the scope of this study to examine these "macro" processes per se; reader familiarity with the historical and social context must be assumed. Our inquiry, as outlined in the preceding section, is deliberately restricted to the "micro" level. We examine individual Vietnamese behavior as a way to understand the organizational dynamics of the PLAF and, in more general terms, institution-building. By so doing, we hope to correct a gap in the literature about this war and to contribute to theoretical understanding of political development. Of course, social, and historical forces do impinge upon individuals and organizations. Insofar as these forces indirectly affected behavior and shaped the operation of the People's Liberation Armed Force, they are implicit in the analysis.

This study does not attempt a *complete* analysis of the "success" of the NLF in controlling the country or in establishing a stable set of institutions capable of governing. Such success depended upon conditions "external" to the organization in addition to conditions "internal" to the PLAF. However, given our focus on a systematic, intensive analysis of behavior within the PLAF, we cannot consider in detail such obviously critical factors as the nature of the Saigon regime (its ability to govern, its legitimacy, the loyalty and support it could engender) or the involvement (political as well as military and economic) of the United States and the Communist nations. A complete understanding of the revolution in Viet Nam will require analyses meshing behavior *within* the organization with behavior *of* the NLF in its environment; we attempt only the former.

Though systematic comparisons would be highly desirable, the study is not comparative except in the sense of drawing upon the relevant literature of other armies, Communist institutions, revolutionary movements, and organizations. The Army of the Republic of Vietnam (ARVN)—i.e., the army of the South Vietnamese government—would have provided a particularly pertinent comparison as would the People's Army of Vietnam (PAVN)—i.e., the army of the North Vietnamese government.[18] Of course, both the PLAF and the PAVN fought in South Vietnam. For the most part, their identity was separate and their units were not mixed during the period considered in this book. However, as with so many aspects of this war, the relationship between the two was more complicated. In many units of the PLAF, the leadership consisted, at least partially, of ex-Viet Minh who regrouped to the North at the time of the Geneva Accords, remained in the service (in various capacities) in the North, and infiltrated to the South. Insofar as they served in the PLAF, these so-called regroupees were treated in the same manner as other soldiers.

The controversial issue of the exact nature of the relationship between the northern government (the Democratic Republic of Vietnam) and the Front (particularly, the People's Revolutionary Party of South Vietnam—i.e., the Communist party) will not be considered because it is not germane to our topic. Though it is quite impossible for one who has been deeply involved in thinking about the Vietnam war to be neutral, our scientific inquiry would be hopelessly muddled if we succumbed to the temptation of speaking out on controversial yet peripheral issues about which we lack adequate evidence. We shall try—insofar as possible—to resist the temptation.

Within the self-imposed restrictions of dealing with internal dynamics of the NLF, we further limit the analysis to the "military" organization. The Front's efforts to control the countryside involved the establishment of a "civilian" (sometimes called "political") infrastructure in the villages that served as a partial government and as a mobilizer of peasant sympathy, provided logistical and financial support, and gathered intelligence. Though the line between civilian and military activities was in this context exceedingly fine, only the latter will be considered. Except in connection with recruitment, the NLF's success or failure in controlling villages, in linking such control to a centralized authority, and in gaining support of the peasants will not be treated; the reader is advised to consult the literature on these significant issues.[19] Moreover, not all "military" activities will be examined. Broadly speaking, the PLAF consisted of the Main Forces, Local Forces, and Guerrilla Forces; soldiers from both Main and Local Forces will be considered as well as full-time members of Guerrilla Forces. There were also military contingents of an autonomous nature not integrated into the regular military structure; these units will not be examined. In short, the analysis will be of full-time, regular army troops. Moreover, due to the focus of this study and to the nature of the primary data, rank-and-file soldiers and middle-level officers (called cadres), rather than the elite political leadership or high echelon commanders, will be examined.

The period of the war considered here starts from the late 1950s and early 1960s to mid-1967 before the Tet offensive of 1968; the primary focus is on the internal dynamics of the PLAF operative from roughly 1963 to 1967 when the organization was mass-based. The reader should be cautioned that after 1967 a number of changes occurred in the war and in the PLAF that might alter some of the details presented. However, these changes do not invalidate the basic analytical thrust of examining the processes of institution-building.

### Data: Problems and Solutions

The "raw" data for the study consist of captured (and translated) NLF documents and translated interviews with former Front members who either became prisoners or defected. The interviews, the primary data, were designed and conducted by The RAND Corp. and The Simulmatics Corp. and, needless to say, without their kind permission to use these interviews, this study would not be possible.[b] The Simulmatics interviews, numbering approximately 100, were conducted from 1966–67 and are all with defectors (ralliers) to the side of the Republic or Government of (South) Vietnam (GVN), under the auspices of *Chieu Hoi* (Open Arms) program.[20] The RAND interviews used for this study, numbering approximately 1,000 and conducted from 1964–67, deal with both prisoners and defectors. For reasons of comparability, appropriate samples of the RAND interviews were used for all quantitative analysis.

Analyzing interview data of the type indicated above poses serious methodological difficulties. Surely the testimony of defectors and of prisoners must be treated with utmost caution. One could ignore these difficulties in the hopes that somehow the errors they cause would not appreciably affect the results; too often scholarly research takes this tact. In this case, however, the difficulties are sufficiently significant that it would be irresponsible not to confront them and not to make the value of the analysis contingent upon their satisfactory resolution. Throughout the course of the study, a variety of qualitative and statistical techniques are employed to analyze the data so that major sources of spurious analysis are overcome where possible, avoided where necessary, and minimized when all else fails. Errors undoubtedly remain. Yet, their magnitude is sufficiently bounded that the results are confidently offered. This section outlines the general approach used in coping with the data problems by discussing in turn the two principal sources of error, sampling bias and response bias. Additional detailed methodological comments are interspersed at appropriate points of the text.

*Sampling Bias*

The prisoners and defectors whose interviews were used in this study do not constitute a representative sample of the PLAF. This difficulty poses problems. But it does not imply the data are useless. Instead, a number of restrictions must be followed. In general, the nature of the sample prohibits offering accurate estimates of the value of some important variables in the PLAF.[c] For example, the proportion of cadre (officers) to rank-and-file soldiers in the sample is not a reasonable estimate of that "true" proportion in the PLAF; moreover, the sample proportions cannot be "weighted" so as to obtain an accurate estimate. Though thus prohibited from making quantitative statements about marginal distributions in the population, conditional statements can be offered about the

---

[b]Microfilm copies of these interviews can be obtained from the RAND Corporation.

[c]The word "sample" does not mean, in this context, probability sample but rather a non-probability selection of respondents from the population.

relationship between two, or more, variables. The latter type of statement is usually of interest for theoretical purposes.

To explore the nature of the sampling difficulties more fully, the following section reviews the sampling procedure employed in gathering the RAND interviews. Since a somewhat different sampling problem exists for prisoners than for defectors, each will be considered separately, beginning with the prisoners.

**Prisoner Sample.**   The sampling process for prisoners may be conceived of as having involved two stages: (1) capture and (2) "selection" by the interviewers. Ideally the population for the first stage, capture, was the entire PLAF, and if the probability of capture for each and every member were equal, then a random sample of the PLAF would have been generated. However, capture was not a "random generating process" since some soldiers were obviously less likely to be captured than others. Very high ranking officers, say battalion level and above, were not likely to be captured; therefore, for this, and other reasons, none of them appear in the sample. Consequently, this study does not cover the military elite of the PLAF.

A second group systematically excluded from sampling were those soldiers who were killed before, during, or after capture; among these were soldiers who died rather than be captured or submit to imprisonment. Though the motivations of this group are neither simple nor uniform, as subsequent analysis suggests, it seems reasonable on a priori grounds to surmise that their motives included feelings ranging from loyalty to fanaticism. Since such sentiments could play a critical role in the operation of the PLAF, the systematic exclusion of soldiers possessing them might profoundly bias the study. The Front did maintain a select number of soldiers whose mission was highly likely to culminate in their own destruction. Few of these so-called "terrorists" were in the sample. Consequently, this study may underestimate the extent of "fanaticism" in the PLAF. On the other hand, a significantly large number of soldiers whose testimony and manner clearly indicated an unswerving loyalty to the Front were captured, interviewed, and included in the sample. The difference between their motivations and those of soldiers who refused to be captured or were subsequently killed may be one of degree. In short, though there may be a sampling bias causing us to underestimate the extent of fanatical belief and, to a far lesser degree, the extent of loyalty in the Front, these potential errors are within tolerable ranges. Factors other than the two discussed here that account for variations in the probability of capture will be briefly discussed in Part III.

The second stage process of selecting interviewees from among the prisoners also was not random. In this stage the population, or if you will subpopulation, was all PLAF prisoners. Prisoners were dispersed in a variety of detention centers controlled primarily by GVN authorities. Due to wartime conditions—and perhaps other reasons—access to detention camps was limited, and it is a credit to the RAND interviewers that they were able to conduct as many interviews as they did. Under these conditions, a probability sample of prisoners was not feasible. Instead, the teams interviewed whomever they could within a roughly established "quota" system based upon attaining an adequate range of Front members and upon maintaining balanced proportions.

The range of PLAF members covered appears adequate with the exception, again, of higher level officers and of terrorists. The interviews comprise both Party members and non-Party members, both political functionaries and fighters, both former Viet Minh Resistance fighters who did regroup to the North and then infiltrated South and those who did not regroup,[21] both old-time veterans and new recruits. Though soldiers from the three major types of military formations, the Main Forces, the Local or Regional Forces, and the Guerrillas, were included, by no means was a soldier from every combat unit—e.g., of battalion size—included; nor were all operational areas of Communist forces represented, though the major allied Corps areas were. In addition to experiential factors, other basic characteristics seem fairly well represented: a wide range of ages from 14 to 65, both male and female, the fairly well-educated and the mostly illiterate, poor peasants and rich peasants, land-holders (though no large landlord) and laborers (though few South Vietnamese urban dwellers). Buddhists, Catholics, Ancestor Worshippers, some Cao Daists, several Montagnards (since this is a conglomerate name for a very wide range of primitive ethnic groups living in the mountainous areas, coverage was not inclusive here) and several Hoa Haos were included. This comprehensive range of various types of soldiers suggests that an acceptable range of the motivations prevalent in the Front were contained in the sample; all one can do is assume such is the case.

The interviewing teams also attempted to maintain a balance of respondents. In particular, they tried to conduct interviews with as many higher ranking cadres as they could, but they also obtained interviews with a roughly equal number of lower ranking cadres and of rank-and-file soldiers. Of course, this procedure introduces a severe sampling bias—there were a higher proportion of cadres in the sample than in the population. However, by purposely overrepresenting cadres, enough interviews were supplied so that post hoc control and comparison becomes possible. In other words, a sufficient amount of data exist in each of the various levels of rank so that conditional relations within a level of rank may be used for inference to the corresponding level in the PLAF and then levels can be compared. In short, by a stratified, comparative analysis, the sampling bias due to disproportions in rank can be controlled.

Ideally, one could arrive at a surrogate random sample by controlling for all relevant sources of bias. However, this tactic is costly in terms of the ability to make reasonably accurate statistical inferences (i.e., degrees of freedom are lost with each new control). In other words, the sample size limits how far one can go in controlling. Therefore, rather than controlling for each bias on each occasion, selective controls can be employed. For example, when considering the conditional relationship between the activities used in recruiting a peasant and the degree of control exercised over his village by the Front, it is reasonable to assume that a control for rank would not be necessary. In other cases, for example, in considering the commitment of a soldier, rank controls would be necessary.

In summary, the approach for dealing with sampling bias will be to limit the population of inference, to deal with conditional rather than marginal distributions, to control sources of biases, and, above all, to make flexible use of reasonable assumptions.

**Defector Sample.**   The population of defectors consists of all those soldiers who left the PLAF of their own accord—i.e., they escaped. However, the sample of defectors available for analysis excluded a large group of leavers—viz., those who deserted from the PLAF but did *not* rally to the GVN. Since one can think of many a priori reasons why deserters might be different from ralliers, this omission might represent a significant sampling bias. Experience suggests, however, that the differences between deserters and ralliers was at most one of degree. Nonetheless, this systematic exclusion should be duly noted.

The sample of defectors used here is not a representative sample of all ralliers for much the same reasons that the second stage sampling process of prisoners did not result in a representative sample of prisoners. Again access to *Chieu Hoi* centers and to ralliers were limited and a rough quota system based upon range and balance had to be followed. Since this was the case, conditional rather than marginal inferences will be made, controls will be instituted, and flexible assumptions will be adopted in all analyses of defectors.

Though defectors and prisoners should be presumed to come from different populations for many purposes, this is not the case for all considerations. For example, all Front members were exposed to similar indoctrination and integration techniques. Defectors may have reacted differently from prisoners—surely an assumption whose empirical validity must be tested—but this does not alter the fact of similar exposure. The point is that for some purposes defectors can and hence will be considered to be a sample of the full PLAF.

In summary, the sample problems for these data, though severe and restricting, are manageable. The way particular biases are handled will depend upon the specifics of the analysis. Therefore, detailed solutions to sample problems will be discussed at appropriate points in the text. Much the same approach will be followed for response biases.

### Response Bias

The possibility of bias due to the responses soldiers gave on their interviews posed serious difficulties for these data. "Systematic" response bias is the primary concern by which is meant that (a) an individual "distorted the truth" and that (b) certain types of individuals tended to distort for the same reason and in the same way. Before sketching the strategy used to cope with response bias, this section catalogues the numerous sources of such error for these data. First, the general context of the interview situation will be briefly reviewed.[22]

**Interview Setting and Procedure.**   The interview situation varied a great deal from respondent to respondent. The interviews generally took place in interrogation facilities of detention camps. Wherever possible, the subject was left alone with the interview team. However, in some cases, Vietnamese guards were present for part and occasionally most of the interview. The interviews were all conducted in Vietnamese by trained, bilingual Vietnamese interviewers; at times, American members of the interviewing team guided the interview, but most often Americans were either silent observers or actually not present in the room. The Vietnamese interviewers were highly educated, urban, and to some extent Westernized. The gap between the status of the peasant soldier and the high status awarded by Vietnamese culture to the educated interviewer could be very great indeed; in some cases, this status differential was enough to inhibit the development of adequate rapport. The subject was told that he was being interviewed for purposes of American social scientists and that his interview would not be used by GVN or Allied military authorities. There was an attempt to avoid an atmosphere of interrogation but, as might be expected, many subjects were skeptical at first.[d] However, the first series of questions, frequently about village life before joining the Front, helped allay some of the soldier's fears, and, consequently, for a great many subjects, confidence developed as the interview progressed.

The nature of the interviews may have mitigated some of the problems of rapport and skepticism as well as other sources of distortion. They were long, more-or-less intensive interviews. Many lasted over four hours with a sizable number continuing for two, and occasionally three, days. Hence, there was an opportunity for skilled interviewers to develop rapport. The questioning itself was not directed towards short-answer responses. On the contrary, though too many questions tended to be leading, the questioning and probing often elicited lengthy replies that followed the subject's natural style. Some peasants, particularly those whom the interviewers, in their written debriefing, characterized as of "low-intelligence," were inarticulate; some, particularly among prisoners, were highly recalcitrant; most were surprisingly articulate. The latter case may

---

[d]Interrogation by the ARVN as well as the conditions of detention were inexcusably brutal far too often. Of course, insofar as such inhumane treatment had occurred prior to the interview, severe distortions were produced. These cases appeared to be not more than 5 percent of the sample, though any such estimate is just a guess. In the usual case, peasants adapted extraordinarily well to prior interrogation and conditions of detention. Though the ex-Front members might not have believed (or understood) the purpose of the interviews, the behavior of the interviewers—courteous and respectful—was essential in allaying their fears.

have been so for several reasons. In this particular sample, the educational level was, relative to the society at large, high. In addition, whereas peasants often would not have been accustomed to analyzing and expressing opinions about their behavior and those of others, their training in the Front required them to do exactly that. Moreover, subjects usually had been interrogated previously by military authorities, and, consequently, the more relaxed atmosphere of this interview situation perhaps was more conducive to a freer unfolding. Finally, some respondents tried to impress the interviewer with their knowledge.

**Conscious and Subconscious Distortion.**   A number of serious, specific potential sources of response bias arose from the context of the interview and the nature of Vietnamese culture. To systematically review these potential biases, the following brief discussion is divided into reasons for deliberate, conscious distortion and to sources of more-or-less subconscious distortion.

Some soldiers on some questions may have deliberately distorted their responses. For example, some defectors seemed to believe they could curry favor with their interviewers and hence affect their future. In numerous cases, ralliers had been exposed, before the interview, to GVN "education" in the *Chieu Hoi* centers; this education provided them with slogans and with clues as to what the "best" attitude was (as well as, in some cases, inducing genuine opinion change). Similarly, there were prisoners who also might have sought to gain favor; these prisoners not infrequently indicated that they had wanted to defect. On the other hand, some prisoners, rather than trying to curry favor, indicated, at times in exaggerated ways, their continuing loyalty to the revolutionary cause. (This also seemed to be the case for some defectors.) At least in a few cases, the respondents seemed to be "double agents" whose stories were replete with contradictions. Some subjects seemed to fear that their testimony might be disclosed to Front agents. (Since, in many detention camps, prisoners had organized themselves in ways similar to their organized life in the PLAF, fear of disclosure can be readily understood.)

At the subconscious level, a number of elements may have promoted distortion. Many of the events that respondents were asked to recollect occurred several years prior to the questioning and, moreover, numerous episodes—some of a traumatic nature such as indoctrination, punishments (and rewards), combat activity, capture or escape, and internment—had intervened. Thus, fuzziness in recollection, rationalization and justification, and repression all could, and indeed did, occur. In addition, the Vietnamese peasant's conception of causalty is sufficiently different from Westerner's propensity to align things neatly in chronological order that distortion, from a Western standpoint, was inevitable. Moreover, there was a tendency for the respondents to show deference to the interviewer and to act in a manner "appropriate to the situation," which not infrequently meant the ex-soldier said what the interviewer wanted to hear. These effects were mitigated somewhat by the sensitivity of the Vietnamese interviewers who could accordingly adjust their line of questioning. Nonetheless, such distortions as an exaggerated emphasis on being "victims of circumstances" and an overplaying of hardships were evident.

**Strategy for Dealing with Response Bias.**   The list of possible, and indeed probable, response bias for these data is imposing enough that the validity of the entire enterprise can be challenged. However, a more reasonable approach than dismissing the interviews altogether is to exercise extreme caution in a selective manner; this is precisely the strategy followed.

Some of each respondent's testimony was less subject to distortion than other parts. For example, a statement of what rank a subject held was probably more reliable (though in several cases this was not true) than his answer as to whether he was criticized or not. In short, doubts about response bias are relevant to individual questions for a given individual rather than for all questions and should be so judged. In those few cases (about 5 percent) where the respondent's entire testimony was questionable, the interviews were excluded from further analysis. In the usual case, the responses to a given subject had to be excluded for only some interviewees; in other cases, not respondents but entire areas of concern had to be omitted from systematic analysis even though they were of substantive interest.

When suspected systematic distortion could not be ignored, control variables were introduced wherever possible. For example, on the issue of the amount of coercion used by the Front in recruitment, as testified to by respondents, it seemed prudent to introduce a control for whether the respondent was a prisoner or defector. Again, reasonableness and flexibility guided the introduction of such controls.

The final hedge against response bias was to be conservative in making inferences. Though qualitative as well as quantitative analysis is subject to response bias problems, quantitative analysis implies additional errors due to processing the qualitative data; these processing errors can cumulate with and mask response bias and, hence, increase the danger of specious inferences. In particular, we content analyzed and coded[e] the translated interview material.[f] The errors introduced by the content analysis will be discussed in detail in the

_____

[e]Frank Denton provided considerable help and encouragement in my preliminary efforts. My debt to him is indeed great. The coders, besides undertaking an extremely difficult and, at times, tedious task and completing it with distinction and sensitivity, were a source of insight into the culture and the interviews. My debt to them is poorly paid by recording their names here: Ardie Betts, Russell H. Betts, Penelope Y. Mendenhall, Dorothy Jane Pratt, and Pho Ba Hai. Reliability estimates will be provided in the text. RAND also coded various portions of the interviews, and this RAND coding was used for analyses indicated in the text.

[f]Significant problems exist in translating Vietnamese into English. This difficulty can be particularly severe in dealing with the symbolic meaning of Front political and ideological appeals. To cope with these problems, we tried (a) to avoid placing too much weight on particular passages and (b) to treat symbolic areas with the utmost caution.

appropriate substantive sections of the text. To minimize these errors, special coding procedures were devised and grosser measurements than ideally desirable were employed. Finally, to guard against faulty inferences from the statistical analysis itself, the analysis was limited to the minimal statistical techniques consistent with the level of measurement and suspected amount of errors. The inevitable result of handling such messy data was a series of analyses that individually are challengeable but together genuinely cope with significant substantive issues.

# Part I
# Mobilization

### Introduction to Part I

Though mobilization is a sine qua non of a mass-based revolution, the general literature on revolutions rarely deals systematically with this complex process. The literature on Vietnam, with the exception of several outstanding studies,[1] views mobilization myopically. One segment focuses on the NLF's ideology and explains mobilization in terms of romantic notions of spontaneous revolutionary movements; an opposite segment sees primarily coercion not revolutionary ardor. These perspectives misconceive mobilization for two reasons. First of all, mobilization is an organizational process involving *both* recruitment activities and the peasant's cognitions and motivations upon entering the Front. Thus, it is necessary to examine the transaction between the PLAF's recruitment techniques and individuals' receptivity. Secondly, mobilization occurs in a cultural context. No matter how trite it may be to note that Vietnamese think, behave, and are motivated in ways very different from Americans, seldom does one find explicit incorporation of these psychocultural factors into the analysis; failure to do so risks profound misunderstanding.

The following two chapters analyze revolutionary mobilization as an organization-building process occurring in its particular cultural context. Though the social science literature defines mobilization as a broad process of social change, we will restrict our examination of mobilization to the recruitment of peasants into the PLAF. The NLF also mobilized villagers into a network of civilian organizations in a variety of ways—e.g., villager participation ranged from full-time membership in the civilian infrastructure to low-levels of activity in "struggle movements." However, though the distinction between military and civilian organizations was far from precise, only the former will be considered. Notwithstanding these restrictions, it will become apparent that induction into the army was, in the cultural and historical context, truly a process of mobilization for it implied both an "uprooting or breaking away from old settings, habits, and commitments" and the introduction of "new patterns of group membership, organization, and commitment."[2]

Mobilization will be analyzed in microstructural terms by examining how and why peasants responded to Front recruitment activities. At the individual level, this process began with the peasant's initial exposure to NLF recruitment and ended with his acceptance (or refusal) of membership. Chapter 3 lays the foundation by postulating core personality characteristics of Vietnamese peasants derived from a reasonably common village culture. These basic traits establish the broad dimensions of receptivity of Vietnamese to Front recruitment. Chapter 4 describes the recruitment activities and examines why, and to what extent, these activities were successful, given psychocultural predispositions, in mobilizing peasants.

# 3 Aspects of Vietnamese Peasant Characteristics

Nguyen Van Ton[a] had been a member of the GVN village militia for just two months when the village outpost he was guarding was attacked and overrun by two platoons of PLAF Local Forces. The attack was apparently cleverly planned and caught the outpost by surprise. Ton had just come into his quarters after playing a volleyball game, "when the VC fired into the room, one of my buddies hid himself under the bunk—he was later killed—and the other took his MAS 36 rifle and fled to the rear of the outpost and into the rubber plantation. I tried to do the same but was hit by a Thompson submachinegun bullet in my left calf and was captured." Ton was taken to a district medic and then, because his wound became infected, to a province hospital where he was treated. During two months of recuperation, "I was visited by the Province Committee Chief [of the Party] and by numerous cadres who talked gently with me and asked me to join the People's Revolution. . . . I agreed and was sent back to operate in my village."

That was in the beginning of 1962. Within three years, Ton had become a member of the Party,[b] advanced to a responsible position as leader of a reconnaissance-intelligence squad, participated in numerous battles against the ARVN, and often attacked outposts similar to the one he had once been a part of. On February 22, 1964, Ton defected to the side of the GVN.

This story of a double "turncoat" may strike readers unfamiliar with the realities of Vietnam as odd. Though it is not a typical story, it is also not atypical. Defections from one side to the other occurred frequently as did shifts in the loyalties of villagers. Rather than attempting to examine this behavior within its cultural context, Western observers have too often labeled Vietnamese as "opportunistic." If the dynamics of the revolutionary organization are to be understood, we must avoid such stereotyping and analyze Vietnamese peasant behavior in terms of their own cultural and psychological characteristics.

---

[a]Nguyen Van Ton is an alias as are all the names of Front soldiers used throughout the study. The stories of these peasants are contained in the interviews conducted by the RAND Corporation or the Simulmatics Corporation. Unidentified quotations refer to these interviews. Diacritical marks are omitted from all Vietnamese words used in this book.

[b]The Party referred to is the Communist party which will be discussed in Chapter 6. Front members invariably called it the "Party."

## Assumptions About Modal Personality

Chapter 2 argued the utility and appropriateness of conceiving of individual behavior as purposive (for the activities of concern here). In particular, we assume Vietnamese peasants seek goals and make choices within the constraints of their environmental situation. To explain purposive behavior—and, in particular to explain how Vietnamese confronted the Front's mobilization activities and subsequently adapted to life in the PLAF—requires an analysis of both the environmental situation and the internal (psychological) characteristics of the individual. The latter is the subject of this chapter. Individuals develop relatively stable, enduring psychological characteristics which we call, for ease of reference, a personality structure. We assume—for reasons to be elaborated—that Vietnamese peasants possess many similarities in their psychological traits. This chapter describes salient aspects of these commonly-held characteristics.

Before proceeding with the analysis, the assumptions and limitations underlying our description require clarification. To begin with, this study will not propose an in-depth construct of the personality of any specific Vietnamese peasant—such a construct is far beyond our present state of knowledge. Instead, we will describe salient, commonly-held traits that students of Vietnamese culture generally attribute to Vietnamese peasants, though not necessarily in the form presented here, and that, as a whole, distinguish this culture from Western, as well as other, cultures. Our intent is not to describe peasant culture per se, but rather to infer psychological characteristics of Vietnamese peasants arising from their cultural experience.

The notion of commonly-held personality traits—sometimes referred to as modal personality or basic personality structure or national character—does not imply that one can predict fully a specific individual's behavior in a given situation on the basis of these traits.[1] Rather a probabilistic concept is intended: modal personality consists of those (culturally-induced) traits held by "most" people in the culture. A statement about Vietnamese peasant modal personality should be interpreted as an hypothesis about psychocultural predispositions or cultural constraints on the kinds of behavior likely to occur. Though similar in critical aspects of personality structure, individual peasants differ, of course, in numerous ways. For example, this chapter postulates a common need for security; however, individuals will vary—due to differences in child-rearing experiences in village life, in intrinsic psychological make-up, in assigned social roles, etc.—in the extent of this need. Such variability within the cultural constraints of a commonly-held characteristic will be partially taken into account in the analyses of subsequent chapters.

The validity of the construct of a modal Vietnamese peasant personality rests on several premises about the nature and dynamics of Vietnamese society.[c]

---

[c]For the description of a modal personality to be useful in explanatory analysis, the statistical properties of the distribution of relevant personality traits needs to be discussed.

The foundation of Vietnamese society lays in its villages and hamlets, where approximately three-fourths of the population of southern Vietnam lived, and from which Front membership was largely drawn. We make three assumptions about cultural variability within villages, across villages, and over time. First of all, the culture within the traditional village was highly integrated and uniform. Secondly, though each village traditionally had constituted its own "little community,"[2] those characteristics of village life responsible for transmitting the psychoculture—child-rearing, family structure, village social, economic and political patterns—were reasonably similar across much of Vietnam. Homogeneity was far from absolute, of course. Even ignoring minority subcultures and religious variations, diversity existed in village life across regions of Vietnam.[3] For example, many writers contrast Northerners and Southerners as do the peasants themselves.[4] Yet, the similarities between Northerners and Southerners are more striking and, at the level of modal personality, more significant than the disparities. (Though literature dealing with village life in the North will be used, the overall synthesis of characteristics presented in this chapter discounts peculiarly Northern traits.)

The third major assumption about village life involves the state of transition in Vietnamese society at the time the Second Indochina War began. Gerald Hickey's fine anthropological study of a Mekong Delta village in the late 1950s and early 1960s concludes that, even in the face of forces disrupting village society, "the essential characteristics of the village way of life persisted" to the extent that "traditional values, practices, and rituals continue to be honored and observed, and they are being transmitted to the younger generation as they were in the past."[5] Generalizing this observation, we assume traditional acculturation patterns persisted during the period relevant to this study. Of course, we do not deny the significant changes in village life caused by French colonial rule and its aftermath. Though these changes eroded traditional political and economic patterns and were thus of high import, they had not negated those cultural mechanisms most responsible for the formation of basic personality structure. For example, this chapter postulates a core status drive among peasants which retained its vitality in the present as well as in the past. French colonial rule and the First Indochina War did not still this drive, but they did produce severe dislocations and uncertainties in village life that altered both the values defining status and the institutionalized means for achieving status. In short, though contemporary village life was in flux, basic cultural patterns persisted.

The notion of a modal personality also presupposes a coherence among the various commonly-held traits. That is, these traits are related as a system, not just a collection of vaguely connected dimensions. The culture, it is assumed, determines this configuration uniquely. This study will not attempt to establish

---

We will argue, in the next few paragraphs, that (a) Vietnamese peasant culture—excluding urban dwellers—had a dominant major mode with minor modes that can be ignored for present purposes and (b) the distribution of traits had low variability.

which particular traits of our description of Vietnamese peasant modal personality are *uniquely* Vietnamese (in the sense that they also do *not* typify other
cultures). Some of these characteristics undoubtedly could be found among
peasants in general or among Chinese or, indeed, among all peoples; consequently, some behavior of soldiers in the PLAF could be explained just by
reference to the way any individual, or perhaps any peasant, might respond to a
situation determined by the organization. On the other hand, some traits will be
peculiarly Vietnamese, *at least in degree*; thus, some behavior within the Front
could only be understood by reference to these Vietnamese traits. More importantly, the configuration of all the personality characteristics taken as a whole
represent an interrelated set that is unique. We trust the reader will realize that it
is beyond the scope of this study to isolate particular characteristics exclusively
Vietnamese.

This study does not claim that the characteristics described here adequately
capture the richness of Vietnamese personality and culture. Though we will
suggest some personality dynamics induced by the culture, we make no attempt
to formulate a "theory" of Vietnamese personality. We will characterize only
aspects of Vietnamese peasant personality structure that are critical for examining organizational behavior.

In particular, hypotheses relating to the cognitive realm will posit selected
primary beliefs especially about the way peasants typically orient themselves
towards action—i.e., how they perceive, structure, and evaluate the environmental
situation and opportunities to alter their habitual patterns of behavior; hypotheses relating to the motivational realm will detail core needs, drives, and values;
hypotheses overlapping cognitions and motivations will specify the peasants'
patterns of interpersonal, particularly primary group, relations and their orientation towards authority. We also will suggest some Vietnamese personality
dynamics involving inner tensions and primary anxieties that are pertinent to
understanding how sanctions were applied in the PLAF and what identifications
were possible and likely.[6] In short, we will lay a foundation for explaining
why peasants adapted to life in the Front in the various ways they did.

The characterizations of Vietnamese peasant modal personality are synthesized from the available anthropological, social, and psychological studies rather
than from the primary interview material with former PLAF members. By
postulating the general modal personality of peasants from independent material,
we can assume that these personality traits characterized peasants *before* they
entered the Front. Therefore, this study can examine the extent to which change
occurred among peasants—a central question in studying a revolution—and the
extent to which the revolutionary organization reflected the Vietnamese psychoculture.

We hope that this attempt to hypothesize salient psychological characteristics of Vietnamese peasants will provoke sorely needed field work from which

more refined, better formulated, and more accurate theories can follow. In the interim, the reader is asked to view the constructs presented here in the same light as the author does—namely, as reasonably valid and useful working hypotheses.

### Orientation Towards Action:
### Pragmatic Fatalism

The Vietnamese peasant's way of thinking about the world and how he relates to it—his primary beliefs, his cognitive processes, his orientation towards action—are so profoundly different from the modernized Westerner's and so pivotal for understanding the villager's response to the Front that this analysis appropriately begins by describing salient characteristics of what Frances Fitzgerald, in her absorbing study, *Fire in the Lake*, calls the Vietnamese state of mind.[7]

Perhaps the dominant characteristic generally attributed to the Vietnamese peasantry is fatalism, an acceptance of life as it is, a stoicism in the face of destiny. "The average Vietnamese," observes Ellen Hammer, "has never been in a position to control his own environment, and he is reluctant to act on his own initiative. (The virtue of free will, as Westerners understand it, is not recognized.)"[8] Many aspects of the culture do indeed reflect fatalism—e.g., the widely practiced ancestor worship, belief in the supernatural, astrological practices, geomancy, and the religious-philosophical heritages of Confucianism, Taoism, and Buddhism.[9] But another psychological strand exists in the Vietnamese orientation towards action which suggests that simply describing peasants as fatalistic, in the Western connotation of the word, is misleading. The usual meaning of fatalism implies a resignation to the inexorability of fate;[10] however, Vietnamese can be vigorous people believing that work, effort, virtue, and learning bring appropriate rewards and that one should accept the opportunities to strive for them. Belief in the efficacy of individual action, on the one hand, and resignation to destiny, on the other, seem logically contradictory. Yet, for Vietnamese peasants they are psychologically compatible.[11]

A clue to the way these seemingly ambivalent tendencies are integrated into a coherent orientation towards action is provided in the following observation by Hickey:

> Although few could articulate it, villagers share a cosmological view
> that is daily manifest in behavior and expressed attitudes. . . . Universal
> order is the essence of this cosmology and from it spring other con-
> cepts, one of which is individual destiny. Villagers believe that one's
> destiny is guided by a particular star—the lucid manifestation of a

cosmic force, augmenting or diminishing it, thus boding good or evil
for the individual, who in this context is <u>predisposed rather than
predestined.</u> (underline added)[12]

Being "predisposed rather than predestined" suggests a structuring of reality distinct from either an acceptance of destiny or from a presumed control over one's
fortunes. Though the underlying dynamics and indeed the deeper meaning of
these cognitions will unfold as the analysis proceeds, several hypotheses characterizing this Vietnamese orientation towards action can be offered now. It is
hypothesized that the peasant's perception of fate, as revealed by concrete manifest signs, serves as a cognitive framework within which individual action occurs.
The peasant tends to react to situations that are created, he *perceives*, by forces
beyond his control—i.e., he tends to act in ways that alter his usual course of
behavior only if the necessity to do so is evoked externally. In short, the
peasant's action tends to be a response to the environment rather than self-
generated initiative: he "bends with the wind."[13] Reliance upon external
forces (attributed to fate, destiny, nature) constrains and narrows an individual's
range of behavior. But such reliance also cuts another way. Since one is forced
to act due to circumstances beyond one's control, then the individual is not only
free to do everything in his power to take advantage of his circumstances but
ought to do so. The acceptance of fate thus legitimizes highly pragmatic behavior.
Vietnamese speak and presumably think in terms of reality calculations that deal
with relatively short-run [14] tactical advantages [15] arising from the concrete
exigencies [16] of the immediate situation;[17] within this cognitive framework, they vigorously seek to attain certain core values (which are discussed
below).

    There is perhaps no single term that adequately captures this Vietnamese
characteristic orientation towards action of inhibited choices yet tactical flexibility, of constrained cognitions yet reality calculations, of acceptance of circumstances yet maximization of immediate advantage, of being part of a larger
destiny yet responding according to the dictates of the situation: the term *pragmatic fatalism* will be used to suggest these features.

    Acting pragmatically is moral for Vietnamese, assuming that the peasant
perceives his situation correctly. Thus, Paul Mus argues that the shifts of villagers'
loyalty reflect their value system and, in this sense, is a "deeply moral reaction
to success. . . . It is piety. Heaven has made its choice. It is a pious way of
obedience to the will of heaven."[18] This characteristic behavior implies several
additional hypotheses conceptualizing Vietnamese cognitive processes. Peasants
tend to structure situations in which they must act into dichotomous choices.
They perceive and evaluate these choices not in the specific, highly differentiated
manner of modernized Westerners that discriminate moral, political, social, and
economic factors into separable dimensions but rather in a diffuse manner that
blends these elements and judges the choices as complete and antagonistic

alternatives which are either proper or improper.[19] The specific constituents of "propriety" will be further clarified as the basic needs, values, primary beliefs, and orientations towards authority of Vietnamese peasants are delineated.

### Security Needs

Of the inventory of values usually attributed to Vietnamese peasants, perhaps the most frequently mentioned are the family, the land, the village, sometimes the nation, and always personal survival. These concerns are all interrelated, of course, arising from common life circumstances, child-rearing patterns, village social structure, and cultural practices and beliefs. For the purpose of the subsequent analysis of how peasant's respond to new circumstances precipitated by their involvement with the PLAF, it is necessary to examine the underlying part played by such concerns in the peasant's personality structure. This section posits a common Vietnamese core need for security and interprets the various concerns listed above in terms of security needs. The ensuing discussion will make apparent that "security needs" represents a complex configuration of anxieties and tensions that the culture both generates and provides inevitably incomplete solutions for. Understanding how security concerns are raised and satisfied in the culture establishes a foundation for the later interpretation of similar problems confronting the soldier in the PLAF.

### Security: Survival and "Fitting-In"

Personal survival is surely a basic concern of Vietnamese peasants. However, its meaning in the Vietnamese context can be misinterpreted if this motivation is equated to a simple fear of death. Death, an ever-present possibility in village life, does not have the same sense of finality as in Western conceptions. Simply put, to die is to enter into a different state of existence. As such, "[d]eath is an exit," Hammer observes "which [Vietnamese] not infrequently choose for themselves deliberately, sometimes for motives of honor but sometimes also for surprisingly futile reasons. Life is all the less valued because the Vietnamese believe in the survival of the individual after death. . . ."[20] In particular, a basic tenet of ancestor worship is that "Death is no real departure from the family—one joins the ancestors to exist as an unseen but nonetheless present member."[21] The crux of the matter—the link between a feeling of security and personal survival—is that unless one dies in a proper way, his future existence may be jeopardized.[22] Thus, the fear of death seems a less psychologically threatening prospect than that the circumstances of death might lead to a discontinuity in immortality.[23]

Of particular relevance for revolutionary mobilization is the belief that dying in defense of the Vietnamese homeland is an honored death. This attitude combines a strong feeling of an identity as a Vietnamese [24] (one bordering on xenophobia) with a sense of martyrdom and seems widely-held among ordinary Vietnamese as well as among elites.[25] Walter H. Slote found, in his intensive psychological study of selected Vietnamese subjects, that the "concept of death . . . constitutes a central philosophical core of the Vietnamese attitude toward life. . . . The rewards for dying in a particular manner are far greater than they are [in our society] . The highest reward is reserved for the martyred hero, and he is celebrated in folklore and mythology. This kind of death assures immortality and is a nuclear element in personality structure."[26] As will be argued subsequently, this attitude played an important part in the appeal, and in the maintenance, of the PLAF.


### Security-Insecurity and Family Relations

The Vietnamese attitude towards death can be placed into cultural perspective if one realizes that "the family more than the individual was the basic unit of Vietnamese society" and that "each member in death as in life was assured his place in this scheme of things, according to his rank."[27] That is, the basis for the Vietnamese sense of security is precisely in fitting into the scheme of things.[28]

To clarify the Vietnamese basic sense of security and to formulate the ways it depends upon fitting-in, primary patterns of Vietnamese social relations and principal psychodynamic characteristics will be hypothesized. In light of the relatively limited research on Vietnam, these hypotheses must be considered as quite tentative; they are intended to characterize salient features rather than posit a coherent theory. The following brief sketch and interpretations rely heavily on the findings of Slote and on analogous characteristics in Chinese culture.[29] The discussion begins with a series of hypotheses about underlying relations in the cornerstone of Vietnamese society, the family. Not only do critical psychodynamics evolve from family relations but, to an extraordinary extent, characteristics of broader interpersonal relationships mirror patterns set in family life.

Two opposing strains, both often observed, exist in Vietnamese child-rearing practices. On the one hand, there are the highly permissive, in many ways indulgent, practices—the suckling and feeding on demand, the immediate response to crying infants by the mother, sibling, kinfolk, or neighbors, the considerable attention and affection paid to young children, the casual toilet training, the freedom to roam about the hamlet and in and out of neighbors' houses, etc.[30] A result of these patterns is a sense of comfort, a sense of belonging and complete nurturance, a sense of security. However, the unlimited nature of these relations cannot be complete in any culture; in Vietnam, limits on behavior take an absolute, pervasive, and particular form: children must conform to a set of highly stylized patterns of respect behavior. Each person in Vietnamese society has a finely differentiated status (discussed below) and the child must adhere to formal rituals of conduct appropriate to the relative status positions. A single phrase imparting the nature of this behavior pattern might be situation-centered role playing.[31] The child, and later the adult, adopts that set of behaviors, expectations, and stereotyped responses prescribed as *proper* in the interpersonal situation. In terms of family relationships, a particularly critical aspect of role adoption is embedded in the notion of filial piety which prescribes the obligations and proper behavior of child to parent.[32] Since the required respect forms are highly stylized, behavior is judged as either right or wrong according to whether the child conforms to the proper rituals. Just by the sheer force of imitation, children learn the correct forms at a very young age.[d] However, any serious violation of form provokes a swift, severe punishment. (Children are rarely punished or even chastised except for improper respect behavior.) Punishment takes the form of humiliation, isolation from the family, and an implicit threat to be cut off from the family.[33] In general, children *passively obey* their parents.

From the above widely *observed* mechanisms—on the one hand, extreme permissiveness and on the other, severe restrictions reinforced by a consonant social structure (which will be investigated shortly)—spring inner tensions in Vietnamese personality whose dynamics can be inferred though not, as yet, solidly established. Evidence suggests an underlying, deeply repressed hostility towards parents and authority figures.[34] Yet, first and foremost, hostility must be strictly avoided. The results may very well be the *denial of emotion* and the *dissociation of behavior from inner feelings* often attributed to Vietnamese. Repression of hostility also may be a source of the sporadic fits of rage, reported by sympathetic observers, to which Vietnamese peasants can be subject.[35]

Walter Slote hypothesizes that indulgence coupled with absolute restrictions may produce, in the Vietnamese context, a core ambivalence involving security-insecurity: a longing for an ideal, totally trustful, completely secure relationship yet a distrust, a recognition of the inability of full gratification. Thus, on the one hand, there exists an extreme dependency upon the mother and father to the extent that, "Vietnamese clearly establish that they cannot function without the support of the parents . . ."[36] or substitute figures; on the other hand, there is a constant anxiety about the relationship breaking-up, about the family staying together.[37] For purposes of simplification, we call this underlying dynamic a need for security.[e]

---

[d]In addition to implicit imitation of behavior, the standard mode of Vietnamese teaching-learning is by *rote*—i.e., by exact repetition of basic precepts (for example, of the filial acts of devotion).

[e]A need for security can be conceptualized as a universal trait, not unique to Vietnamese, of course. The task of this section is to describe various aspects of the way this

There are then two levels of functioning, one external and the other internal, which are nonetheless both realities. In behavior, there is conformity to proper rules, passive obedience, filial piety and devotion, a sense of security and comfort, a merging of one's identity in the family. Underneath and unexpressed except indirectly, there is hostility, disassociation, distrust, and a feeling of insecurity. When faced with new situations, the tensions involved in this need for security can be expected to play a crucial role in determining the choices made by Vietnamese peasants.

### Interpersonal Relations in Village Life: Community and Conformity

The patterns of behavior in family relations are reinforced and extended in interpersonal relationships in the village. After the family, the village, or as it has been appropriately called the "commune," traditionally constituted the fundamental social and political unit.[38] Though the impact of French colonialism, of modernization, and of war has affected village life in diverse ways, it is hypothesized that many of the basic patterns of interpersonal relationships still continued during the time period considered in this study.[39] For convenience, these relationships can be divided into close, primary group relationships and into more general relationships in village life.

The complete nurturance found in the parents' relation with the child extends to other immediate groups. Not only do parents and siblings care for the children, but so do neighbors and kin.[40] Moreover, a sense of comfort and normality in a group setting is a dominant pattern of adult social relations both among kin and among other members of the village who share daily activities:

> While the household group is the most basic unit of village society, the small kin clusters . . . share the same primary group characteristics. It is at this level that one finds face-to-face relationships, unqualified mutual aid, and common participation in celebrations. There also are non-kin households in some of the clusters, and consequently proximity sometimes supersedes kin ties as a basis for strong social bonds.[41]

Thus, a naturalness in group relations, a group spirit, indeed a feeling for group solidarity characterizes the village culture.[42]

Adult ties with the primary group echo the security-insecurity tensions associated with early family-life. Security lies in integrating into the group. By this merging of the self into group life, "there is," Paul Mus suggests, "a self-

---

"need" is manifested in Vietnamese psychoculture. The term "need for security" should be understood as a suggestive phrase connoting a complex set of characteristics and dynamics. Considerable more research on Vietnamese personality must be accomplished before a theory of these dynamics can be elaborated.

realization and self-awareness that frees one from the doubts, the violence, and the depressions that characterize introverted and subjective ways of living."[43] Yet, the integration of the individual into the group is so profound that the peasant's sense of himself—his identity—rests upon these relationships; hence, he is dependent and vulnerable.

Perhaps the best indication of dependency upon the group is suggested by the notion of "loss-of-face" which is the primary means of social sanction in Vietnamese society. Hu defines "face" as

> the respect of the group for a man with a good moral reputation: the man who will fulfill his obligations regardless of the hardships involved, who under all circumstances shows himself a decent human being. It represents the confidence of society in the integrity of ego's moral character, the loss of which makes it impossible for him to function properly within the community. (underlining added)[44]

The closest Western expression of the effect of "loss-of-face" is the feeling of shame that the self does not live up to the standards of proper behavior prescribed by the group. However, two cases must be distinguished: (a) where the standards of the group are internalized, i.e., where the group is the individual's identity group and (b) where the standards are not internalized but the external signs of approval and disapproval are important. "Loss-of-face" in the first case implies both guilt and shame; it can cause anxiety about being rejected by the identity group. The threat of such rejection in light of the need for security in the group is a profound threat indeed; it will be called *identification shame*. Mus sensitively describes this aspect of Vietnamese culture:

> The French were constantly surprised at the number of cases in which loss of face resulted in murder and, even more, in suicide. This violence occurred because "face" is not just another word for vanity or social pretention; it is the very character of one's being.[45]

The second case involves shame without guilt. It too is deeply felt but its effects depend upon the situational context; it will be called *situational shame*.[46]

*Orientation Towards Authority in Village Life:*
*Avoidance of Conflict and Hierarchy*

Though the peasant possesses positive attachments towards his village, the primary group with its sense of solidarity and complete trust among members does not extend fully to all villagers. People who are not members of one's primary group can be treated with distrust and suspicion.[47] Indeed, perhaps because of distrust and anxiety that one's own inner hostility will be released, conflict is seen as an inherent possibility in relating to others. But, as in family life, conflict in interpersonal relations should be avoided.

No theme is more basic in the psychoculture than avoidance of conflict. Its centrality is evident in the philosophical-ethical-religious belief system where it is conceptualized by the notion of harmony. As Nguyen Huu Chi notes:

> The most striking characteristic of the Vietnamese . . . culture is the strong emphasis on harmony as an ideal way of life. . . . Both Confucianism and Taoism view the cosmos as the result of a harmonious evolution. . . . [H]armony is the foundation of life . . . [and] . . . there are only the Right Way (*Chinh Dao*) which leads to [harmony] and success, and the Wrong Way (*Ta Dao*) which certainly leads to . . . disharmony . . . death, disintegration. Harmony in nature brings good crops. Harmony in man brings peace and calm.[48]

The maintenance of harmony, the avoidance of interpersonal conflict, is not simply an abstract ideal.[49] Social practices of village life, buttressed by family and kin relationships, instill and enforce—in a word, institutionalize—three patterns of interpersonal behavior for maintaining and restoring harmony: (1) a hierarchical social structure with an associated code of proper behavior and ritualistic conformity, (2) extension of the primary group, or (3) consensual agreement. These regularized patterns constitute the implicit, institutionalized political order of village life from which peasants acquire many of their primary beliefs about the nature of legitimate authority.

The hierarchical pattern is the predominant means of maintaining harmony in Vietnamese villages:

> The village was profoundly hierarchical in social structure, and a man's life, in all the many practices and rites that knit the village together, was determined in infinite detail by his rank and function in the society.[50]

This order should not be equated (for reasons discussed subsequently) to a class structure, a caste system, or a sharply distinguished social stratification system. Status distinctions are finely drawn with the key element being who is superior and who is inferior. To the superior, deference in the form of proper behavior must be shown. The pervasiveness of this social ordering based upon status distinctions can be seen in the formalistic code of proper behavior for dealing with others to which all villagers conform. Nguyen Dinh Hoa's analysis of Vietnamese language clearly reveals how thoroughly integrated the notion of proper respect behavior is in the culture:

> Vietnamese society has a tightly woven culture. The dominant theme expressed through the language is "to take one's proper position among other members of the community." Names should be correctly used.

> An individual has a pathological fear of offending other people and of losing face. . . . Apply the "correct name" . . . in social intercourse is the concern of everyone.[51]

Thus, Vietnamese society copes with the possibility of conflict by establishing ritualistic order. Conforming to the proper rituals, i.e., playing the role prescribed in the situation, assures recognition of each person's status. On the other hand, violation of conduct appropriate to the given status situation can invoke a loss-of-face and can, for serious transgressions, raise the threat of isolation from village life. New interpersonal situations in which a proper set of relationships have not yet been formed leads to uncertainty over how one "fits in."

This hierarchical pattern with its code of proper behavior and ritualistic conformity imply dominance-submission relationships, somewhat akin to the father and son relationship as embodied in the ideals of filial piety. People in positions of high status in the traditional village had the privileges of deference but they also had obligations (which we will elaborate subsequently) and they too were bound by rules of propriety, e.g., arrogance or the arbitrary use of power and position was inappropriate.[52] Though superior and subordinate were unequal in terms of rights, they were equally embedded in and adhered to—for moral and pragmatic reasons—a village order that prescribed what was proper and right.

Another social mechanism for avoiding conflicts in interpersonal relations is the "extension" of the family in the formation of friendships.[53] Such friendships between males are of intense quality akin to a love relationship within which emotion, loyalty, solidarity, complete trust, equality, and a lack of concern over status are the ideals. In a very real sense, the friend becomes a brother, a member of one's primary group. Yet, these friendships are rare in Vietnamese society and, thus, may be more a fantasy wish than a reality.[54]

Perhaps because distrust is so deep, perhaps because of an over reliance on the formal mechanism of conflict avoidance, the ability to *resolve* conflicts by bargaining and cooperation is not well-developed. Despite the ideal of harmony, disagreement and violence arising from disagreement do occur.[55] In Hickey's study of a village of approximately 3,000 people, he recorded sixty to ninety cases of disagreements that had to be brought to the Village Council for arbitration in the period from August 1956 to May 1958. Nine of these cases involved direct physical violence. The traditional process of settling these conflicts is more significant than their frequency. Unable, or unwilling, to settle things by mutual agreement and compromise between themselves, the villagers resort to a village body which sits in arbitration rather than judgement. The proceedings symbolically brings to bear the weight of the village in the common interest of harmony. [56] The "solution"—often pragmatic and symbolic rather than based on abstract principles of justice—is an agreement to which both parties consent and thereby preserve "face." (Failure to agree would not be proper.) Thus, by a process of agreeing to abide by the "village consensus," the conflict is defused and the facade of harmonious relations restored.

The highly integrated order described above represents the structure of authority as practiced *within* traditional villages. Consequently, it is reasonable to infer from this pattern elements of the peasant's primary beliefs and values about the nature of authority (which we call an orientation towards authority). The Vietnamese sense of security resides in fitting-in to a proper and prescribed role in the family and in the village hierarchy. The peasant was brought up to believe that ritualistic conformity to proper behavior led to security, that deference was given to those in authority, that interpersonal conflict should be avoided. His self-identity depended upon a collective ordered life, the only life he knew, and the life without which he could not function.[57]

### Status Drive

Some writers describe Vietnamese peasants as completely passive, lacking initiative, and even lazy. This characterization distorts active, goal-seeking aspects of peasant personality. Vietnamese possess strong drives towards attaining a variety of values. These positive motivations are distinct from the anxiety-reducing motivations discussed under the heading of need for security in the preceding section, though they intrinsically influence each other. For reasons to be advanced, these positive motivations underlying Vietnamese peasant behavior will be subsumed under and referred to as a status drive.[58] This section explores the nature of the status drive in Vietnamese peasant culture.

Dealing with goal-seeking behavior in a transitional society poses serious difficulties. In a stable society, there is a balance between the goals and values considered as legitimate by the culture and the means institutionalized within the society for achieving them.[59] The traditional village culture of Vietnam had a close fit between goals and means. However, French colonial rule profoundly eroded institutionalized means, diminished cultural sanctions, and distorted goals to the extent that Vietnamese society was thrown "off balance." It is beyond the scope of this study to review the history, or indeed the impact, of these changes in patterns of landholding and taxation, in economic incentives and administrative controls, in political and social organization. For present purposes, the critical assumption is that, even in those regions of southern Vietnam where colonial impact was severe, the psychocultural sources underlying status drives persisted and, indeed, may have been exacerbated. In short, the status drive remained a major component in Vietnamese personality at the time of the NLF's efforts to mobilize the peasantry.

As the preceding section suggests, Vietnamese are extremely sensitive to status. Village society was hierarchically structured in terms of subtle gradations of status ranking each villager in relation to others.[60] Yet, this comprehensive structuring did not preclude change in social status. On the contrary, social mobility within the village hierarchy was possible in fact and widely believed as an ideal.[61] Aside from age and sex, social status depended primarily upon *achievement* rather than ascribed characteristics. Vietnamese believe that one's social situation is not immutable, that people differ only in their ability and the luck granted by fate, and that the individual should strive to improve his position in life.[62] Nguyen Dinh Hoa aptly summarizes these sentiments: "consciousness about social differences . . . was taken for granted, accepted as the order of things. It sometimes engendered hatred or jealousy, but always gave birth to a healthy emulation, a wholesome earnest desire to climb the social ladder rung by rung . . . in order to reach a better status."[63] In short, Vietnamese peasants possess a well-developed drive to achieve status.

It would be a misinterpretation of the culture to conceive of the peasant's belief in the possibility of individual achievement and his desire for improvement as indicative of "individualism" in the Western sense of the word or as a sentiment divorced from and unconstrained by a collective, organized life. On the contrary, for three related reasons this motivation needs to be viewed in terms of those group relations so fundamental in the culture. First of all, the individual's attainments were judged by the group and thereby given social recognition— respect, honor, prestige—that placed him, at least traditionally, within the status hierarchy of village life. Secondly, the individual's rank not only afforded him privileges and rights vis-à-vis others but also entailed obligations to those below him and to the community. Thirdly, the values sought were those sanctioned by the community and the means used had to be proper in the cultural context. Each of these points can be clarified by briefly reviewing values highly regarded by the culture.

Besides certain ascribed characteristics—age, sex, and the unique prestige accorded to patriotic heroes and their patrilineal descendants—the traditional values that determined the individual's social status could be achieved: wealth, land, education, certain prestige positions, political positions, and "virtuous" behavior. Hickey found, in his analysis of a contemporary Mekong Delta village, that peasants possessed a "strong motivation for economic gain."[64] Economic well-being was sought not only for reasons of subsistence and as a hedge against bad times but also as a means of improving or strengthening one's status. Thus, economic differences were highly related to social status and, moreover, the village elite and the upwardly mobile villager spent a considerable portion of their wealth in prestige symbols (substantial houses, elaborate family celebrations, etc.). Men of wealth carried the responsibility of noblesse oblige and were expected to contribute to civic and religious ceremonies, lend money to villagers, and generally support the community in times of need. Such obligations combined with the practice of divided inheritance prevented, at least in traditional times, the accumulation of great wealth and the development of an economic based social class. Even in those areas where colonialism led to landlordism and

gross economic inequalities, landlord-tenant relationships often retained
traditional, though sometimes tragically exaggerated, elements of rights and
obligations.[65] Land has often been cited as fundamental to the peasant's sense
of security both for reasons of sheer economic survival and stability and for the
highly important ritual value of linking the peasant to the ancestral lineage.
Beyond the subsistence level, land was also sought for reasons of social mobility.
Again quoting Hickey: "An increase in landholding, preferably by purchase
rather than rental, is essential to upward mobility. . . . Once a villager has acquired
some land by inheritance or purchase, he is motivated to accumulate more—an
amount sufficient for the succeeding generation to maintain the status of the
family."[66] As in traditional times, education continues to be highly valued not
only for the sake of knowledge qua knowledge but for the social advancement
and prestige it brings.[67]

We suggested that the efforts to achieve status were circumscribed traditionally by moral notions of correct behavior. In the closely-knit setting of the
traditional village, community sanctions (of the social type suggested earlier)
could be applied to violators of proper conduct. However, the role played by
moral considerations goes beyond constraints and negative sanctions; it also has
positive qualities. The culture honors a set of ideal behaviors expressed in the
notion of *virtue*:

> One sure way to achieve a good name [that is, respect and prestige] . . .
> is to keep the right path of virtue. . . . The *Quan-tu* [the virtuous
> man] is distinguished from the mass not by his intellectual qualities but
> by certain specific moral virtues such as righteousness, the cult of
> honor, disdain for material comfort and financial gain, leniency, and
> modesty. One of his constant preoccupations is self-examination with a
> view to improving his moral self.[68]

The village elite, in particular, are expected to act in a virtuous manner, and, by
so doing, they both retained and enhanced their prestige.

Another area traditionally serving as a legitimate goal and providing institutionalized means of achieving higher status were political-administrative positions
in the village. As our introductory chapter suggested, the village in the traditional
political system had considerable autonomy from the weak central dynastic state
and was largely self-contained and self-governed. Positions of elite power and
status, the high venerables, coincided with political offices. However, colonialism
created a centralized administration that established bureaucratic offices within
the village. These bureaucratic positions tended to be divorced from the power
positions accorded legitimacy within the village.[69] It is beyond the scope of
this study to detail such disruptive effects except to note that, at the time of NLF
mobilization, many villages had experienced an erosion of the traditional social-
political institutions: the opportunities and means of achieving social mobility

in the traditional ways of rising within the closed, autonomous status hierarchy of the village were in doubt.

The above characterization of aspects of the modal personality of Vietnamese peasants forms a background for our analysis of the PLAF. We will see that the beliefs and motivations described by pragmatic fatalism, by security derived from fitting into an organized, collective life, and by the drive to achieve social aspirations defined the peasant's receptivity to mobilization and predisposed the way he would adapt to life as a member of the Front.

# 4

## Recruitment and Acceptance

How does a revolutionary organization mobilize peasants? Under what conditions can it be successful? These questions may be analyzed from several different viewpoints. One might deal with the broad sweep of social conditions and wrenching changes that set the stage for revolution; or examine the historical development of the organization and of its leadership; or investigate the military-political balance of forces. A combination of all these approaches will ultimately be necessary for a richer understanding of this complex phenomena. However, this chapter focuses on just one aspect of mobilization: why peasants became members of the revolutionary organization. We will examine the ways in which the NLF's recruitment activities affected the lives of peasants and thus resulted—given their cognitions and motivations—in them joining the PLAF.

The Front employed a variety of organizational activities directed towards creating an environment conducive to mobilization; by so doing, the organization restructured the life situation confronting villagers. In addition, the Front offered incentives to peasants that were, we will contend, necessary for their acceptance of membership. However, the restructuring of village life and the incentives were effective only insofar as they were in accord with Vietnamese basic personality characteristics. In this sense, the psychocultural characteristics described in the preceding chapter defined the parameters within which mobilization operated.

The first section of this chapter provides a brief overview of the recruitment strategy, tactics, and organizational techniques of the NLF. The second section investigates several case histories of the entry of Vietnamese peasants into the Front. By exploring the stories of former PLAF members in some detail, we hope to portray the realities confronting peasants and the manner in which peasants perceived and acted upon these realities. The third section leaves the details of individual histories to examine patterns of acceptance of membership using quantitative evidence.

### Recruitment Activities

The National Liberation Front engaged in a variety of recruitment activities ranging from kidnapping to enlistment drives, from drafting eligibles in entire villages to carefully planned and protracted propagandizing of single individuals, from overt threats to patriotic and nationalistic appeals. The techniques were so varied from area to area, individual to individual, one phase of the war to another, and even from one season to another that before illustrating specific techniques for particular individuals, several observations about broad patterns in Front recruitment are in order.

Political-military developments in the course of the war, e.g., American involvement, GVN drafting and military efforts, the Strategic Hamlet program, pacification programs, etc., caused major strategic shifts in NLF recruitment policies. Though reader familiarity with these developments is assumed, it is pertinent to recall briefly the phases of NLF growth leading from a select, covert operation to a mass-based organization. In the early years of forming and solidifying, from roughly 1957 to 1962—the years called by Pike "the social movement propaganda phase"—considerable emphasis was placed on persuasion and voluntary enlistment of carefully selected recruits. The "political struggle movement phase" from early 1962 to late 1963 resulted in a change of strategy leading to less selective recruitment.[1] In the years from 1964 to 1967 (the end of the period considered in this study), the level of conflict and the need for new recruits greatly increased. PLAF recruitment activities often became harsher, involved more coercion, and overt compulsory drafting.[2] The revolutionary organization had become mass-based.

These strategic shifts in policy as well as the numerous changes in content and emphasis of recruitment were centrally planned and controlled by the Front's organizational apparatus. However, this strategic centralization did not imply, by-and-large, a rigid system of induction. On the contrary, considerable tactical flexibility was exercised at local levels on the who, how, and when of recruitment. Careful planning, involving detailed dossiers on individuals in a village, permitted an approach tailored to village situations.[3] Front agents were particularly alert to personal difficulties that would increase the susceptibility of potential recruits. As W.P. Davison observes: "If a man was experiencing family problems, had gone badly into debt, was in trouble with the law, was about to be drafted into the army, or had been mistreated by government officials, this was likely to come to the attention of watchful Viet Cong agents, who would approach him and ask him to join their movement."[4] In addition, peasants were recruited to serve different functions in the NLF, e.g., as part of the civilian organization, or in different branches of the military, or corvee labor, according to their capability. The net result of this localized approach is well summarized by Jeffrey Race: "the revolutionary organization ensured that critical decisions . . . were made by local people, with relatively more flexibility and with some sensitivity to the demands of the particular situation."[5]

Thus, the command structure of Front recruitment can be summarized as centralized planning with decentralized implementation. Such a structure placed prime responsibility on low-level cadre.[6] Indeed, since peasants judge a system in terms of personal behavior of its representatives, one would expect that the manner in which recruitment cadre dealt with villagers was crucial to whether the

peasant accepted membership. The next section shows that the cadre's conduct
was in fact crucial. However, at this point in the analysis of the PLAF's structure,
a systemic question needs to be raised: did the decentralized reliance on low-level
cadre for the complex task of persuading villagers produce erratic, highly
unreliable recruitment that perhaps distorted overall goals and principles of the
organization? By-and-large, no. Though variability did exist, the behavior of
cadre was extraordinarily uniform in carrying out the spirit of the revolutionary
organization.[7] They had adopted a role and developed identification with
organizationally prescribed behavior; moreover, they had internalized elements
of a revolutionary ideology that not only contributed to their motivation but
also provided a common set of ideas enabling the implementation of general
instructions.[8] (Part II analyzes how, why, and to what extent such identification actually developed in the Front.) Thus, decentralized implementation
worked not only within a structure of centralized planning and control but also
within an ideological context of commonly accepted beliefs about how to treat
villagers and persuade them to join the Front.[9]

Another major factor in recruitment was the circumstances of village life. As
suggested in the preceding chapter, social-political-economic institutions in the
countryside were under erosion prior to the beginning of the Second Indochina
War. Without attempting to analyze the state of village life, three observations
are particularly pertinent. First of all, a major impact of the Viet Minh war was,
as Jeffrey Race convincingly argues, "the overthrow of the power of the local
elite, which the French had employed to carry out the functions of the central
government in the countryside."[10] By the time the NLF began mobilization
the de facto government operated by powerful landlords in large areas of the
Mekong Delta or by the religious sects had disappeared or were tenuous.[11] This
lack of coherent government facilitated the Front's access to the village and to
the individual (as well as affecting his cognitions and motivations in ways to be
discussed). Secondly, the Front actively attempted to disrupt and destroy village
organization and replace it by their own.[12] Thirdly, considerable variability
existed across southern Vietnam both in the Front's success in controlling village
life and in the erosion of village social organization.

"Control" was the word employed by military people to describe the
variability in NLF influence indicated above.[13] The allied classification of VC
controlled, GVN controlled, or contested—paralleled by the NLF classification
sometimes called "extended liberated zone," "temporarily liberated zone," and
"weak zone"[14] —suggests the very different conditions of access to the peasant
exercised by the Front. In liberated zones the Front maintained such complete
control that in effect they were the sole governing body: a social-political
Communist infrastructure existed, taxes were collected, no GVN functionaries
were present, communication and mobility to other areas were controlled. Of
course, in this environment the peasant was exposed to numerous forces which
shaped his cognitions and socialized him. In the contested areas, Front control

was not complete or fluctuated. It was "temporarily liberated" for NLF presence could be very real if not as constant as in the liberated zones. Often a political infrastructure existed although at times covert; taxes were collected; recruitment activities went on; GVN functionaries might be present or at least could enter the hamlet during the daytime perhaps with armed forces. Even in government "controlled areas," or the "weak" zone as the Front termed it, NLF presence might exist in the form of a covert infrastructure or sporadic propaganda visits.

It is obvious from this brief overview of recruitment activities that the dynamics of mobilization necessarily depended upon the NLF's ability to control the circumstances of village life. The next section turns to an analysis of these dynamics from the perspective of individuals.

### Perceptions of Authority and Opportunity

The large-scale variations in recruitment patterns were irrelevant from the viewpoint of the individual. He had to respond to a specific situation, and he did so in terms of his perceptions and motivations. To portray the process of recruitment from the individual's standpoint, several concrete case histories will be explored.

The first case concerns the story of Nguyen Van Ton who joined the GVN militia, was captured by the NLF, and decided to become a member of the PLAF. We will detail *his* account of the situation so that a richer sense of Vietnamese realities can be conveyed. Particular attention will be devoted to interpreting Ton's decision to participate in the revolutionary organization in terms of the interplay among Vietnamese modal personality characteristics, Ton's life situation, and the NLF's recruitment techniques.

*Basic Personality Characteristics and Joining*

**Joining the Militia.**  Nguyen Van Ton's father left his home in North Vietnam with his family after the end of the Japanese occupation to work as a laborer for a French rubber plantation owner in Cambodia. Following several fluctuations in fortunes, the family settled at the close of the Resistance in Thanh-Luong, a small village not far from the province capital of Binh-Luong where the father became a barber.

The family did fairly well. The father earned about one hundred piasters a day from cutting hair and selling small items in his shop allowing the family to save some money each month. By the time Nguyen Van Ton was 17, he was busily employed. "I worked as a rubber tapper in the morning from 6:30 am to 2:30 pm and as a barber in the afternoon. As a rubber tapper I earned 44 piasters and 800 grams of rice each day and a bonus of 50 cents for each liter of rubber gum. This bonus amounted to one to three hundred piasters per month. I worked six days a week as a rubber tapper and seven days a week as a barber." As a dutiful son, he contributed to the maintenance of the family unit. "My wife and I lived with my father and mother. My wife and my sister were also rubber tappers. My mother stayed at home to do the housekeeping. My three little brothers went to school."

Ton, who had completed elementary school before the family moved to Thanh-Luong, said he felt satisfied with his life and had no special worries. He was not unambitious, however. "I wanted to remain a barber, to save enough money to buy myself a barbershop in the City." The war intervened.

By the end of 1961, war pressures were being felt in Thanh-Luong. "At the time I left, my village was under GVN control. It was peaceful . . . ," as far as Ton then knew. "I did not pay any attention to politics; all that the people wanted was to be left alone to work for their living and not to be oppressed . . . The village authorities and the militiamen were all inhabitants of the village, they were all relatives of the villagers and they did their best to help them with their birth certificates, their authorization requests, etc. . . . They were very kind to the people . . ." The Front, however, was becoming active, though Ton at this time was not aware of the activity. "I learned later [while serving in the Front] that the Front already had an agent network in my village. . . . The Front had already established in my village a Party chapter composed of five or six members. The mission of the Chapter was to collect taxes to establish contact with the civilians, to distribute Front leaflets." There was as yet no overt military presence in the form of Front guerrillas. "At that time my village was ordered by Mr. Diem to form a militia unit to defend the village against a VC attack . . ."

Why did Ton join the militia? "I joined the militia because I was afraid of being drafted into the regular ARVN. . . . Everybody who . . . served as a militiaman for two years would be exempted . . . from the ARVN draft. I was afraid of the draft and my father urged me to join the village militia for two reasons: (1) the militia did not have to fight the Viet Cong; they were only doing police work in the village; (2) the militia remained in the village and I could stay near my family during these two years. Therefore, at my father's urging, I volunteered to serve in the militia thinking I would get rid of my obligations in two years and would return to my work."

His reasons seem clear enough. However, by decomposing this simple act into its various elements, we can illustrate aspects of Vietnamese peasant behavior.

Ton's orientation towards action can be seen in this decision. From Ton's perspective both the necessity to decide and the alternatives themselves were determined by forces beyond his control. Recall his testimony, "all that the people wanted was to be left alone to work for their living. . . ." Ton considered two alternatives: (1) be drafted by the ARVN, or (2) join the militia. Both alternatives were disagreeable. He chose that alternative whose consequences were least disagreeable. This orientation towards action—the decision evoked externally, alternatives constrained, and rational self-interest in selecting alternatives—illustrates pragmatic fatalism.

Ton judged these alternatives in terms of three interrelated values. First of all, there was personal danger—"the militia did not have to fight the Viet Cong"; secondly was his family—"I could stay near my family"; thirdly was village life—"I . . . would return to my work [in the village] ." These preferences all reflect, and would satisfy, the major need of personal security.

There were indications in his hopes for the future—"I wanted to . . . buy myself a barbershop in the City"—that Ton was "ambitious." Such "ambition," however, reflects a status drive. In this decision, the desire for status did not enter; it did, however, play an important part in Ton's later decision to join the PLAF.

Ton's cognitions and orientations towards social relations in his village and towards politics are only partly revealed in his testimony. Though he was young, he was fully integrated into his family unit and into village life. Both the family and the village seemed to be tightly-knit. The former was an extended family unit to which every member contributed. The village constituted a community where officials "were all relatives of the villagers and they did their best to help them with their birth certificates, their authorization requests, etc. . . ." Ton had a "subject" orientation towards governmental official, to borrow Almond and Verba's apt phrase.[15] The villagers were certainly aware of government, they had no other choice. Yet, they were "output oriented": "all that the people wanted," Ton said, "was to be left alone to work for their living and not to be oppressed." To Vietnamese, *authority which oppresses or cannot prevent oppression loses its legitimacy*. Ton himself was not a participant, "I did not pay any attention to politics."

These characteristics of Ton—his pragmatic fatalistic orientation towards action, his concern with security and status, his integration into family and village social structures, and his subject orientation towards government—also were evident in his entry into the Front.

**Ton's Entry into the Front.**   After having served for three months in the Militia, Ton was wounded in an NLF attack on his post, taken away to a Front hospital for treatment, and two months later decided to join the "People's Revolution." Ton's capture did not involve a decision, at least not one that can be fruitfully analyzed. Yet, unless he was captured, he might never have entered the Front. Ton's experience in the militia caused him no discontent. On the contrary, "it was a very pleasant time. When not on guard duty I stayed with my family. I took my meals at home; therefore I received my full pay which was nine hundred piasters a month." Hence, he might have been content to serve out his time in the militia. However, the capture placed him in a radically altered situation: fate had again moved to present him with another decision. The outcome of this decision-problem—"joining" the PLAF— was opposite to the outcome of his choice some six months earlier but many of the same factors underlying his previous behavior can be seen at work here.

The Front treated him in a "proper" manner when he was captured and during his hospitalization; such behavior is singularly important to Vietnamese:

> I could not find anything to complain about the attitude and behavior of the VC during that period [when captured and interrogated]. No one could be nicer to me than the Front cadres. Their only purpose in capturing me was to find out if I were a spy, or if I had done harm to the population. If not, I would be released after a period of reeducation. I told them the only reason for me to join the Militia was that I had wanted to avoid the ARVN draft. I also told them I was a new recruit with no training at all, therefore I could not do them any harm.

The various facets composing "proper conduct" as viewed by Vietnamese cannot be fully exposed in this straightforward testimony but several aspects can be suggested. An important dimension of proper behavior is the avoidance of improper conduct by superordinates, particularly the excessive use of power. Rather than acting arrogantly, the cadres embodied by their conduct the image of virtuous authority: "I was visited by the Province Committee Chief and by numerous cadres who talked *gently* with me." Such behavior by cadre was not idiosyncratic nor unusual. As Part II describes, the Front explicitly socialized their members to show respect, to be virtuous, to avoid arrogance with power or the arbitrary use of physical force, to "treat civilians as members of their family, to include them within the circle of their trust and obligation."[16] Proper conduct by the Front made Ton receptive to persuasion.

The cadres in no way condemned Ton for having been an enemy. They understood and accepted the pragmatic reasons he cited for being in the Militia; they did not hold him morally culpable. So, far from being treated as a war criminal, the Front who now controlled Ton's future began to "reeducate" him. After a month and a half of reeducation—a process which will be analyzed subsequently—Ton was asked to join the Front:

> Then the cadres asked me to choose between the two paths laid before me. They asked me to fulfill my duty toward the people and they let me know that the Front was in critical need of young men like me. . . .

> At the end of this period [the reeducation] I could have returned to my family, but I did not. The cadre asked me whether I wanted to join the Revolution. He warned me not to work for the GVN again in case I chose to leave, and he told me how grateful my country would be to me when the day of liberation came. I did not want to return home because I would certainly be imprisoned for having lost my gun to the enemy and besides I was won over by the aims of the Revolution. Therefore I decided to join the Front.

Despite a number of obvious and highly significant differences, major similarities existed between this decision and Ton's early one. Again the external environment—the situation controlled by the PLAF—evoked the decision problem. Moreover, the alternatives themselves were constrained and prescribed by the situation. As before, Ton structured his alternatives in a polarized fashion in the sense that choices were thought of as sharply distinguished and the consequences of one were the opposite of the other. However, this binary choice situation resulted from NLF persuasion that was directed toward narrowing the alternatives to two extremes; one choice being the correct path because it was proper and because it was better; the other path being the bad, ignoble, improper choice as well as less advantageous.

The tactical approach to reality calculations also clearly emerges. Ton aligned the disincentives against the incentives associated with each choice. He could presumably return home—family considerations and personal security were key motivations in Ton's earlier decision to join the militia. Yet, now these goals could not have been achieved because the situation had changed. If he tried to work for the GVN, he would be imprisoned (Ton said he believed) for losing his gun. Moreover, if he did return to the GVN, the Front would consider him an enemy subject to harsh punishment. Ton could only be expected to act in his self-interest; what constituted self-interest had changed.

Would Ton be violating filial piety and devotion by going with the Front? On the contrary, according to Ton, "I thought my family would be proud of having a son who had contributed to the liberation and would benefit from my accomplishments." Perhaps Ton was, in response to subconscious drives, breaking away from the family and the confines of village life; but there is no evidence of this in his testimony. That the family "would benefit from my accomplishments" should be understood primarily in the sense of prestige. In this indirect way, Ton was expressing his hope of realizing social advancement both for himself and his family by being a member of the Revolution. By saying that the "country would be grateful," he was indicating his personal ambition in an appropriate manner sanctioned by the culture.

By saying that he would be fulfilling his "duty towards the people," Ton indicated that he felt the cause of the Front was a righteous one. However, this feeling clearly did not exist before he was exposed to Front propaganda. Ton was "won over by the aims of the Front" as a result of a process of persuasion:

At the hospital, they were even nicer. I was the only prisoner in a room of twenty patients. At first, when my condition was very bad, I was given chicken soup to eat. Later when my condition improved I was given rice with beef sauce. Every day [for over a month] the Propaganda and Indoctrination cadres would come to lecture to me in particular and to my roommates in general about the meaning of the present war of liberation. . . .

> . . . Besides the lectures of the Propaganda and Indoctrination cadres, I
> was visited by the Province committee chief. I talked with my room-
> mates and with the female nurses. I read their information bulletin, and
> I listened to Radio Hanoi on a Philips battery-operated radio.

Before examining the content of this propaganda, it is important to appreciate
the environment under which persuasion took place. Ton was undergoing invol-
untary reeducation. The informational environment was controlled and closed
to outside, possibly discrepant, sources. A variety of communication media were
employed—the radio, written material, informal conversations with roommates
and female nurses, the formal but personal lectures of the cadres, and a personal
visit from a man of high status. All of these techniques reinforced each other and
led to a sense of self-esteem. As Ton put it, "I was treated very nicely both from
the material standpoint as well as from the spiritual standpoint. Consequently I
volunteered to stay with the Front."

The major message of the lectures reiterated day after day by the cadres,
was a political one:

> They said the North Vietnamese people were trying to help their South
> Vietnamese brothers chase away the American imperialists and to win
> back their independence. They showed me how rotten the Diem regime
> was; Diem and Le Xuan (Mme. Nhu) were dictatorial and were selling
> the South Vietnamese people to the Americans for their own family's
> profit. The Americans were false friends; they did not come to Vietnam
> to help the people but rather to take over the country. Then they talked
> about the aims of the People's Liberation Front which were to liberate
> South Vietnam from the domination of American imperialism and from
> the Nhu family, and to lead the South Vietnamese to Socialism as in
> North Vietnam, where no one was exploited and where everybody was
> free and everybody was master of his tools and his land.

This testimony is unusually articulate. (Ton later worked as a member of an
Armed Propaganda Team where his job was to persuade villagers to assist the
Front or to participate in Civilian Struggle.) Nonetheless, these themes, and variations on them due to different stages of the war (e.g., after Diem's death the
propaganda had to change), appear in most of the former PLAF's stories. The
ideological content of the message is simple and personalized and thus appropriate
for peasants. The specific content of the propaganda themes need not be analyzed
here except to note that the nationalism, the xenophobia, the attack on the mis-
conduct of persons (Diem, etc.) rather than on institutions, the betrayal of trust,
the symbolic expression for socialism, the image of a future "where no one was
exploited" all strike responsive cords in the Vietnamese common belief system
and served to legitimize the NLF.[17] They did for Ton, at any rate, for, when
queried, he said, "The aims of the Front were more important in my decision

than fear of prison. The cadres had succeeded in arousing my noblest feelings."
Of course, Ton may have been rationalizing and glorifying the reasons why he
joined. But insofar as he thus rationalized *when* he joined, it too was part of the
persuasion process.

In sum, underlying the process of "volunteering" was the Front effort to
convince Ton that his security needs would be satisfied in the PLAF. By demon-
strating proper behavior, by enhancing his self-esteem, by offering his a well-
defined role in a stable organization ("the Front was in critical need of young
men like me"), the NLF promised him a secure future. Indeed, the very nature
of the strong authority relations in the Front suggested security to the Vietnamese peasant, as will be shown in detail in Part II. Moreover, his personal ambitions could be realized in the organization. These motivations when combined
with the circumstances that were compromised due to Front manipulation and
when combined with the latent sentiments of nationalism and heroism that were
activated by Front propaganda justified pragmatic fatalism and caused Ton to
accept membership.


### Propriety and the Use of Force

In Nguyen Van Ton's story, elements of necessarily complex dynamics
appear: coercion mixed with persuasion, implied threats coupled with personal
incentives, control of the peasant's circumstances joined with an appeal to volun-
tarism based upon patriotic sentiments. However, one individual's case history
does not provide a sufficiently comprehensive view of the full process. In succeeding sections, several case histories, including some in which mobilization was
unsuccessful, will be analyzed and compared. Each section focuses on selected
dynamics of the overall process beginning with the NLF's use of force in recruitment.

The Front captured Nguyen Van Ton, kept him in captivity for an unusually
long time in terms of Vietnamese medical standards, reeducated him, and asked
him to "volunteer" making him well-aware that he had compromised himself.
Force was used in two ways. First it was used openly to gain access to the individual, to control him so that the process of persuasion could be carried out.
Second, it was used in an implied manner that was part of persuasion itself.
Recall Ton's statement, "He [the Propaganda Cadre] warned me not to work for
the GVN again. . . ." The first use of force—gaining access to, and in this case
complete control of, the individual—did not prejudice the persuasion process.
Ton accepted his "captivity." As far as the way force was used in persuasion, it
was minimal—though clearly existent—applied properly from his standpoint, and
again did not seem to prejudice the Front's case. The best measure of this is
that Ton felt he joined of his own volition.

To investigate these points comparatively, we will contrast Nguyen Van

Ton's story to that of Dong Van Kiet. Kiet was a poor farmer who lived with his wife and baby in his family's village in Quang Tin province. The insurgency intruded upon his village in 1961 when the GVN decided to introduce the strategic hamlet program. Kiet, who was 23 at the time, joined the GVN militia but since the area seemed secure, he asked for, and received, a discharge from the militia after having served for six months and returned full time to his farming. For two years Kiet continued the usual life of a peasant, "I led a happy life with my family. I was not dissatisfied about anything." He paid as little attention as possible to politics and the war. "At that time, I never stopped to think about the [GVN] government. I was only worried about my work. I didn't think anything bad about the government." These are stereotyped answers. Kiet was well aware of politics at the village level. When asked about the behavior of the Village Council, Kiet replied,

> the Village Council sometimes caused difficulties for the villagers. They were unfair, and consequently a few of the villagers were discontented. . . . The Village Council members accepted bribes also. Later on they were demoted and replaced by new members [these were elected] who were better than the old members.

The strategic hamlet program also interrupted the normal peasant existence and caused some difficulties. Yet, the villagers and Kiet went along with it and he felt that "Generally speaking they [the villagers] were not dissatisfied. Some of the villagers were discontented about it, but they were in the minority." As far as the Front was concerned,

> the villagers were more sympathetic to the GVN than to the VC, for they could see for themselves that the people who had led a happy life in GVN controlled areas before these regions fell in the hands of the VC were now leading a miserable life, because they had to pay taxes to the Front . . . [and] . . . had to do forced labor.

As far as the ideology of the Front (what it stood for, how it worked), Kiet said simply, "I didn't know anything about communism. I led a happy life. I just ate and then enjoyed myself. I didn't hear anything about life in the Front."

At the beginning of 1963, when Kiet was 25, fate intervened so that he could no longer avoid the political struggle.

> One night the VC infiltrated . . . [my] . . . hamlet and took me and two other villagers away. The VC were armed. The two other villagers were old. They wept and begged the VC to let them go back to the village. The VC released them but took me away because I was young.

So, as with Nguyen Van Ton, the Front gained access to Dong Van Kiet by overt force. They then proceeded to indoctrinate him but their attempts were less successful.

[When taken away] I was afraid I would die because they took me
deep into the jungle. . . . [They] put me in a course on politics to
reform my thoughts, to make me break away completely from the
GVN and understand fully the policy and line of the Front. . . . They
reformed me for three months and then mobilized me to join their
army. They mobilized our spirit, but actually it was tantamount to
forcing us to join. If we refused they would kill us. So all of us had to
"volunteer" to join their army.

One of the rituals followed by the Front, particularly in the years up to
1966, was that of "volunteering." [18] In the case of Nguyen Van Ton this
ritual had meaning: he did indeed volunteer. For Dong Van Kiet, he too was
propagandized:

I was told that the Revolution of the South was being carried out by
the South Vietnamese people themselves. The Revolution did not spring
up in the North. The purpose of the Front is to bring material welfare
to the people, and to divide land to the poor.

But he was not persuaded. The interviewer asked, "Did these aims appeal to you
personally?" Kiet replied, "No, not at all. I was forced to join the Front. I had no
choice but to stay with the VC to pass away the time."
    Thus, both men adapted to the situation in which they found themselves.
One, however, was persuaded to join; the other claims he stayed under duress.
Though both men eventually defected, Ton did so several years later after having
risen to cadre; however Kiet left in less than a year and did not fully accept membership in the revolutionary organization.
    By deliberately comparing these two cases that (a) are similar in that both
respondents were captured and (b) are different in that one accepted membership whereas the other did not, we can control—at least partially—the initial
access phase of recruitment and contrast the final phase of acceptance. What was
it about the circumstances, the motivations, or the coercion-persuasion mix in
these stories that explains the success of mobilization in one case and the failure
in the other?
    Though force had been used in both cases, Ton had been captured whereas
Kiet was kidnapped. The distinction is not simply a legalistic point; it is a matter
of the legitimate exercise of force as perceived by the peasants—a matter of
propriety. The Front clearly used overt force which, from Kiet's standpoint, was
excessive and improper. Kiet agreed to stay in the PLAF because, assuming his
testimony is accurate, he feared "they would kill us." This is surely a pragmatic
reason. But it is not pragmatic fatalism. He did not see his self-interest being
served in the Front for several possible reasons: (a) the improper use of force
perhaps raised Kiet's anxieties about whether he could trust the Front with his
future; (b) unlike Ton, who was younger, Kiet had established his own family in

a separate household and perhaps felt less restless, more secure, and less willing to take risks; (c) like Ton, he had no prior interest or knowledge of politics outside the village, but, unlike Ton, latent sentiments of nationalism and heroism were not activated. In short, the mix of personal motives and incentives as well as the disincentives and compromised circumstances were not sufficient for Kiet to truly become a member of the PLAF. In a very real sense, he did not accept membership in the Front. He in fact escaped as soon as conditions permitted.

In sum, these contrasting cases suggest several observations. First of all, mobilization did not end with the physical induction of a recruit and his willingness to comply because of force; it ended with his acceptance of membership. Even though peasants were predisposed towards acquiescence, coercion did not guarantee their acceptance of membership. Secondly, culturally defined bounds of legitimate behavior existed and though acting within these bounds might not have been sufficient to cause acceptance of membership, acting outside of them, i.e., acting illegitimately, might deter acceptance. These hypotheses will be explored further in the following sections.

### Persuasion and Control of Village Life

The peasants in the above cases were impressed into service. The more frequent process of mobilization involved the NLF's attempts to control the circumstances of village life. Three cases of voluntary enlistment will now be explored illustrating the process of persuasion in which a central role was played by the Front's manipulation of the village environment.

Le Van Chop was the oldest son in a family of seven who lived, in 1965, in a small village in the province of Vinh Long. His parents were tenant rice farmers and by working long hours, particularly during harvest time, they managed to provide an adequate living off this rich land.

Chop was illiterate. His father had sent him to school when he was young, but, as Chop said, "I preferred guarding buffaloes." When Chop reached his teens, he began to work the land with his parents. Except for the restlessness of boys typical in Vietnam, Chop, at the age of 17, had accepted the peasant situation. When asked how he felt about his personal life, whether he was satisfied or dissatisfied with it, he replied, "I worked on the land with my parents. Some years the harvest was good, other times it was bad; but I had no worries."

Chop's village was "controlled" by the GVN who had organized it into three strategic hamlets and a military post containing about thirty soldiers who were members of the Self-Defense Forces or militia. According to Chop, the villagers liked and respected the GVN soldiers and village officials, one of whom, a hamlet chief, was Chop's uncle. But "control" in Vietnam was seldom absolute. NLF agit-prop teams came to the village at night in mid 1964 and again in 1965 just before Tet.[19] The team consisted of a number of soldiers sufficient to

deter an attack from the nearby GVN post, a group of entertainers, and probably—although Chop makes no mention of him—an agit-prop cadre. On the visit
in January 1965, the Front staged entertainment. Chop enjoyed it a great deal:

> The day the dances were held many [VC] came but I do not know how
> many. They invited the people to come to see the dances. Many families
> were afraid so they did not dare go; others went and enjoyed themselves.
> . . . My younger brothers, sisters and I [went]. My parents were afraid
> to go. We loved the excitement. . . . We liked the dances very much . . .
> We [Chop and some friends] got excited and decided to join right
> there and then.

The interviewer asked: "Did you go to the VC and ask them to accept you?"
Chop replied:

> Some of my friends suggested I join the VC with them because we
> would be able to learn the dances. I left with them that night without
> letting my parents know about it.

It is quite possible that one of Chop's friends was covertly working for the NLF.
In any event, Chop clearly entered the PLAF voluntarily with little coercion
involved in the persuasion process, although the Front did use force to gain
access to the hamlet and to insure an audience for their propaganda.

Ngo Sanh Ngai also lived in a contested area, but in his case the influence of
the Front was more complete. In 1957 in the Thoi Binh district of An Xuyen
province where Ngai's village was located, the forerunners of the NLF were clan-
destinely moving to establish its organization. During this building period, they
primarily relied on maintaining contact with, and as far as possible mobilizing,
ex-Resistance fighters. Many families in Ngai's village had been Resistance
families, and, in particular, Ngai's oldest brother had been one. Ngai's brother
regrouped to the North in 1954 and was still there in 1957 when Ngai began his
involvement:

> When I was 16 years old, I asked for permission to quit school and
> return home to help my parents. I fished in the swamps. In 1957, the
> VC cadres were operating clandestinely. I met one cadre . . . [who
> introduced himself as an ex-Resistance fighter] . . . in the swamps who
> asked me to go and liberate the nation, restore peace and achieve
> national re-unification. At that time, I knew nothing about the GVN
> and readily believed him when he said that my mission of liberating the
> nation would be a glorious one. I was young and enthusiastic and wanted
> to join the movement. . . . I met [the cadres] every day and they edu-
> cated me, so I believed what they said. *The Village Council members
> simply considered me as a high school student.* (Emphasis added)

Ngai did not actually become a full member at that time. There perhaps was no particular need for him then. He served as an "informer" on GVN movements and supplied food to the cadres. In 1958 he became a youth leader and in 1959 a part-time village guerrilla when his village became liberated. At the end of 1961, Ngai was sent away from his home as an infantry fighter in a Local Forces Company. He had become a full-time revolutionary. He joined the Front of his own volition after persuasion. No duress was involved. Easy access, though not completely free, along with the slow pace of events at that time permitted a prolonged recruitment process.

Nguyen Huu Tinh's village in Dinh Tuong province was "contested" in 1961. Of the seven hamlets constituting the village five were controlled by the GVN.[a] Tinh lived in one of the two hamlets where the Front exercised a great deal of influence. In 1960 and 1961, the Front had "executed" ten people in the village "three of them were hamlet chiefs and the remaining seven were agents in the GVN's pay." In Tinh's village no hamlet chief or GVN officials were present. Occasionally GVN troops would come into the village but, by and large, GVN influence was minimal. A semi-overt infrastructure existed and part of their activity was recruitment. Tinh's recruitment was similar to many other youngsters in his hamlet:

> There was one inhabitant of my hamlet who often came to see me and talked about the Front. He was a Front cadre. He explained to me that the Diem government, aided by the Americans, had only exploited the people and rendered them more and more unhappy. The Front was then set up in accordance with the people's wish. Its aim was to drive out the Americans and crush the Diem government so as to bring the people freedom and happiness.

In addition to this personalized, face-to-face persuasion activity, the Front organized a recruitment meeting which most villagers attended. As Tinh recalled it, the cadres "explained to the population where the right path lies and exhorted the youths to join the Front's ranks. It was in the work of this meeting that these youths, myself included, decided to enlist in the Front forces." Tinh was fourteen.

The above cases were selected so that the critical variable of control of village life might be explicated. Control, which connotes the extent to which the Front influenced the immediate environment facing villagers, ranged in these examples from the sporadic presence of agit-prop teams in Le Van Chop's hamlet to the sustained, covert infrastructure in Ngo Sanh Ngai's village to the virtual Front government in Nguyen Huu Tinh's hamlet. The degree of NLF control

---

[a]Villages in southern Vietnam are usually a collection of hamlets which are sufficiently separated that the Front could control some hamlets but not others.

defined the setting for the process of persuasion. In Nguyen Huu Tinh's hamlet, the Front forcibly replaced the GVN and became an effective, indeed legitimate, political system. In joining the PLAF, Tinh was going along with his friends.

In Ngo Sanh Ngai's village, the Front did not replace the GVN but provided an alternative to the traditional system. Ngai was assigned small tasks that both tested and involved him. More importantly, these minor activities gave him a sense of self-importance and self-esteem. Indeed, although Ngai cites political appeals, the key to his motivations is best revealed by his statement, "The Village Council members simply considered me as a high school student." The NLF offered him an opportunity to achieve status, an opportunity unavailable in the traditional way of rising within the village hierarchy.

In both Tinh's and Ngai's case, the act of joining implied not only their acceptance of new opportunities provided by the Front but also their acceptance of the Front's authority. Indeed, Tinh was in the NLF for five years before being captured and Ngaï remained a member for four years until he defected. In contrast, Le Van Chop's entry into the PLAF illustrates a situation in which the Front's control was not sufficient to establish their authority and Chop's willingness to volunteer did not imply an acceptance of authority.

The PLAF's appeal to Chop was the "dances," the breaking away from the boredom of village life as well as from its responsibilities. The night he impulsively left with the recruitment cadres Chop walked in "the mud and cold" to territory where Front troops could stay in the villagers' houses during the day. After a week or so, he was given "a red stock rifle" and taught how to aim at targets (he was not allowed to fire the rifle). For several months Chop's unit visited various villages in the region distributing propaganda leaflets. In April, they engaged in what was apparently an ambush that involved few, if any, casualties. As Chop recollects it, however, "It was a big battle and after that I escaped." Why did Chop leave the PLAF after three months? His own words tell the story:

> I thought if I joined the VC, I would be able to learn to do the dances. They told me that if I joined them they would put me in the entertainment group. But after I joined them they did not let me learn the dances, instead they gave me a gun and told me to fight. I could not endure the hardships so I escaped. . . .

Chop felt deceived. Though he had volunteered, he never accepted the Front's authority and, thus, did not complete the final stage of mobilization, full membership in the PLAF.


### Decision to Participate

Abstracting away from the specifics of the case histories investigated thus far, we can interpret the dynamics of each peasant's decision to participate in terms of a simple model of peasant choice. Vietnamese peasants behaved purposively within psychocultural constraints. The traditional tendency to accept one's fate implied an inertia that the Front could break by a combination of disrupting village life, on the one hand, and offering new opportunities, on the other hand. The peasant weighed his alternatives in terms of his concerns for security and his social aspirations. Unless the Front could convince him that his best interests would be served in the PLAF, the peasant would not fully accept membership. However, the process of persuasion was constrained. The Front could not act illegitimately but had to operate in ways broadly consonant with beliefs of the traditional culture.

### Patterns of Acceptance

These briefly sketched cases suggest a number of hypotheses about the recruitment-acceptance process. To further examine these hypotheses and to gain a comprehensive view of the range of circumstances and motivations involved in peasants' entry into the Front, the interviews were content analyzed.

In almost all the interviews respondents were asked specifically what their reasons for entering the Front were. Except for a few cases in which little information emerged (e.g., for some ex-Viet Minh who regrouped to the North, details of their initial recruitment in the forties had faded from their memory), the answers were relatively rich in detail. These discussions were coded by a team of analysts.[b] Table 4-1 presents the result of the coding—viz., a list of the variety of reasons indicated by the interviewees as *their* reasons for entering the PLAF.

Before turning to a discussion of the content of table 4-1, some methodological notes are in order. Since Chapter 2 reviewed various general sources of bias, it suffices in this chapter to note problems specific to joining. Indeed, that portion of the interviews dealing with the circumstances of joining and with the respondents' self-described motivations was particularly subject to distortion.[c]

---

[b]Our coding of perceived reasons for joining followed a two-stage procedure. In the first stage, the coders were asked to indicate specific reasons cited by the respondent. For example, a coder would transcribe that the "Front had promised land if he joined" or that he had been promised "decreased taxes for his family." In the second stage, the analysts were asked to code which one of a series of more general categories the specific reason might be assigned to. For example, both of the reasons given above would be categorized as "Incentives for Joining." This two-step coding process was followed for two reasons. First, we wanted to be assured of a full spectrum of reasons. It is easy to attain a highly reliable coding by specifying few categories of a gross nature; however, in doing so, the full variety of reasons could be forced into an artificially limited classification. Secondly, insisting upon the specifics provides both a check upon the validity of the taxonomy and a means for attaining reasonably reliable categories by aggregation.

[c]Since Chapter 2 deals with general problems of the validity of the answers, we only will note several problems unique to the issue of the respondent's entry into the Front. There seemed to be a considerable amount of distortion on this subject. In particular, there was a tendency for subjects to emphasize their susceptibility to Front propaganda, to the

Therefore, rather than risk spurious quantitative analysis arising from statistically untrustworthy data, only limited data analysis was undertaken. In particular, the coding was sufficiently valid and reliable in two areas. First of all, the range of circumstances and motives listed in table 4-1 represents a reasonably comprehensive coverage for the sample. In other words, these "reasons" include most of the reasons why peasants entered the PLAF even though the relative importance of each reason cannot be estimated in quantitative terms.[20] Secondly, since in most cases the circumstances of entry (as perceived by the subjects) were probed consistently and intensively, it was possible to categorize a "perceived mode of entry" which will be discussed shortly.

### Coercion and Acceptance of Membership

The first category listed in table 4-1 is that of force. As already detailed, overt force, either actual or explicitly threatened, was often used in PLAF recruitment. Nguyen Van Ton's case represents an example of a captured militia man. A surprising number of ex-GVN people who were captured—or, in the case of local officials, arrested—served in the NLF. Dong Van Kiet's case illustrates kidnapping (which had become more frequent by 1967, the last year covered by this study). Forcible conscription, similar to kidnapping, was sometimes employed in "liberated" areas in those situations where the villagers refused to be drafted. Drafting, even without the usual preparatory agit-prop work, became more frequent in the later years. In some cases, rather than physically forcing a peasant into service, individuals were explicitly coerced by threats of violence. For example, a son would be told his father would be shot or taken away to the jungle (or the mountains) to be "reeducated." In a number of cases of overt coercion, persuasion was not employed and no positive motivations were indi-

---

circumstances, to social pressures, etc. Though some interviewers probed deeply enough so that other appeals became exposed, the probing in many cases appeared to be insufficient with the result that susceptibilities were overemphasized. Such exaggeration could have led to inflated relative frequencies. Similar remarks apply to other areas—for example, to political appeals. That political sentiments often serve more as rationalizations than as strongly motivating forces is both true and significant. However, it obviously makes an important difference as to whether the respondent learned and was motivated by political appeals before he entered the Front or after. Since most PLAF soldiers were indoctrinated after entry, the tendency to cite political motivations was probably accentuated and only sensitive probing could hope to disentangle before and after. Due to these sources of error, coding into general categories proved quantitatively unreliable and, hence, quantitative analysis based on this coding had to be limited. There were very few errors of *omission* at the specific level of transcription. However, since specific statements usually could be interpreted in several ways, the coding of the more general categories became unreliable. By adopting a more complicated coding procedure (e.g., one that recorded patterns within the responses), the difficulty might have been overcome. But such procedures were not justified on two counts: (1) their cost would far exceed their marginal usefulness and (2) the validity of the answers given by the respondents was too questionable to warrant complex coding.

**Table 4–1**
**Reasons for Entering the PLAF**

1. Force
    captured, arrested
    kidnapped, forcible conscription
    threats against self, family, or property
    drafted

2. Social pressures and circumstances
    all his friends were joining
    pressures from family and village
    had to (in the sense of duty), everyone's duty
    felt trapped, couldn't do anything else

3. Emotional appeals
    "taken in" by propaganda
    young and enthusiastic
    hatred

4. Personal susceptibilities
    personal problems (in family, conflict in village, debts)
    dissatisfied with village life

5. Pragmatic Reasons: personal or family rewards/penalties
    i.   rewards
        social advancement, prestige
        honor and glory, would be hero
        promises of land, decreased taxes, special privileges
        education in Front
        could stay near home, easy life
        adventure, entertainment

    ii.  penalties if not join
        would be drafted by ARVN
        would be arrested by GVN
        would be harassed by NLF

6. Arrogance and Injustice
    member of family, or friends, killed by French or ARVN
    abuses to self, family, or village by GVN or ARVN
    corruption, or injustices, of local officials
    lost land
    strategic hamlets

7. Political-social appeals
    nationalistic sentiments
    ideological goals

cated for joining the Front. However, in a number of other interviews involving drafting, capturing, and explicit threats, positive motives were also mentioned.

To explore the variabilities in the use of force, the circumstances of initial access and entry into the Front as revealed in the interviews were coded in a manner similar to that described for the data of table 4-1. Each respondent was classified into one of three groups (plus an unknown category): (1) coerced—those who claimed they were forced into becoming a member of the PLAF and indicated no other reason for entry, (2) mixed coerced and volunteered—those

who indicated an element of coercion was involved but who also cited a willingness to join due to some appeal, and (3) volunteered—those who said they were
not forced into becoming a member of the PLAF. By being conservative toward
the mixed category, this aggregation proved sufficiently reliable. Table 4-2 (Part
A) shows the frequency of responses in the sample for the perceived coercion
involved in entry into the PLAF.

Two methodological reservations concerning this tabulation must be raised
immediately. First of all, since the sample is not statistically representative,
the proportions shown do not accurately estimate the extent of coercion in
recruitment into the PLAF. However, these data can be used to examine conditional relationships that provide indirect evidence on the conditions of
coercion. Once such relationship is displayed by table 4-3 which cross-tabulates
perceived coercion with the control of the soldier's village at the time of his
initial involvement. These figures support the contention that the Front tended
to use overt force in liberated areas more than in contested areas.[21]

A second methodological note of caution concerns the validity of the categorization into coerced, volunteered, and mixed. Though this aggregate classification is probably less subject to bias than the classification of table 4-1, this
measurement still is vulnerable and must be treated with care. A major source of
systematic bias is the presence of both prisoners and defectors (ralliers) in the
sample. By controlling for this bias, several cautious conclusions can be drawn.

Table 4-2 (Part B) compares prisoners and ralliers on the distribution of
perceived coercion involved in recruitment. A systematic measurement error for

**Table 4-2**
**Coercion in Entry**

**A. Perceived Coercion Involved in Entry into the PLAF***

|  | Number | Percentage |
|---|---|---|
| Coerced | 82 | 30.6 |
| Mixed | 71 | 26.5 |
| Volunteered | 115 | 42.9 |
| Total | 268 |  |

**B. Perceived Coercion Involved in Entry Controlled for
Detention Status***

|  | Prisoners | Ralliers |
|---|---|---|
| Coerced | 39.5% | 23.8% |
| Mixed | 27.5% | 24.4% |
| Volunteered | 33.0% | 51.8% |
| No. of Interviews | 102 | 166 |

*Regroupees not included.

Table 4–3

Coercion Involved in Entry as a Function of Village Control

| | Village Control | | | |
| | GVN | Contested | Front | Total |
| Coercion Involved | % | % | % | % |
|---|---|---|---|---|
| Coerced | 18.0 | 27.8 | 40.2 | 29.7 |
| Mixed | 21.3 | 28.7 | 27.6 | 26.6 |
| Volunteered | 60.7 | 43.5 | 32.2 | 43.7 |
| No. of Interviews | 61 | 115 | 87 | 263 |

ralliers might be expected in that defectors might have deliberately claimed they were forced to join the Front. However, the data show that half the ralliers said they volunteered without coercion. Fifty percent is not a reliable estimate of the "true" figure in the PLAF for there are two severe sampling errors. One is the exclusion of deserters who (except for a small number captured in sweeps) were not included; they might have been likely to have been coerced. A second gross bias is the disproportionately high percentage of cadres in the sample; they might have been likely to deny coercion. Even if this estimate were 30 percent too high, it is quite obvious that many of those people who defected, and *thus might be presumed to claim they were forced into joining*, say they joined voluntarily. In short, volunteering did not guarantee that the peasant stayed.

For the sake of avoiding response bias from defectors, just the prisoner sample can be examined to see if, in fact, coercion existed in their recruitment. Included in the sample of prisoners were a number of ex-PLAFs who were similar to defectors in many ways except that they did not defect; this group can be called "Potential Defectors." Since such prisoners might give biased answers on how they joined the PLAF, their influence in the sample was controlled. Based upon discussions in the interviews about the subject of defecting (for example, often respondents were asked directly "Did you think of rallying?"), it was possible to classify prisoners into Potential Defecting Prisoners and other prisoners, who for convenience will be called Hard Core Prisoners. This classification was undoubtedly biased in the direction of overestimating potential defectors. Nonetheless, the distinction is useful for control purposes. Table 4–4 (Part A) presents a cross-tabulation comparing Potential Defecting Prisoners with Hard Core Prisoners for the various types of recruitment. Approximately one quarter of the sample of Hard Core Prisoners said they were coerced into joining. Thus, even among those soldiers *least* likely to distort their answers as to how they entered the Front, a sizable percentage claimed they were coerced.

Again the above conclusion is weak. Yet, these two weak findings suggest that there was a degree of substitution between forcing people to join and persuading them. In other words, as previously argued, even though some soldiers

Table 4-4
Coercion and Detention Status

A. Comparison of Potential Defecting with Hard Core Prisoners on
Perceived Coercion Involved in Entry into PLAF

|  | Hard Core Prisoners | Pot. Def. Prisoners | Total Prisoners |
|---|---|---|---|
| Coerced | 27.0% | 46.2% | 39.2% |
| Mixed | 16.2% | 33.8% | 27.4% |
| Volunteered | 56.8% | 20.0% | 33.4% |
| No. of Interviews | 37 | 65 | 102 |

B. Prisoner Status as a Function of Perceived Coercion Involved in
Entry into PLAF

|  | Coerced | Mixed | Volunteered |
|---|---|---|---|
| Pot. Def. Prisoners | 75.0% | 78.6% | 38.3% |
| Hard Core Prisoners | 25.0% | 21.4% | 61.7% |
| No. of Interviews | 40 | 28 | 34 |

perceived themselves as having been coerced, they accepted membership and became members of the Front.

Table 4-4 (Part B) shows the same cross-tabulation as table 4-4 (Part A), but with the nominal classification of Potential Defecting Prisoners and Hard Core Prisoners as a dependent variable. The data analyzed in this way provides crude evidence of the effect of recruitment. Assuming Potential Defecting Prisoners were less dedicated than Hard Core Prisoners, the cross-tabulation indicates that the manner of recruitment did matter. One-fourth of the soldiers who claimed they were coerced were Hard Core Prisoners whereas over 60 percent of the volunteers were Hard Core. In short, being coerced increased the liklihood of defection. Though this result is statistically significant (using a chi-square test), the figure of 25 percent contains too many potential biases to be trusted as a useful estimate for the PLAF. Nonetheless, it seems clear that coercion was a costly form of recruitment.

Some further significant evidence supporting the above conclusions can be garnered by examining the relative frequency distribution of the length of service of defectors as shown by table 4-5 and illustrated by figure 4-1. A glance at these figures reveals the very different distributions of frequency of length of service for the three categories of recruitment. The median length of service for the coerced is only 7.5 months whereas for the volunteers it is three years. Within the first year over 60 percent of the coerced defectors had defected whereas after two years 60 percent of the volunteers who eventually defected still had not. (These results are significant at the .01 level using a one-way analysis of

Table 4–5
**Frequency Distribution of Length of Service of Defectors, Comparison of Coercion Involved in Recruitment**

| Length of Service (in months) | Coerced % | Mixed % | Volunteered % |
|---|---|---|---|
| 3 or less | 23.1 | 19.0 | 4.8 |
| 4–6 | 15.5 | 4.8 | 5.9 |
| 7–12 | 23.2 | 26.8 | 10.9 |
| 13–24 | 12.7 | 16.8 | 16.6 |
| 25–48 | 18.1 | 21.6 | 22.6 |
| over 48 | 7.4 | 12.0 | 39.2 |
| Total | 100.0 | 100.0 | 100.0 |
| No. of Interviews | 39 | 42 | 85 |
| Median | 7.5 mo. | 12.0 mo. | 36.0 mo. |

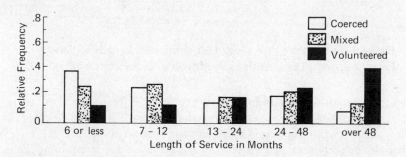

**Figure 4-1.** Histogram of Length of Service of Defectors, Comparison of Coercion Involved in Recruitment.

variance $F$-test.) Since the sample is not representative of all defectors, these figures are not suitable estimates. Nonetheless, these data make clear what is obvious from examining the interviews: many Vietnamese peasants were forced into the PLAF and left as soon as escape was possible.

This gross assertion hardly needs the data displayed to support it. However, the data also reveal a more refined conclusion. Figure 4-2 plots the relative frequency density distribution of the length of service for the different types of recruitment. The curve for the coerced depicts the large proportion who defected as soon as possible. The rate of defection drops rapidly within the first year although maintaining a high level. After a year and a half, the frequency of defecting is somewhat stabilized at a low level. There are two slight modes, one at roughly two years and the other at roughly four years service; however, these may represent sample fluctuations ($n = 39$) and a tendency for the respondent to be somewhat fuzzy about the month he joined. The curve for the volunteered

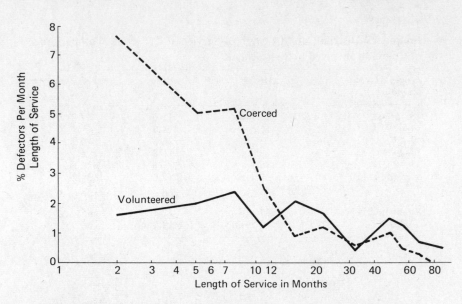

**Figure 4–2.**   Relative Frequency Distribution of Length of Service of Defectors, Comparison of Coercion Involved in Recruitment.

shows the great difference within the first year in defection rate and in the absolute level of defection as compared to the coerced. Thereafter, there are two modes, one at roughly a year and a half and the other at about four years. (It is statistically unlikely that these patterns in the curve are due to sampling fluctuations.) Thus, this curve suggests that, among the volunteered defectors, there were three periods of increased defection: one early one, a middle one, and a late one. Moreover, if people who served less than one year from the sample are excluded, then no significant difference exists between the coerced and the volunteered in terms of their distribution of length of service.

These data support our earlier observations that (a) for some of the coerced the circumstances of their joining may not have affected their career in the Front, (b) entry in the Front was a process and acceptance of membership need not have begun with the moment of entry but perhaps took between three months to a year depending upon the circumstances, and (c) those Vietnamese who were forced in and left as soon as possible, did not complete the recruitment process and never became full members.

### Perceived Reasons for Joining

Mobilization was thus a process whose completion required more than the initial control of the environment by force: positive attractions were essential.

The case histories previously examined suggested a number of different motives and explored their interconnections for each individual. To obtain a more comprehensive view, the range of reasons for joining detailed in table 4–1 will be briefly reviewed. Out of necessity, these perceived (or at least reported) reasons will be discussed one at a time. However, seldom was only one reason cited; the overall pattern was rather of mixed motives and circumstances.

The second category listed in table 4–1, "social pressures and circumstances," though related to force, is clearly a separate matter. The NLF usually employed coercion in a purposive, differentiated manner. By developing agents and an infrastructure (sometimes covert and at other times widely-known though still secret), by selective assassinations, and by repeated visits, the NLF could control the environment of village life and establish their authority to the extent that joining the Front became what was expected of young people. Nguyen Huu Tinh's story illustrated such control. Especially in sympathetic and "liberated" areas the Front could mobilize family and village to pressure eligible peasants. Considering the importance of the collectivity in Vietnamese life, such pressure was difficult to resist without losing face. In a number of cases, "the choice," as Pool observes was "not whether to get involved but merely on which side to do so. Young men [knew] that they [would] be drafted by one side or the other." [22] Many respondents—perhaps more than was justified by the situation—simply said they "had to" join, they had "no other choice." Although many such interviewees seemed to lack positive motivations for entering the Front, a sizable percentage indicated—particularly when probed—other motives (which, however, were not always fulfilled by their service in the Front).

The third category listed, "emotional appeals," represents positive motivations containing nonpragmatic elements. Respondents who indicated they were susceptible to emotionalism acknowledged that they were drawn to the Front but, at the same time, disclaimed responsibility for their action. They were "taken in" by propaganda; the Front was at fault. They were young and enthusiastic so could not be expected to be rational. Hatred was "aroused in their heart" so their mind could not judge correctly. This denial of responsibility for action is acceptable in the culture and, thus, there may have been a tendency on the part of interviewees to magnify the pull of emotionalism. Yet, it would be a mistake to devalue its real importance in the persuasion process. The most effective emotional appeal seemed to have been the arousal of the usually repressed feelings of hatred. Hate was stimulated not simply by the content of Front propaganda but by the combination of content and the manipulation of passions in organized demonstration meetings.[23] Normally repressed emotions when aroused in Vietnamese can indeed cause impulsive behavior, as the preceding chapter suggested.

"Personal susceptibilities," the next listed theme in table 4–1, included personal problems that often involved conflicts in the family or village; the Front offered such respondents an escape from their difficulties. The subcategory of dissatisfaction with village life, listed under personal susceptibilities, was a rather rare complaint (approximately 5 percent of the sample). The usual answer given by Vietnamese peasants to questions about how one felt about village life was a stereotyped reply—"I led a happy life," "People were not dissatisfied," etc. Therefore, the few cases indicating dissatisfactions deserve special note. The basis of their discontent seemed to be with the life in the village—its restrictions, its dullness, its low opportunities for advancement. Such discontentment is usually repressed and, thus, may have been more widely held than the sample showed. Compared to respondents who indicated they were satisfied, the discontented were much more likely to have said they joined for reasons of social advancement and prestige (80 percent of the discontent so indicated). The data also show that a high percentage of the discontented accepted membership in the Front and rose to cadre status.[d]

"Pragmatic reasons" for joining is the next theme listed in table 4-1. Rewards and penalties are both placed in this category for they were often linked together in respondents' stories in that pragmatic weighing of incentives and disincentives illustrated by Nguyen Van Ton's testimony. As observed for that case, though an "objective" analysis of the situation might indicate that Ton was entrapped, he said he joined of his own volition. In some cases, of course, the respondent felt he was entrapped. Le Van Chop's story illustrated deception wherein the respondent learned only after entry that Front promises of rewards could be false. Such complaints sometimes arose for promises of land and special privileges for the family, of staying near home or an easy life, and of adventure. On the other hand, the Front could offer—and, indeed, fulfill—rewards of social advancement and prestige. As the preceding section suggests, the NLF created, in many areas, institutionalized opportunities for rising in a legitimate authority structure. As Pool observes, becoming

> a Viet Cong army officer or tax collector or village or district secretary is an entree into the small rural middle class which also includes the school teacher, the local storekeeper or the government bureaucrat. . . . [o]n the side of what they call the Viet Cong Government (because the Vietnamese do not generally have the Western notion that there is only one legitimate government) they can make a career as professional *can bo* [cadres]. . . . Cadre is recognized as one of the standard professions today.[24]

---

[d]These quantitative assertions draw upon the coding of the categories of table 4.1. Considering the significance of this category, even though its quantitative importance was slight, all of the cases (31) were checked. The numbers indicated in the text should be treated as rough, "ballpark" figures; we frankly do not know whether they overestimate or underestimate the comparable percentages in the PLAF. The discontented will be considered again in Part II when we consider adaptation to Front Life.

Those interviewees who indicated they joined for reasons of social advancement were relatively few but were likely to have accepted membership and risen to cadre status.[e]

The next listed reason for joining is called "arrogance and injustice" and it involves impropriety of behavior on the part of authority. Some interviewees indicated that they or their family had experienced personally some form of maltreatment by French or ARVN troops, GVN officials, or village leaders. (At the time of the war considered here, there was little contact between American troops and villagers.) These abuses took many different forms, but they often left a deep resentment that could be exploited by careful propaganda. For Vietnamese, the objective facts of the incidents weighed less heavily than the impropriety of the act. The stealing of chickens or fruit, an oft mentioned complaint against marauding ARVN troops in the early years, was serious not primarily because of the property involved but because of the sense of violation of home. Higher on the scale of improprieties was an insult, such as a slap, indicating an arrogance of behavior on the part of GVN officials. In contrast, the conduct of NLF cadres was usually exemplary—no cursing, no rudeness, no physical abuse, no lack of respect, no arrogance. The contrast even extended to the use of violence. One peasant tells of witnessing two ARVN soldiers shoot a farmer in his field for target practice. It was not only the death of the farmer which disturbed the peasant but the senselessness of the act. The NLF employed assassination and terror. Yet, it was usually controlled, deliberate, and explicitly "justified" to the villagers (by publicizing the assassinated official's "crimes.") [25] Those few respondents (in our sample) who had been directly and personally victimized by the GVN or the French, e.g., the killing of a member of the family by the ARVN, eventually became highly dedicated members of the PLAF.

Political-social appeals of the Front (the last item listed in table 4–1) were frequently cited in the accounts of entry. In many cases, latent Vietnamese sentiments of nationalism and selflessness were activated and such sentiments legitimized the peasant's decision to join what he perceived to be a proper organization. Legitimation was important. Indeed, it may have been an essential element in the process of accepting membership. Yet, seldom did it alone suffice to cause a peasant to join the PLAF. Of the few cases in which respondents insisted they had joined only for political-social reasons, their discussions so mirrored Front ideological language and thoughts that one could not discern whether this consciousness was present before entry into the PLAF.

---

[e]Those respondents who said they joined for reasons of social advancement were fewer in number than anticipated on the basis of the analysis of Chapter 3. This motive was indicated less frequently than might have been the true case for there is a cultural tendency not to speak of these drives in direct ways. As a consequence, this category was coded unreliably in terms of inter-coder consistency; those coders most familiar with the culture tended to find a concern for status signaled in many indirect ways.

## Conclusion

Douglas Pike is both partially right and profoundly misleading when he observes,

> One of the most persistent questions asked about the NLF follower was "Why did he join?" The implication in the question is that for one or more rational or emotional reasons the individual Vietnamese decided to enlist in the cause, did so, and thus entered as a believer. . . . [A]lmost the reverse was the case. . . . [N]ot motives but circumstances must be considered in understanding the recruitment pattern.[26]

He is right in two ways. First of all, in virtually all cases known to this author, the Front was the active agent; it sought out the peasant, not vice versa. This was true even for those cases in which the individual felt dissatisfied or had a personal grievance. Secondly, the Front did not hesitate to use coercion—that is, to force the circumstances. Without this activity, there would have been no PLAF.

Yet, this recruitment must be placed into the perspective of the Vietnamese peasant culture. The Vietnamese orientation towards action in the *initial* phase of evocation of a decision is passive: there is a marked tendency to wait and see. Therefore, that the Front had to come to the villagers and had to force the circumstances is not surprising. Once the circumstances were manipulated, even by means of overt force, many peasants seized the opportunity—or at least accepted fate—and entered the PLAF. Thus, active recruitment, including coercion to gain access to the villagers, was necessary.

It was not sufficient, however. The data clearly demonstrate that many peasants who "entered" the Front did not remain long enough to be considered members of the revolutionary organization. In short, they did not accept membership. This was likely to be the case for those who perceived their entry as solely due to force but it also held for some who volunteered. Once initial access had been achieved, persuasion had to convince the candidate to accept membership.

Persuasion included coercion in many cases, and numerous peasants remained in the Front because they felt they had to. Nonetheless, it would be a gross mistake to discount the "rational" or "emotional" reasons cited by the soldiers as their reasons for joining. Persuasion had to reassure peasants that their personal security interests were best served in the PLAF. The Front accomplished this both by controlling and changing the reality of village life and by convincing peasants of the changed circumstances. Unless the Front could portray an image of strength and propriety, villagers would be unlikely to accept membership. Once the conditions under which pragmatic fatalism became operative were thus established, the appeals of the PLAF became real and meaningful. Opportunities created by the Front to achieve status in ways analagous to yet replacing the traditional means of rising within a closed, autonomous village hierarchy could be sought. Peasants thus accepted membership and completed the last stage of mobilization into the revolutionary organization.

This analysis of the mobilization of Vietnamese peasants into a mass-based revolutionary organization challenges several preconceptions about revolution. Were peasants who accepted membership "rebelling"? To be sure, grievances existed, but a general sense of oppression did not; ideological and political appeals served as legitimating elements, but not as sufficient motivations; the NLF elite may have suffered from blocked ambitions, but feelings of "relative deprivation" did not activate villagers. Peasants were mobilized by an organization. They acted within the framework of their circumstances and within the constraints of their psychocultural predispositions to improve their security and their future. The effectiveness of mobilization lay not only in what the revolutionary organization said but how it was said and what the organization did. The organization had to train and motivate cadres so they behaved within the culturally prescribed bounds of propriety *and* the organization had in fact to create a new reality for the peasant, a new set of life circumstances, a new institutionalized means for achieving status and security.

The above analysis of the microstructural dynamics of recruitment-acceptance discounts commonly defined elements of revolution to the extent that one can ask whether recruitment into the mass-based organization constituted a revolution. It did not per se. It did constitute mobilization, the sine qua non of revolution. The peasant was placed in a setting that wrenched him away from his traditional circumstances, that embedded him in an environment demanding new responsibilities and obligations, that prepared him for a new role and a new identification. The next essential step in the revolutionary process is the integration of peasants into these new institutions; that is the subject of Part II.

# Part II
# Integration

## Introduction to Part II

For whatever combination of personal fears and ambitions, of political beliefs and acceptance of authority, of being forced and of volunteering that resulted in peasants entering the Front, all new recruits had at least one element in common: they were not, upon entry, committed revolutionaries. Their primary loyalty continued to be to the family; their views of the world still derived from village life; their identity remained that of peasants. Mobilization accelerated the breaking down of these traditional patterns by, as subsequent discussion shows, changing the circumstances of the individual's life. The goal, however, was not simply destruction of tradition, for this would lead only to anomie, disorder, anarchy. The goal was to establish a new order, to integrate individual's into a political organization which commanded obedience and loyalty, which altered the peasant's perceptions, which created a basis for a new identity and role in society. This process of institutionalization is the underlying subject of this section.

Communists possess a vision and a strategem, a theory and a practice, for developing and maintaining a nation-state. It is, as Franz Schurmann suggests with reference to the Chinese Communists, based upon two elements: ideology and organization.[1] In terms of organization, individuals participate in an all encompassing network of hierarchical organizations that are centrally controlled and politically interpenetrated. In terms of motivation, complete obedience is required though not from fear of punishment, at least not in the ideal, but rather from an awareness, a "revolutionary consciousness": in short, obedience is to stem from an ideologically-based commitment. This is theory, of course. The reality deviates from these ideals in critically important ways. But all political systems create myths and possess ideals that fail to be fulfilled in practice. Thus, the fundamental issue is not simply to expose the myth but rather to investigate how, why, and to what extent the political institutions—as they operate in reality—can create the moral consensus, channel the self-interests, and command the compliance and loyalty that integrate individuals into a nation-state.

To examine the above inquiries for the specific case of the PLAF, this study focuses on the individual and examines why, in what ways, and to what extent peasants obeyed the Front. In terms of the analytical conceptions outlined in Chapter 2, we shall focus on the development of patterns of compliance, the

79

establishment of authority relationships, and the integration of individuals into the organizational structure.

The PLAF sought compliance by insisting upon an ideologically-based commitment among its members. The organizational ideology, i.e., the set of norms (demands) constituting commitment, served as the model that the peasant was expected to emulate and the efforts to instill these ideals so permeated Front life that virtually all aspects of organizational dynamics reflected it. Thus, the first phase of the analysis, Chapter 5, characterizes the demands placed on the soldier by describing the norms of commitment in the People's Liberation Armed Forces.

Our initial treatment presents the ideal, i.e., the theory rather than the actuality, of commitment in the Front; what the leaders sought not necessarily what they achieved. There are three reasons for proceeding in this manner. First of all, the Front's efforts to instill commitment were so pervasive that, even though commitment often failed to materialize in the soldiers, these efforts defined the parameters of the situation confronting the peasant when he entered the PLAF. These norms of commitment were given force and meaning on a day-to-day basis by the Front's mechanisms of compliance—the command structure, social system, rewards and sanctions, indoctrination techniques, and organizational milieu; Chapter 6 will describe how these socialization and control mechanisms were designed to operate. The second reason for dealing with the PLAF's model of commitment and its associated ideal mechanisms of compliance is simply that commitment did eventuate in some soldiers. Chapter 7 will analyze why, given the hypothesized Vietnamese personality characteristics of Part I, the Front's socialization techniques might produce commitment. Thirdly, the ideal-type analysis suggested above gives us a base point from which to gauge the success of the Front's socialization efforts.

Chapter 8 examines the reality of life in the Front and finds that soldiers adapted to Front life according to their own motivations and experiences. Within the boundaries set by the PLAF's structure and processes, a mix of various patterns of adaptation, of reasons for compliance, of areas of acceptance of authority coexisted. Since a variety of patterns of adaptation prevailed in the PLAF, Chapter 8 analyzes how successful the Front was in integrating and controlling soldiers with diverse patterns of motivations.

# 5

### Organizational Ideology: Commitment

The PLAF had an explicit doctrine of organizational compliance: it sought, indeed demanded, "voluntary conformity" based upon "ideological commitment."[1] Commitment denotes a pattern of adaptation in which the individual complies with the organization because he has internalized its norms and values to the extent that his self-identity becomes inextricably merged with the organization;[2] this sense of commitment was precisely the Front's objective. In particular, the norms of the PLAF were based upon a conglomerate Marxist-Leninist-Maoist ideology which provided attitudes about political, social, and economic issues as well as prescribing the "correct" way to reason about historical processes underlying them. All soldiers were to learn the doctrine, to be politically "aware," to develop a "revolutionary consciousness." However, the Front's organizational ideology was not limited to abstract political ideas, as this chapter shows.[3] All soldiers were to follow a proper code of behavior regulating relations among cadres (officers) and men, among comrades, and among Front members and villagers. This code, highly moralistic in character, was fully linked to the demand for a revolutionary consciousness in that violation of "proper" behavior was attributed to "incorrect ideological thinking." Commitment then was to be total—encompassing thought and action—and complete—one had to be absolutely "sincere"—and based upon Front ideology. In short, the soldier's self-identity was to be an ideologically committed revolutionary. Then, and only then, would the soldier, as Mao Tse-tung's famous quotation expresses it, be "able to understand completely why he fights and how he must obey."[4]

Commitment was an ideal. In reality, commitment was not fully realized and different patterns of compliance emerged in the PLAF. Yet, this ideal served as a model and, hence, established a range of demands on each soldier; furthermore, as the next chapter documents, much of the organizational structure, processes, and environment stemmed from the Front's efforts to instill and maintain commitment.[5] In short, the concern with ideological commitment constitutes a major defining characteristic of the People's Liberation Armed Forces. Therefore, this chapter will describe the nature and spirit of the Front's norms of commitment.

One method of determining these norms would be to conduct a content analysis of the "theoretical writings" of NLF documents intended for internal indoctrination.[a] Though this technique has considerable merit, it also can be

---

[a]The NLF produced little original theoretical writing. What there was came mostly from the North Vietnamese Communists who in turn used other Communist parties—

misleading for it tends to focus on theoretical doctrine and ignores the complex role that beliefs play in determining the individual's behavior. Ideology affects action insofar as individuals internalize it. Therefore, rather than analyze the specific substance of the Front's ideology, this chapter describes elements of the belief system of peasants who fully internalized the organizational ideology.[6] That is, we shall draw a portrait of a committed Front revolutionary—his definition of himself, his orientation towards authority and action, his perceptions of and sense of trust towards others. To do so as well as to communicate an impression of the spirit of commitment and its sense of totalism,[7] we shall let the words of former revolutionaries speak for themselves: a composite image of a committed soldier will be presented by piecing together verbatim statements, interspersed with interpretive and connective comments, from interviews with former members of the PLAF. The resulting image will not be of a "typical" soldier but of the *ideal* NLF revolutionary whose self-identity is one of commitment. This ideal embodied the norms to which peasants had to adapt.

### Ideal Belief System of Commitment

*Orientation Towards Authority: Obedience*

No refrain was more evident in the testimony of committed soldiers than the spirit of self-sacrifice to the revolutionary cause. For example, the following response of a soldier to a question of why he fought well in combat shows this spirit and dedication:

> To restore the rights and privileges to the people, to restore peace and happiness to the people quickly and seeing that the people were miserable, I was willing to sacrifice my life to put a quick end to their miseries.

The committed were willing to devote their entire life to the revolution. "I made up my mind to fight until I died," said a cadre who had been wounded and taken prisoner while unconscious, "I would have served in the Front until we won, and the Americans had left the country, and the people were protected."

The possibility of death was an ever-present reality for a combat soldier, and, thus, the willingness to die was not an abstraction. Yet, the sacrifice of the body was only one aspect of the required dedication. Commitment implied absolute obedience. According to a captured NLF document used for indoctrination purposes, "The liberation army is a fighting army and therefore must be highly centralized, with inferiors obeying superiors. . . . There must be discipline."[8] Obedience meant accepting any assignment, including terrorism. But

primarily the Chinese—as their source. A large number of documents have been captured in GVN and allied military operations. In addition, a reward was given to people who turned in NLF documents.

obedience meant more than following orders; it involved the sacrifice of one's personal interests, a willingness to "sacrifice unhesitatingly . . . individual interests and bow to the over-all interests of the revolution and the Party."[9] The committed thus felt that personal desires were selfish and wrong:

> How did you feel when you were not promoted as you had expected?
> I was not disappointed at all. The expectation for promotion was only one of my immature thoughts. The promotion depended on the capability of each individual concerned.[b]

The sacrifice of the self became complete only when obedience was, in Mao's phrase, "self-imposed," a feeling that, as a committed soldier stated, "I would never let myself be captured because it was contrary to my virtue."

"Virtue" was a fundamental term in the NLF ideological lexicon of commitment:

> Before being admitted into the Group, I had to make a six-sentence affirmation in front of the national flag: to sacrifice everything to the fatherland, never to surrender to any force of the enemy, to fight with determination unto my last drop of blood, to preserve always the virtues and the behavior of a revolutionary fighter, etc.

Virtue was on a par with self-sacrifice and complete discipline. It extended belief beyond political attitudes and obedience beyond standard military concerns to the internalization of a moralistic code of proper behavior. For instance, one cadre in the PLAF recalled that the indoctrination sessions which occurred almost every day "were tiresome but were useful. They helped clarify our minds and improve our virtues. They helped us overcome all our previous bad habits like swearing and prostitutes." This moral sense of proper behavior was so basic to commitment that it was a criterion for membership to the Party:

> I had proven my progress [in order to be admitted to the Labor Youth Group] in knowing who was the enemy. Those who were lazy or reckless in their duty could never be admitted to the Group, only those who had shown virtue and high spirit in combat and missions.

In addition to the Americans, the GVN, and the landlords, the "enemy" was laziness and recklessness among other soldiers but, more significantly, within oneself. As the soldier exorcised these enemies from himself, he would be virtuous and fit for the Party.

"The Party is just," went the catechism repeated in many interviews, "nothing can be done properly without the leadership of the Party." In so saying, the committed indicated their submission to the leadership of the revolutionary

---

[b] Unidentified quotations are from the interviews with former members of the PLAF.

organization. The willingness to sacrifice for the revolution entailed total obedience to the organization itself. Thus, Gabriel Almond's characterization of the ideal "Communist militant" also applies to the ideal committed member of the PLAF, "The cause to which the Communist is ready to sacrifice everything is the 'revolution,' and the 'party of the revolution.' Since the party is the only vehicle of the revolution, dedication and readiness to sacrifice all for the revolution is synonymous with dedication to the party."[10]

### Interpersonal Relations: Unity

To the elements of commitment thus far sketched—the willingness to sacrifice oneself to the cause and the complete submission of oneself, at all levels of action, thought, and values, to the leadership of the Party—must be added another basic component: how a committed individual perceived himself in relation to others. NLF ideology prescribed the nature of interpersonal relations in terms of the concept of unity.

"There must be unity," declared a Front indoctrination document, "between cadres and men, between army and people. . . ."[11] The notion of unity in the Front reflected many of those themes that characterized the traditional ideal of family and community relationships in Vietnamese culture. For example, unity implied *equality* among members of the PLAF, in part through the exercise of "democratic centralism" in the command structure:

> I was cheered up only by the freedom that was everywhere. No one
> could oppress me. No one could use his high position to look down on
> me because I would expose his attitude to the community. We had a
> sentence that read, "the community rules, the individual leads." The
> leader should gather all the community and expose his decision. Then
> everybody, regardless of his position, would contribute his ideas. The
> best idea would be selected by the community.

Unity also implied *harmony* with the people, as one soldier indicated in responding to a question about what he liked in the NLF, "the Front makes people of different religious and different social classes live together happily, no conflicts or misunderstandings, no unemployment." By the practice of carrying off its dead from the battlefields, the Front demonstrated a component of unity referred to as *mutual love* in the following remarks of a cadre, "When the fighters are living, they fight with us, when they die, they should be brought back and buried in an appropriate manner. This is mutual love in the VC ranks." Moreover, mutual love was not limited to relations between soldiers of equivalent rank. There was an ideal of officers being unified with their soldiers which Ho Chi Minh articulated in a speech to his troops, "Divisional commanders down to group leaders must share joy and hardships with the soldiers, take care of, help, and treat each other like blood brothers."[12]

Analogous to the ideal of family and friendship relationships in Vietnamese society, unity in the Front implied total trust. When asked whether they had confidence in their cadres, the committed invariably said they had "complete trust" in their leaders. In the following passage from an interview with a former member of the PLAF, we see that the ideal revolutionary trusted his immediate cadre not primarily because of the cadre's personal characteristics and behavior but because the cadre was chosen by the revolutionary organization in which the committed had complete faith:

> Do you think the right persons in your unit were selected for promotion?
>   I think they deserved to be promoted because they were not afraid of difficulties or danger during combat, and they strictly observed the rules and regulations. It is because they were outstanding elements that they were promoted to cadre positions, if they hadn't been good, how could they have been chosen?
> Did you have confidence in the new cadres who had been assigned to your unit from somewhere else?
>   Only the company cadres were transferred and replaced by new cadres. I certainly had confidence in them because if they were cadres, it meant they were capable people.
> Do you think Nguyen Huu Tho is the right person to lead the Front?
>   I was way down in the hierarchy of the Front, so of course I was confident that he was the right person to lead me. If all the high echelons in the Front were confident in him, it is only natural that I was confident in his leadership.

The granting of such total trust to the revolutionary organization constituted the unlimited acceptance of authority necessary to "self-imposed" obedience.

### Orientation Towards Action: Politization

Thus, the components of ideal unity in the Front were based upon equality, harmony, and mutual love among the soldiers and total trust of men for cadre and for the organization itself. In addition to these perceptions and sentiments, the revolutionary's orientation towards outside forces, history, himself, and fate also defined his identity. The committed spoke in politicized terms with a basic orientation that was highly active.

The committed felt omnipotent, and enthusiastically so:

> How did your comrades react when they learned of the bombings?
>   Nobody said anything. I myself wished that the Americans would bomb the North more extensively and land troops there . . .
> The United States is a powerful country. Do you think it will sit back and allow the North to crush its forces so easily?

> . . . There are two camps in the world: the socialist camp and the capi-
> talist camp. So, if the GVN and the Americans use force to attack the
> North, the North will use its strength to counter-attack. And this
> means the Resistance will become general. We'll be fighting both in
> the North and in the South, and we will thus be able to solve the
> problem more speedily. The two regions will protect each other, and
> if the North is annihilated by the capitalist bloc, the socialist bloc will
> be threatened, Red China most of all. For this reason, the socialist
> bloc will not allow the North to be taken over.

However, the feeling of omnipotence did not come primarily from reliance on great powers but more from complete confidence in the forces of history. This confidence was stated simply, and forcibly, by a revolutionary, "The revolution comes from the people and will succeed."

Inevitable as victory might be, the committed believed it would not come without determined effort. According to Ho, "We must be determined to fight, to endure hardships and difficulties, to overcome them, and be determined to implement the policies of the Central Committee and the Government. In other words, in our behavior, mind, deeds, and fighting, in everything big or small—we must be determined to win success."[13] The ideal revolutionary felt, "The Front will win. It will not win with weapons, but it will win with morale and hatred for Americans." In short, motivation not weapons was the key to victory.

The revolutionary believed he could not be properly motivated, i.e., have high morale and fighting spirit, unless he understood *why* he fought; to understand, the soldier studied doctrines sent down from the "higher echelons" that explained the "correct" position.[14] As a common slogan said, "know your enemies, know yourself—one hundred battles, one hundred victories." Soldiers who did not "know" the enemy had "ideological difficulties" that could only be overcome by learning the "correct" attitudes and thus gaining an inner determination:

> What do you think would happen if three American divisions were sent
> to the delta?
>> The fighters have been in the delta and never encountered the Ameri-
>> can troops. They don't know the American tactics. At first they
>> would have *ideological difficulty*. But this would be overcome.
> How would these difficulties be overcome?
>> By our resolution. We would have stronger determination in all our
>> activities. It has been said that "thoughts are the father of all our
>> activities."

The significance of the belief that resolution could overcome outside forces must be viewed in the perspective of a traditional society in which peasants tend to resign themselves to fate. In saying, as one committed soldier did, that, "out-

side difficulties could be overcome by inner determination," the ideal revolutionary revealed an orientation towards action distinct from Vietnamese peasant
characteristics. Rather than allowing external forces to define the situation, the
revolutionary believed faith could master fate:

> (Villagers who did not join the Front) these villagers were afraid of gun-
> fire. I think everyone is frightened of the war. I am frightened of the
> war myself. . . . But that didn't mean that I wanted to retreat. I would
> fight with whatever I had till I got killed. . . . I couldn't surrender or
> resign myself to fate. I had to fight back or my country would be lost.
> I didn't know what the outcome of the war would be. But I always
> believed that the revolution would be successful. When you do some-
> thing, you have to believe in the thing that you do, you have to believe
> that what you do will be beneficial.

## Summary

This discussion was intended to portray an image of the ideal NLF revolutionary—his politization, enthusiasm, confidence, zealotry, rationality, fervor,
love, hate. Even though the ideological content was simple, the committed
soldier spoke in the language of a totalistic ideology and insofar as he internalized
the ideology, he thought and acted as a revolutionary.[15] Since the Front
sought to instill commitment, the elements composing the ideology served as
organizational norms that soldiers were expected to emulate. The analysis in
succeeding chapters will investigate the role played by these norms in socialization and examine the extent to which these ideal characteristics were internalized.
For the sake of summary, the norms of commitment will be organized around
the categories unity, obedience, and politization: unity suggests solidarity with
comrades and total trust in the cadres and the organization, obedience implies
absolute devotion to the cause, the spirit of self-sacrifice, and complete submission to the Party; politization connotes "ideologized" beliefs and thoughts and a
sense of power over others, over fate, and over oneself.

The nature of commitment in the Front suggests several observations which
foreshadow subsequent analysis. The complete revolutionary would appear to
have an identity quite different from that of the peasant in the village setting.
Critical dimensions of the Vietnamese modal personality would had to have been
transformed: rather than acceptance of nature, there is mastery over fate; rather
than denial of emotion, there is hate, enthusiasm, zealotry; rather than political
apathy, there is politization; rather than self-interest, there is self-sacrifice;
rather than devotion to the family, there is commitment to the organization.
Analyzing the dynamics of this transformation—how, why, and to what extent it
occurred—occupies much of the next three chapters. Yet, another strain also
emerges from these norms. There was a marked consonance of some revolution-

ary ideals with Vietnamese primary beliefs and values: unity contained over-tones of familial relationships; obedience suggested filial piety; themes of proper behavior, virtue, equality, and solidarity all had their counterparts in the traditional psychoculture. The tension between change and continuity is an inherent dilemma of revolutions; upon its resolution rests the establishment and maintenance of legitimate institutions. The way the NLF dealt with the dilemma and the way it became settled in the reality of this revolutionary organization will be a recurrent theme as the analysis unfolds.

# 6

## The Formal Organizational Structure, Processes, and Environment

The PLAF's doctrine insisted upon revolutionary commitment to insure compliance. Yet, new recruits were still peasants possessing neither revolutionary commitment nor any deep sense of loyalty towards the Front. From the standpoint of the NLF, they were raw material that had to be molded. The PLAF expended considerable internal resources in its attempt to imbue its members with the proper sense of revolutionary commitment. Indeed, it would hardly be stretching matters too far to argue that the nature of the organizational structure from its authority system to its prescribed group social structure, from its indoctrination techniques to its rewards, from its interpenetrating political and military command apparatus to its discipline and informant system hinged on putting this "theory" into "practice."[1]

This chapter describes the formal structure, processes, and environment of the PLAF. For the moment, the concern will be with the design of the organization—the ideal, not necessarily the actuality. Detailing the formal characteristics of the organization is a first step in understanding the forces impinging upon the soldier. Insofar as these forces were sustained over time, they could induce a regularized set of demand-response behavior, i.e., a pattern of adaptation, characteristic of the soldier. In short, the formal structure, processes, and environment can be analyzed as socializing agencies—the approach taken in the present chapter—regardless of whether commitment or, in fact, other forms of compliance were instilled (an issue dealt with by Chapter 8).

The formal organizational structure served functions other than socialization, of course. Subsequent chapters will show that a characteristic of the PLAF was the extraordinary extent to which the structure set the context and established the parameters within which all behaviors occurred. Thus, the detailed description presented in this chapter also lays the foundation for considering the organizational structure as a mechanism of control and integration.

### Organizational Structure

The following statement, quoted by Pike from a captured NLF indoctrination document, outlines the primary organizational principles of the PLAF:

1. Organization must conform to political lines . . .
2. The liberation army is a fighting army and therefore must be highly

89

centralized, with inferiors obeying superiors. . . . There must be
discipline. . . .
3. The army's political tasks are fundamental: There must be unity
   between cadres and men, between army and people. . . .[2]

These principles—politization, obedience, and unity—were examined in the last
chapter in terms of norms; this chapter describes their implementation in the
organizational structure. It will become apparent that the organizational ideology
and the formal structure meshed.

### Command Structure

The first organizational principle deals with the political nature of the PLAF.
The People's Liberation Armed Force was an integral part of the overall National
Liberation Front organization. Although its overt combat functions and, to a
lesser extent, the particularities of its military structure distinguished the PLAF
from other divisions of the Front, it clearly was an instrumentality of the
centralized NLF command.[3] In the sense of overall operation, the Army was
politically controlled. More significantly, the PLAF was politicized down to the
lowest level of organizational functioning, the individual soldier.
    The PLAF had a command system of parallel military and political struc-
tures. At each level of command within the military hierarchy down through the
Company and Platoon level, there was a political officer (leader, commander, or
commisar) who served functions distinct from those of a parallel military
commander. The former was responsible to a different command system even
though the latter frequently had a higher designation (for example, the military
officer might be a Company Commander whereas the political officer might be
an Assistant Company Commander).[a] Rank-and-file soldiers as well as officers
understood these distinctions.
    The basis for the political commissar's autonomy was his role in the Party
structure which intermeshed with the military command system. The structure
of the People's Revolutionary party was typical of Communist parties:[4] a
hierarchical command structure headed by a Central Committee; various sub-
echelons each in turn headed by a committee that was integrated by having
vertically overlapping memberships, the lowest unit in the hierarchy being a cell
of party members.[5] The political commissars were Party members, sat on a
Party committee at and above their own echelon, and received orders from the
Party command system. They were responsible for indoctrination and criticism

---

[a]Designated ranks in the formal sense did not exist; instead officers were referred to in
terms of their functions. This must be understood as symbolic of a doctrine of egalitarianism
in the Front. The highly status conscious Vietnamese both appreciated this symbolism and
acted according to the realities of status differentiation.

Table 6-1
Status in the Military Structure and in the Party

| Party Status | Military Rank | | | |
| | Non-Cadre | Low-Cadre | Mid-Cadre | Total |
| --- | --- | --- | --- | --- |
| | % | % | % | % |
| Not in Party | 89.9 | 62.5 | 22.0 | 66.9 |
| Prospective Member | 5.8 | 18.7 | 7.7 | 8.7 |
| Party Member | 4.2 | 18.7 | 70.3 | 24.4 |
| No. of Interviews | 189 | 64 | 91 | 344 |

Chi-square = 162.913 with 4 $d.f.$ (significant at .000 level).
Gamma = .835.

and self-criticism sessions. Moreover, they served a surveillance function of checking the conformity and political awareness of the military leaders and the men in their unit. They also had responsibilities for dealing with complaints of Party members and for recommending promotions to Party membership.

Although this dual system of command occasionally seemed to be a source of conflict, the structures were intermeshed since cadres were almost always Party members, as table 6-1 indicates. This table compares rank in the military structure to status in the Party for the sample of interviewees (including both ralliers and prisoners). Party status is grossly categorized into three levels: full Party membership, Prospective Party membership,[6] and nonmembership. Table 6-1 classifies status in the military hierarchy into three levels: the non-cadre, low-level cadre, and middle-level cadre. For the purposes of coding, low-level cadre corresponds to the equivalent ranks of assistant squad leader and squad leader, whereas middle-level cadre include assistant platoon leader to the highest ranks in the sample.[b] The table suggests how closely related the two status systems were: for members of the sample, 70 percent of those who were middle-level cadres were Party members whereas 90 percent of the non-cadres were neither Party members nor Prospective Party members. This relationship probably held, at least approximately, in the PLAF for the time period covered by this study.[c]

---

[b]The sample does not contain any very high ranking officers, as Chapter 2 noted. The coding of Party membership is the RAND coding. The inter-coder reliabilities are 90–96 percent. Both codings represent the status of the soldier when he left the Front. Though a finer classification of rank would have been desirable, several difficulties prevented this. For example, the PLAF used functions instead of formal rank designations. Thus, a platoon leader of a reconnaissance unit had more status than a platoon leader of a training camp. Moreover, Main Force designations did not always carry the same status as Local Force designations. We were able to circumvent these difficulties by the gross classification described above.

[c]The percentage of middle-level cadres in the sample is higher than was the case in the PLAF. However, though the marginal percentages in table 6-1 most emphatically can *not*

Table 6–2

**Status in the Military Structure and in the Party, Comparison of Prisoners and Defectors**

A. Prisoners Only

|  | Military Rank | | | |
|---|---|---|---|---|
|  | Non-Cadre | Low-Cadre | Mid-Cadre | Total |
| Party Status | % | % | % | % |
| Not in Party | 92.5 | 87.5 | 12.9 | 73.3 |
| Prospective Member | 6.2 | 4.2 | 6.5 | 5.9 |
| Party Member | 1.2 | 8.3 | 80.6 | 20.7 |
| No. of Interviews | 80 | 24 | 31 | 135 |

Chi-square = 90.326 with 4 *d.f.* (significant at .000 level).
Gamma = .892.

B. Defectors Only

|  | Military Rank | | | |
|---|---|---|---|---|
|  | Non-Cadre | Low-Cadre | Mid-Cadre | Total |
| Party Status | % | % | % | % |
| Not in Party | 87.6 | 47.5 | 26.7 | 62.0 |
| Prospective Member | 5.7 | 27.5 | 8.3 | 10.7 |
| Party Member | 6.7 | 25.0 | 65.0 | 27.3 |
| No. of Interviews | 105 | 40 | 60 | 205 |

Chi-square = 85.497 with 4 *d.f.* (significant at .000 level).
Gamma = .776.

Some further checks on the reliability of the relationship shown in the table is worthwhile. Although some interviewees may have lied about their Party status or about their rank, this source of measurement error does not seem significant. However, since the total sample contains both prisoners and defectors, the possibility of bias introduced by the defector subsample needs to be examined. It is possible that a discrepancy between status in the Party and in the military ranks caused the defection of some PLAFs. Insofar as this conjecture holds, the total sample would underestimate the closeness of the two structures. To guard against this source of error, the subsamples of prisoners and defectors were examined separately with the results shown by table 6-2. The prisoner

be taken as representative of the actual proportions in the PLAF, the conditional relationships cited above are less subject to sampling bias. The statistical strength of this relationship, taking into account the sample size and assuming that these categories constitute ordinal measurements, is indicated by a gamma statistic of .835.

sample, which may provide a more reliable estimate of the state of affairs in the PLAF, shows an even stronger intertwining between the military ranks and Party status: 80 percent of the middle-level cadre were Party members whereas over 90 percent of non-cadres did not belong to the Party (the gamma statistic is .89[7]). An examination of the defector sample relationships shown in table 6–2 (Part B) indicates a weaker relationship, although still a strong one. Among defectors there is a greater divergence between rank and Party status, particularly due to some higher ranking people who were not members of the Party. The obvious implication is that this discrepancy may result in defection, a point investigated in detail in Part III.

The interpenetration of the Party and the military structures was especially significant because selection to the Party was based upon one's progress towards, and prospects for, becoming committed. To quote from a former cadre:

> The admission into the rank of the Party members was based upon
> three criteria: virtue, steadfastness and achievement. The Party
> member should hold steady under every hardship. Therefore he should
> be thoroughly indoctrinated.

The soldier either became a Party member or was continuously in contact on a face-to-face basis with Party members. In particular, his primary group was likely to contain Party members which was one of the means used to insure politization of the group itself.

### Primary Groups

The hierarchical command structure of any army tends to embed its primary groups—i.e., the small, face-to-face social group in which one's primary activities take place [8]—in the organizational structure;[9] in the PLAF, this formal integration held to an extreme extent. The primary group was anchored in the PLAF chain of command by means of the three-man cell. Each soldier belonged to a cell and all his activities, both in combat and in everyday living, took place in the context of the cell in accordance with the prescribed doctrine, the principle of "shared responsibility in fighting and performance." "Unity" in the Front started at this basic level, as the following official description from a Radio Liberation broadcast (quoted by Pike) makes clear:

> [Cell members must] build their cell into a three-member collective,
> glue-welded on the basis of comradeship and mutual life and assistance,
> stemming from a thorough revolutionary spirit, a noble class spirit, and
> good revolutionary virtues. To this end each cell member must tell his
> colleagues facts about his private life. . . . They must consider their
> [cell] and their [cell members] as brothers. . . .[10]

The idea of group solidarity was thus an explicit norm demanded by the organization, but it had to "stem from a thorough revolutionary spirit," i.e., from
ideological commitment.

   Though the cell was a fundamental building block for primary group
relationships, the outer boundaries of the primary group were squads (or even, in
some units, platoons).[d] The cell was integrated into a squad usually consisting
of three cells. A great deal of a soldier's political activities—including formal
indoctrination meetings, criticism and self-criticism sessions, and "cultural" activities—took place in group meetings consisting of the squad. The organization
delineated the boundaries of primary relations by imposing restrictions on
activities outside of one's squad and by granting awards to, and leveling punishments against, squads as a whole.

   The organizational principles of politization, unity, and obedience came
together in the ideal of "democratic centralism," viz., "the community decides,
the individual leads." This principle was employed, as far as doctrine had it, at all
levels of command. The practice at the squad level began with a policy directive
from the next higher level. (The squad leader usually "participated" in policy
discussions at the platoon level.) The directive had, of course, to be followed.
However, insofar as latitude existed in execution, free discussions among group
members occurred. Ideally, these discussions culminated in concrete policy
which everyone obeyed. The squad leader (the cadre) guided the discussion along
"correct" lines. That is, the basis of the decision was to be derived from ideology.

### Cadre

   "Unity with the cadre" suggests how fundamental the cadre was in the ideal
design of the organizational structure. The cadre was selected according to two
criteria: ideological commitment and leadership ability. Leadership ability
implied that one had passed through a testing period and had shown "excellent
accomplishment and good execution of orders." Moreover, the potential cadre
had to show he could win the respect of his comrades, as the following remarks
of a former cadre indicates:

> Before you can become a [cadre], you have to show that you are wor-
> thy of the honor. When you are in your unit, you have to set good
> examples for others to follow. You have to be first in your work, first
> to volunteer for a mission and first to finish it. You have to treat the
> people under your charge in such a way that when you leave them, they
> will miss you. You have to treat the people under your charge in such

---

[d]This variability reflects the different forces in the PLAF. The cell was probably the
most central in the more autonomous operations of guerrillas. Activity at the platoon level
was perhaps greatest among combat units of the Main Forces.

a way that they respect and trust you. . . . A person who treats the
people badly so that they don't dare complain about him in front of
him but do so behind his back, will never be accepted.

The cadre ideally advanced politization and commitment in the primary
group in two critical ways. According to research on group dynamics, an
individual may exercise considerable influence in a group even if he does not have
organizational designated authority. One term used to describe such exercise of
leadership is "informal leader."[11] In the Front, the principle of "unity with
cadres" implied the merging of the informal leader with the formal leader in the
person of the cadre, thus checking the formation of an autonomous informal
group; it implied that the cadre demonstrated "talent" in all three of the areas
that group theorists believe define leadership ability, viz., "activity," "task
ability," and "likability."[12]

The second way cadre were to advance commitment in the primary group
was by "setting good examples," i.e., providing a model of proper behavior.
In the next chapter this aspect will receive further analysis. At this juncture, the
important point is that since the cadre (frequently a Party member) was selected
because of his high commitment, the model he presented for emulation was—in
the ideal—one of ideological commitment.

### Rewards and Punishments

The system of sanctions was another interrelated agency of socialization in
the PLAF. To a large extent, rewards were granted for signs of progress towards
ideological commitment and punishments were administered for violations
of commitment. The totalistic nature of commitment implied that all behavior
was interpreted by the PLAF as a reflection of ideology. "Thoughts are the
father of all our activities" was one of the slogans the PLAFs committed to memory. To violate discipline is to do wrong. Not doing one's job, for example,
could cause accusations of being lazy: it revealed a lack of virtue, a sign of political weakness, of low revolutionary spirit, of selfishness, of insincerity, of lack
of faith in the Party, of the need for reeducation.

A large variety of specific rewards were employed. Commendations were
awarded to both units and individuals. Alexander George suggests for the Chinese
Communist Army, where a similar system of awards was employed, that this
system permitted "a very wide distribution of decorations while retaining . . . a
basis for competition and status differentiation."[13] The most important
rewards, however, were promotion in the military ranks and especially advancement in the Party. Party membership was considered a high honor by both
the organization and the soldiers.

Discipline was strict and was most often invoked for violations of the organizational norms. However, punishments involving physical force were rare, if not

prohibited. Criticism in criticism-sessions or in larger meetings was the frequent penalty inflicted. Such criticism involved public shaming, which in the Vietnamese context can be quite severe, as the next chapter discusses. Another punishment was "reeducation," which, by its very terminology, suggests violations were attributed to a deficiency in ideological training. For cadres and Party members discipline and penalties were more severe than for non-cadres, ranging from official reprimands to demotions to expulsion. In theory, these penalties could be reversed if the soldier proved himself reformed.

The various agencies of socialization thus far discussed—the organizational structure and its politization including the interpenetration of political and military status system, the primary group and the extent to which it was embedded in the organizational structure, and the sanction system—defined the environment in which specific indoctrination training, programs, and techniques took place. Now PLAF indoctrination designed to lead towards commitment can be examined in more detail.

### Indoctrination and Organizational Environment

One connotation in English of the word "indoctrination" suggests forcible teaching of alien principles. Though some of the methods used by the PLAF involved elements of "coercive persuasion," the ideal spirit of indoctrination in the PLAF was one of education.[14] The following quotation from Ho Chi Minh indicates the "correct" attitude:

> To overcome all difficulties . . . , the most important question for our army this year is . . . to carry out the political remolding campaign, to raise higher the political consciousness of the whole army, . . . and to bring the political and ideological level of the army nearer to the demands of the revolutionary task. . . . In carrying out the ideological remolding, we must firmly stick to the principle of educating and raising the proletarian ideas, overcoming wrong ideas, highlighting the good points, and correcting the weak points by patiently educating, convincing, and promoting the self-consciousness of everyone.[15]

In theory, the soldier was not only to learn but also to understand. However, the process of education was pervasive with the ultimate objective being complete "milieu control."[16]

### Basic Training

Training and indoctrination occurred in an initial intensive period and thereafter on a regular and a continuous basis. Most recruits went through an initial period consisting of military and political training sessions, day-to-day routine activities, and special activities. This period was analagous to basic training in most armies with the critical exception of the intensive political indoctrination, called "study sessions." These sessions taught the history, the nature, and the mythology of the revolution from the NLF's ideological perspective. The specific content of the sessions, which varied, was not as important as the methods of education employed. Simple slogans—frequently from the writings of Mao Tse-tung and Vo Nguyen Giap—were emphasized and constantly repeated following rote learning techniques. Often, the political cadre, who conducted these group study sessions, used the device of free questioning from the students. Questions would be solicited, and indeed expected, and the recruits' answers would be in terms of the slogans—that is, the "correct" answers. The preceding chapter exhibited some of these stock phrases. The PLAF had to learn these slogans and employ them in group meetings. In short, the soldier was taught an ideological language and was expected to use it.[17]

Significantly these slogans were not limited to political topics. Or to put the point into the perspective of the Front, education did not recognize a boundary between what was, and was not, political—for all was political. As previously discussed, a great deal of emphasis was placed upon conforming to a code of proper behavior in interpersonal relations—towards comrades, cadre, and the people. This code, highly moralistic and ascetic, stressing courtesy and control over oneself, was justified in political terms. And this too was part of the language.

The thoroughness of PLAF education in the initial training period—its duration, the balance between military and political training, its execution—varied greatly according to the training personnel, military exigencies, the designated assignment of the recruit, and the stage of the war in which the recruit entered. In the early years—from 1959 to 1963—training was prolonged and emphasized political indoctrination. In later years when the Front had instituted a draft and relied heavily on recruitment by coercive means and when the pace of the military aspects of the war had accelerated, initial training was more erratic and less political.

## Career Training and Group Sessions

Indoctrination continued after basic training. For example, shifts in assignments probably played an important role in indoctrination, particularly an assignment to an agit-prop team [18] where one had the job of educating and persuading villagers. In purely cognitive terms, teaching others can be an effective device for convincing oneself. But in addition an important cognitive spill-over effect could occur: the individual could become, in Almond's phrase, a "power tactician."[19] This theme will be considered further in the next chapter.

Additional indoctrination occurred with career advancement and was important not only because it reinforced previously learned values, but also because the individual was selected out from the rank-and-file—a significant symbol of status. With this new status, new and more important information was learned. This was particularly the case with admission into the Party, where the individual was exposed to more theoretical ideology and to the "esoteric" doctrine.[20]

In addition to career related training, indoctrination was conducted on an episodic basis, often by the company political officer. Meetings occurred when a change in doctrine was being promulgated or when morale was felt to be low, particularly after a battlefield defeat. Common practice also called for indoctrination sessions—akin to pep talks with a strong element of political exhortation—prior to battle. Partly for disciplinary reasons but also as part of recuperation and revitalization, "reeducation" and "reorientation" stressing indoctrination themes was conducted for entire units in safe areas away from combat zones.

Whereas initial and periodic indoctrination were significant, particularly in providing a consistent language and image throughout the NLF, perhaps the most crucial aspect of indoctrination occurred on a continuing basis. A former cadre recalled,

> From the spiritual point of view, we had to work all day. Any leisure
> time was spent in indoctrination sessions. The sessions usually began
> at 7 P.M. Saigon time; everybody exchanged views on the work done
> during the day, recalling the accomplishments as well as the defects in
> order to learn how to improve future work. The sessions lasted about
> an hour followed by collective amusement sessions, i.e., songs and
> music to make us think less about our families.

These general discussion (*sinh hoat*) sessions were held in group meetings often at the platoon level. Mutual and self-criticism sessions (*kiem thao*[e]), conducted on a continuing basis usually at the squad and cell level, formed a critical aspect of indoctrination. In contrast to the indoctrination meetings, criticism sessions were highly individualized involving each soldier in examining his own behavior as well as those of his comrades. Active participation was compulsory.

### Milieu Control

Monopolization of information was also a central aspect of indoctrination, although complete monopolization was not achieved in practice. To attain

---

[e]Kiem thao is the phrase used by Pike and others to refer to these criticism and self-criticism sessions. Actually, kiem thao in Communist usage refers only to criticism sessions. The NLF uses "pha binh va tu phe binh" to refer to criticism and self-criticism. My thanks to Carl Thayer for pointing this out to me.

uniformity and orthodoxy, the "correct" Party line was formulated by agencies of the Central Committee and disseminated to cadres, usually Political Officers, by means of directives, broadcasts from Radio Liberation and Radio Hanoi, clandestine newspapers, pamphlets, and special meetings. In turn, soldiers were informed by cadres in the context of group sessions, usually at the squad or cell level, where face-to-face communication is effective. The rank-and-file soldier also had limited access to authorized newspapers, leaflets, and booklets, and occasionally to radio broadcasts. These news sources were deliberately designed for internal propaganda purposes. Military news for the soldier spoke only of victories never of defeats, greatly exaggerated enemy losses while minimizing Front losses, and stressed heroic deeds of the common soldier and of combat units.

In addition to these direct "news" sources, "cultural activities," e.g., meetings of group singing and entertainment in the form of plays, storytelling, dances, and songs, were held frequently. These activities, as with the news, were carefully designed for indoctrination purposes. Directives to cadres make this point clear: "songs, music, and dances must be used in accordance with our policies, and only correct songs should be used."[21]

Not only was information designed, coordinated, and controlled, alternative sources of communication were prohibited, which is essential if monopolization were to be meaningful. Thus, listening to Radio Saigon or picking up airdropped leaflets from the GVN would subject a soldier, and especially a cadre, to criticism and disciplinary measures. Attempts also were made to prevent soldiers from hearing ARVN loudspeaker calls for defection. A primary source of information in peasant society is by rumor and the PLAF attempted to control rumor in two basic ways: (1) fraternization with villagers was restricted, except in liberated areas and (2) discussions among soldiers, which were generally confined to members of a unit, had to avoid certain taboo areas. These restrictions were enforced by the surveillance principle that soldiers, particularly Party members, should report indications of low morale, improper behavior, etc. Such reports would subject the erring soldier to criticism or even public reprimand.

## Summary

Thus, the Front expended considerable effort in the socialization of the soldier. This attempt to achieve compliance by ideological commitment involved much of the activities of the soldier and encompassed all aspects of his life in the PLAF. The command structure, the imposed and politicized primary group, the system of sanctions, and the indoctrination techniques all combined to fully emerse the soldier in an ideological environment, a controlled milieu. The soldier was embedded in an imposed primary group whose leader, the cadre, was in turn embedded in a highly centralized, hierarchical command system; the control system penetrated down to the lowest rank-and-file soldier; there was little autonomy for soldier, primary group, or cadre. Though subsequent chapters will show that deviations from this formal design existed, it was within this context that demands were placed on the soldier to which he had to adapt.

Since the last two chapters describing the ideology and structure of the Front were intended to record the situation facing the soldier, we avoided interpretive comments. Nonetheless, some observations suggest themselves. First of all, the organizational ideology and structure reinforced each other to an extraordinary extent: the ideological concerns of unity, obedience, and politization were complemented by such structural elements as the embedded primary group, democratic centralism, and a controlled milieu. Secondly, the structure (as well as the ideology) constituted a new set of life circumstances for the peasant. Such Front techniques as the criticism and self-criticism sessions were not within the cultural experience of Vietnamese. On the other hand, many elements of the PLAF's structure had traditional counterparts, e.g., reliance on the group and the mode of learning. As with the norms of commitment, the formal structure of the revolutionary organization combined change with continuity.

# 7

## The Development of Commitment

How does revolutionary commitment develop? The preceding descriptions intimate fragments of a necessarily complex answer. By mobilizing peasants, the Front removed them from their old surroundings and thus prepared them for accepting a different role. Upon entering the PLAF, the recruit confronted new life circumstances in the form of an organizational structure, environment, process, and doctrine designed to produce an ideologically-based commitment. But the peasant is not infinitely malleable; he acts purposively within the constraints of his psychocultural predispositions and his individual cognitions, motivations, susceptibilities. Thus, describing socialization techniques per se cannot adequately explain why commitment develops. In addition, the analysis must examine the psychological dynamics of commitment, i.e., why peasants *might* adapt to the new life circumstances created by the Front in such a way as to merge their identity with that of the organization and thereby become an ideal revolutionary. This chapter undertakes such an analysis.

This chapter assumes ideal conditions. Namely, that socialization techniques were executed perfectly. Of course, in practice socialization deviated from the formal ideal and, consequently, patterns of compliance other than commitment developed; the next chapter analyzes that reality. First, however, we wish to examine the "pure" case—why commitment might have developed if all the elements of socialization operated the way the Front intended. Proceeding thusly allows us to establish the *limiting case* of the effects of socialization. Using the limiting case as a base, subsequent empirical analysis considers patterns of adaptation other than commitment to have resulted from deviations from the ideal.

### Consonance and Centrality Hypotheses

To analyze the development of commitment under ideal conditions, we use a microstructural approach. That is, we examine why peasants having the modal personality characteristics (described in Chapter 3) and subject to Front socialization (described in Chapter 6) might internalize organizational norms (described in Chapter 5). Since neither the theoretical literature nor empirical research have produced a definitive analysis of commitment, our approach must necessarily be eclectic, exploratory, and more speculative than we should like.[1] Moreover, though commitment represents an integrated pattern of beliefs and behaviors, the analysis must proceed piecemeal by dealing with the details of various organizational processes and the individual's cognitions of and motivations towards them. Two overarching themes will help organize these separate micro-explanations—namely, the notions of consonance and of centrality.

Whether in the form of ideas embodied in the organizational ideology or of prescribed norms of behavior defining the individual's role as a revolutionary, some demands placed on the soldier were *consonant* with his pre-Front personality characteristics whereas other demands were *dissonant* and still others were neither consonant nor dissonant but simply *noncomparable*. Consonance refers to the fit, congruence, or compatibility between the Front's institutional characteristics (as revealed by demands) and the individual's prior cognitions and motivations.[2] Though the problems of defining "consonance" in operational terms are exceedingly difficult and have not been resolved in the literature, subsequent analysis will judge the extent to which the details of the Front's social structure, reward and penalties system, indoctrination techniques, authority structure, and ideology were consonant with traditional peasant personality.

A new idea, value, or norm of behavior may be either internalized, not internalized (rejected), or internalized in a modified form. The focus in this chapter concerns the ideal case of internalization; subsequent analysis will address the latter two possibilities. For the sake of simplification, we shall say that when consonant demands become internalized, they *increment* the existing belief system; when noncomparable demands become internalized, they *expand* existing beliefs; when dissonant demands become internalized, they *replace* pre-existing beliefs.

The second theme that will help set the stage for the analysis involves the *centrality* of a trait; that is, how basic and deeply-held a trait is to the individual's personality structure. Following Milton Rokeach, the individual's personality structure may be conceptualized in terms of centrality—viz., (1) a central (or core) region composed of primary beliefs, needs, drives, (2) an intermediate region which "represents the beliefs a person has in and about the nature of authority and the people who line up with authority, on whom he depends to help him form a picture of the world he lives in," and (3) a peripheral region comprised of specific cognitions.[3] The peasant entered the PLAF with an organized set of cognitions and motivations which we call his pre-Front personality structure; if he became totally committed as prescribed, he internalized, i.e., incorporated into his existing structure, the Front ideology (the ideas, norms, values, sentiments characteristic of a revolutionary). Using this terminology, the pre-Front Vietnamese peasant modal personality may be characterized in the following way. At the center were those elements of cognitions and motivations summarized, by Chapter 3, under the headings pragmatic fatalism, security needs, and status drives. In the intermediate region were those beliefs and behaviors derived from the role occupied by the individual in the village hierarchy. In the periphery were the specific knowledge and elements of concrete experience.

It seems reasonable to presume that the ease with which a Front demand might be internalized depended upon consonance and centrality. Namely, (1) the more consonant a demand, the more likely it would become internalized; in particular, incrementing would be easiest, expansion next easiest, replacement most difficult, (2) the more central a demand would be, the less likely it would become internalized, (3) centrality and consonance interact, i.e., the more central and the less consonant a demand, the less likely it would become internalized; in particular, replacement of primary beliefs would be most difficult, incrementing peripheral beliefs easiest.

Our scheme for analyzing the development of commitment is structured around these hypotheses. We will detail the elements of the prescribed Front norms that were consonant with the peasant's pre-Front beliefs and present explanations of why such consonance might have lead to internalization of Front norms given the centrality of the demands and the peasant characteristics associated with security, status, and pragmatic fatalism. Front notions that were neither consonant nor dissonant but were nonetheless beyond the usual range of peasant cognitions need to be analyzed somewhat differently. If such ideas did not fit into normal peasant perceptions of reality, the recruit might be reluctant to internalize them and either reject or modify them into a form consonant with previous cognitions. In short, such ideas lack a sense of legitimacy and provoke uncertainty. Therefore, we will investigate the ways in which PLAF socialization might have assured recruits that conditions of security and status were fulfilled so that new norms and behaviors could be accepted.

Some revolutionary norms were dissonant with peasant beliefs (as this chapter will detail); thus, their internalization implied replacement of preexisting cognitions and motivations. For example, full commitment to the Front was, in the ideal, so demanding and so total that it virtually excluded self-identities other than being a revolutionary; in particular, it was incompatible with strong family identifications. Therefore, for a peasant to have adopted the revolutionary identity would have required the replacement of his dependency upon family identifications. To effect such replacement, we assume that prior beliefs and sentiments had to be first broken-down. Consequently, the analysis will investigate both specific PLAF institutional mechanisms and characteristics of the new life circumstances that fostered the weakening of traditional attachments.

### Mobilization and Susceptibility

Mobilization of peasants into the PLAF paved the way for commitment in the most direct way: it unequivocally altered the life circumstances of the villager. When they entered the PLAF regular forces, many recruits confronted an alien, though perhaps benevolent, environment. They had to adjust to an atmosphere of constant and routine activities, of indoctrination and exhortation, of discipline and moralism, of criticism and self-criticism and of a lack of privacy, of deprivations and of the danger of combat. Not only was the soldier's life space new and strange, but the break with the comforts of his old environment was dramatic. Many recruits, with their deeply rooted ties in their family and village and accustomed as they were to the traditional and relatively static existence of the peasant, felt homesick. Both confronting the new and breaking with the old combined to cause uncertainty which, for ease of reference, will be called *situational uncertainty*. Perhaps the major cause of anxiety for Vietnamese in situational uncertainty arises from dealing with others; until interpersonal relations could be ordered, until a new role could be accepted, one could not feel secure. In the extreme, situational uncertainty could provoke anxiety to the point of identity-diffusion and render recruits susceptible to commitment.

Another aspect of the susceptibility of new recruits was their age. Recruiting youth was a deliberate policy of the Front. Douglas Pike, based upon his study of numerous captured internal NLF documents, reports that "for recruitment the NLF was interested only in the young. . . . [A] strong pattern [was followed] of recruiting the 16 to 20 age group first, the 21 to 25 age group second, and little interest was shown in those over 25 unless they demonstrated some special talents."[4] The data support this observation. The median age at the time of entry into the Front for a sample of 270 ex-PLAFs is approximately 21.0 years with a standard deviation about the median of 5.9.[a] For those who said they were coerced into joining ($n = 79$), the median age of entry is 21.7 years; whereas for those who said they volunteered ($n = 115$), the median is 19.8 years and one-third of them had joined the NLF at 18 years old or younger. It is difficult to say whether these figures underestimate or overestimate the corresponding population parameters for the time period considered by this study. Nonetheless, they are accurate enough to indicate that many recruits were indeed young. The importance of this recruitment policy, for present purposes, is that some young people may not have settled into stable patterns of self-identity; their identity-formation may have been uncompleted making them vulnerable to having their self-definition crystallized according to the norms of Front socialization. "It stands to reason," Erik Erikson observes, "that late adolescence is the most favorable period, and late adolescent personalities of any age group, the best

---

[a]This sample excludes ex-Viet Minh. Ex-Viet Minh were either "regroupees" (Viet Minh soldiers who went to North Vietnam at the time of Geneva Accords and were infiltrated back into the South) or living in the South when recruited by the NLF. These soldiers played a critical historical role in the formation of the PLAF. Most of them became cadres, particularly middle-level cadres. Though many were ideologically committed, the discussion of identity-formation does not analyze these soldiers.

subjects for indoctrination; because in adolescence an ideological realignment is by necessity in process and a number of ideological possibilities are waiting to be hierarchically ordered by opportunity, leadership, and friendship."[5] Insofar as Erikson's observation applies to the Vietnamese context, then young recruits might have been especially susceptible to adopting the revolutionary role prescribed by the PLAF.

For some Vietnamese youths, the lack of a stable self-identity may have been exacerbated, perhaps to the point of "role confusion,"[6] by disruptive changes occurring in the village society prior to and during the Second Indochina War. Chapter 3 briefly suggested that one of the effects the erosion of the village hierarchy may have had was the creation of uncertainty, the raising of severe doubts about one's self and one's future. It could have lead, as McAlister and Mus put it, to "the lack of any really precise identity within a declining village community that also had lost its own identity. How did one establish his distinctiveness under such circumstances? There no longer were examinations in Confucian learning to set a standard for achievement."[7]

Undoubtedly, some recruits—particularly those aspiring for status in the Front—were "losing their sense of identity with their traditional ways of life and [were] seeking restlessly to realize a modern way."[8] Yet, how extensive was this effect? Available data do not conclusively answer this question. The Mus-McAlister argument is compelling for surely village society had undergone vast and traumatic changes. But part of the amazing historical resilience of the Vietnamese culture resides in the strength of family ties. Ironically, the disruption of village order could have resulted in a greater reliance on the family for identity.[9] On balance, the evidence suggests (a) that the disintegration of the traditional social life surely promoted mobilization—by, as Chapter 4 argues, permitting NLF access, facilitating the establishment of the Front as an alternative authority, and allowing the NLF to create a new opportunity structure, and (b) that where disruption was severe, susceptibility to adopting the new role offered by the Front increased.

Thus, youth's vulnerability, disruption of village society, and situational uncertainty could have resulted, separately or especially combined, in magnifying security needs. Insofar as such anxiety existed (there clearly was variability), the soldier was susceptible to becoming committed.

However, susceptibility did not guarantee commitment since the peasants' need for a secure identity could have been satisfied in other ways. Given such susceptibilities, the task remains of explaining how Front socialization mechanisms exploited these vulnerabilities to instill commitment. The discussion will be organized around the three major themes of commitment—unity, obedience, and politicization. Lacking a suitable theory of personality development (particularly for Vietnamese), the following sections offer a series of loosely-connected, micro-level hypotheses that taken together "explain" the ways PLAF socialization might have led to commitment.

**Unity and Primary Group Identification**

Unity was a fundamental theme in commitment and basic to the Front's notion of unity was the integration of the soldier into the imposed primary group of the squad and its cells. Integration of a group can result from diverse motivations.[10] However, for the front "unity" implied integration based upon solidarity, "mutual love," total trust, treating each comrade as a "brother." The ideology proclaimed solidarity as the norm and PLAF's socialization attempted to foster it. From the standpoint of the individual adapting to his circumstances, how and why might he develop a feeling of solidarity? The answer, in broad terms, is that solidarity could develop because of the basic Vietnamese need to minimize insecurity and maximize security. Let us turn to detailed reasons for this proposition.

A basic characteristic of Vietnamese personality is its group orientation. Vietnamese naturally think, respond, and identify themselves in terms of groups and group situations. Therefore, integrating into the Front's group life fit the soldier's expectation of proper social relations. But in addition to simple integration, solidarity could develop for several reasons. Many recruits were anxious over their own identity because of the uncertainty of this new situation. Such situational uncertainty could arise due to an insecurity over relating to others, a mistrust of others, a desire to avoid interpersonal conflict. A Vietnamese method of coping with such insecurity is to go to the opposite extreme of avoidance, complete intimacy. The new comrades became "brothers" bonded by complete trust and mutual love, i.e., by solidarity. Thus, the recruit could gain a sense of his own identity by identifying with his primary group.

Many other aspects of Front life reinforced the soldier's cultural predisposition towards identifying with the primary group. The new environment was confusing and uncertain at the purely cognitive level. As Schacter observes, "ambiguous situations or feelings lead to a desire to be with others as a means of socially evaluating and determining the 'appropriate' and proper reaction."[11] This conclusion seems particularly valid for the Vietnamese peasant whose concern over ambiguous interpersonal relations can best be relieved by following proper rules of conduct as prescribed in the social situation. In addition, many soldiers were faced with the threat of personal danger and the constant reality of severe hardships in daily life in the Front. These stresses can foster solidarity, as Irving L. Janis, drawing upon studies of soldiers in combat and of medical patients, argues, "It has long been known that when people are exposed to external stress they show remarkable increase in group solidarity."[12]

Thus, the new life situation facing the recruit contained many elements of insecurity; he could minimize that insecurity, and concurrently begin the road to identity-formation of the ideal revolutionary, by accepting the solidarity of group life. However, group life in the Front also offered positive attractions whose elements are discussed next.

Pragmatic fatalism is a major characteristic of Vietnamese peasants. Chapter 4 argued that some recruited Vietnamese accepted membership and others did not. Those who did were acting in accord with pragmatic fatalism: they accepted their situation as ordained by forces beyond their control and, hence, were free to behave in a way best suited pragmatically to their interests. They could then devote considerable energy in applying themselves to immediate tasks, of which the PLAF provided a great many, and seek the rewards—education, excitement, intrigue, and ultimately status and acceptance—that the Front offered. This spirit, one of acceptance and enthusiasm, was strictly channeled by the PLAF, of course. Maximizing status under the constraints of the situation defined by the Front required active participation in group life. Once the primary group began to function, the rewards for becoming part of the group could be immediate and reinforcing. A sense of community, a source of security for Vietnamese, and self-esteem could follow.[13]

Thus, the potential for satisfying basic needs and gratifying basic drives existed in entering primary group relations on the basis of solidarity. However, another critical element was present in the Front that may have integrated these forces and may have played a principle role in identity-formation along prescribed lines, viz., unity with the cadre.

The cadre, Chapter 6 notes, was ideally the "great man" leader who combined "activity," "task" ability, and "likability." He, according to the doctrine of unity of soldiers with cadre, "must share joy and hardships, take care of, help, and treat each other like blood brothers."[14] The soldier's ideal relationship to the cadre is indicated by the following recollection of a former NLF member:

> After working hours, we could joke with them [the cadre] and considered them as equals. But things were different during working hours. I was confident that they could lead the unit in combat and *protect my life*. If the fighters didn't have confidence in them, how could they lead their unit? (Emphasis added.)

The cadre could become an older brother (or perhaps a father surrogate). Hence, the soldier could satisfy his own security—"protect my life"—by identifying with the cadre. Such identification had a particular significance in its own right, as we shall discuss shortly. In addition, it provided what may have been a critical link in primary group solidarity. Freud, and others following Freud,[15] argued that members of the group set up a leader as a model and that bonds of mutual trust and affection develop by means of this source of identification. In Freud's words, "a number of individuals . . . have put one and the same object [the leader] in the place of their ego ideal and have consequently identified themselves with one another in their ego."[16] Freud considered this mechanism to be the basis of group solidarity: "Many equals, who can identify themselves with one another, and a single person superior to them all—that is the situation that we find realized in groups which are capable of subsisting."[17]

## Obedience and Filialism

The preceding section hypothesized some of the reasons why the ideological norm of unity could have been incorporated into the soldier's self-identity by means of identification with the primary group. However, such identification could be dysfunctional from the standpoint of the organization. One widely-supported conclusion of research on groups and organizations is that solidarity "does not necessarily increase or decrease the productivity of a group. Rather, [it] . . . serves to heighten the susceptibility of group members to influence from other members."[18] Thus, solidarity could retard or foster commitment depending upon the extent to which the norms of the primary group matched the formal norms of the PLAF. To prevent the development of informal norms that might deviate from prescribed values, the Front sought to embed the primary group in the organizational structure. Whether or not it was successful in doing so ultimately rested upon the soldier's willingness to obey PLAF authority.

Obedience implied, in the Front's ideal, absolute conformity to a strict code of proper conduct and total submission to authority; without these ingredients commitment could not be complete. This section explores why obedience could have eventuated.

Pragmatic fatalism was perhaps a cornerstone of the soldier's acquiescence to the PLAF's strict obedience. Insofar as the soldier accepted membership, the situation became defined and controlled by the Front. He perceived no other alternative but to act in compliance with Front demands. Moreover, given that he accepted his "fate," he could energetically proceed to advance himself within the prescribed constraints of the system. The first, and foremost, ways to advance, i.e., maximize his status in terms of self-esteem, promotion, awards, and membership in the Party, was by "execution of the superior's orders." These rewards followed compliance directly and hence were self-reinforcing.

However, obedience implied more than complying with commands; it demanded constant conformity to a strict code of proper behavior. Conformity to a formalistic code of proper role relationships is a central characteristic of Vietnamese culture. The traditional structuring of role relationships was hierarchical with an individual, in any specific interpersonal situation, being either superior or inferior. The individual in the inferior position showed deference to the superior. Thus, the Vietnamese peasant entered the Front with a primitive belief that hierarchical role relationships were the natural order. The prescribed role relationships in the PLAF were similar in nature to those of the culture; they were, of course, hierarchical. Though formality seemed to be somewhat deemphasized, the PLAF's practice of not observing formal ranks was consistent with the Vietnamese penchant to determine status in symbolic, subtle ways. In short, given the soldier's basic acceptance of membership, conformity to the prescribed authority relationships was in accord with his basic beliefs about the nature of legitimate authority; adopting a prescribed role could be expected and would be welcomed.


### Channeling Filialism

According to Front doctrine, obedience had to be total: deference alone was inadequate, submission was required. Whereas congruence with his belief system might be a sufficient explanation of the soldier's compliance in role relations, submission to authority involved a deeper level of psychic functioning. The parallel in the soldier's cultural experience was less in general role relationships than in the ideal of family relations, filial piety. The Vietnamese son was expected to be filial throughout his life; to be filial was to be obedient, loyal, devoted, reverent to the parents. "Nor was this to be a token response," Lifton observes for the traditional Chinese culture, "since if it did not stem naturally from his inner being, he was not being truly filial" [19]—i.e., he was not being "sincere." [20] The problem for the Chinese Communists, Lifton argues, was to turn a filial son into a "filial Communist." [21] Similarly, the NLF did not have to create the sentiments of absolute submission, loyalty, spirit of self-sacrifice that constitute the core of filialism. Insofar as commitment to the Front evolved, the emotions of filialism had to be channeled into identification with the organization and the object of filialism—the family—had to be replaced.

Though the emotions and drives associated with filialism are characteristic of Vietnamese personality, some important sources of variability deserve comment for they affected the likelihood of commitment. Evidence collected by Slote indicates Vietnamese repress extreme hostile feelings towards their parents. [22] It is reasonable to speculate, in lieu of further evidence, that the way these emotions worked themselves out varied among the young Vietnamese peasants recruited into the Front. At one extreme, some Vietnamese could have rebelled against the culturally prescribed ways, refusing to submerge hostile feelings aroused by the demands of filiality. This rebelliousness might have been associated with an identity crisis, particularly one arising in the context of a disrupted social order. By adopting the identity of the committed soldier, the rebel could establish a status separate from the family while simultaneously accepting a role that provided him the security that resided in filiality.

At the other extreme was the usual situation of Vietnamese who had adapted to the demands of filialism, deeply repressing hostility towards their parents. They had developed the roots of self-identity in their family. If they were to become committed, a breaking down of family identification would have had to precede a transference of filialism. The radically altered life situation in the Front may have had such a breaking down effect for some recruits. Not only were the soldiers being cut off from their roots in village life; they were also being cut off from their family. Though such physical separation does not necessarily imply a psychological rupture, it might have for some soldiers, particularly in light of the very real possibility of dying away from home and proper family burial grounds.[b] Furthermore, the Front, by treating a reliance on the family as a sign of weakness in commitment, promoted a breaking away. Insofar as ties to the family were broken down, the consequent anxieties could be minimized by the soldier's submission to authority—thus regaining the threatened filial relationship in a surrogate fashion.

### Criticism and Self-Criticism

The acceptance of the authority structure and the adoption of prescribed behavior by the soldier relied on a combination of consonance and of nondissonance with pre-Front beliefs and thus incremented or enlarged the peasant's belief system. However, the channeling of filialism to the organization required replacement of more central values. A potentially important technique for effecting this replacement was the criticism and self-criticism session.

At the core of PLAF emphasis on ideological commitment was the belief that "thoughts are the father of all our activities"—if one has the "correct thoughts," then he will act properly. How would the Front know whether an individual had "correct thoughts," i.e., had internalized the ideological norms? By observing his behavior.[23] The converse—if he did not act properly, he had bad thoughts—also held and was employed as the basis of the *kiem thao* sessions. In these sessions, the soldier was forced to criticize his behavior as being improper ("unvirtuous") and to trace the cause of his impropriety in mistaken ideological thinking. No aspect of behavior nor of one's inner life was immune from examination. The essence of self-criticism was a confession, not so much of the fact of the wrongdoing but of wrong thinking, coupled with a determination to "rectify" one's thoughts.

Assuming for the moment that some soldiers confessed "sincerely," in what ways would such confessions induce submission and identity-formation along the prescribed lines? The act of confession itself was an act of "symbolic self-surrender."[24] Moreover, by denying the rightness of his own "inner" thoughts, the soldier would be challenging the roots of his own identity. The result might be a heightened sense of uncertainty and of identity-diffusion. The attendant anxiety and confusion could be alleviated by submitting to the clear and "correct" thinking offered by the Front. The soldier thus exposed himself in a primary group atmosphere in which others were similarly submitting; as Lifton observes, this "sharing of confession enthusiasms can create an orgiastic sense of

---

[b]The PLAF tried to ease these intense Vietnamese feelings by its policy of carrying its dead off the battlefield for proper burial and subsequent notification to the parents. These policies were not always carried out, and this caused some soldiers great dissatisfaction.

'oneness', of the most intense intimacy with fellow confessors and of the dis-
solution of self into the great flow of the Movement."[25]

Of course, the sincerity of confessions in criticism sessions cannot be so
easily assumed. On the contrary. Suppression of emotion and saying what is
proper in a given situation rather than what one might believe are deep-rooted
characteristics of Vietnamese; confession could be invoked because it was
required, not because it was sincere. Thus, internalization of "correct thinking"
would not take place and commitment would be thwarted. However, several
elements in the socialization situation might have countered this cultural
tendency.

Some soldiers had positive motivations. They were eager to become "educated." They found the sessions, in one former PLAF's words, "tiresome but
useful . . . [for] . . . they helped us overcome our bad habits like swearing and
prostitution." Being sincere was a way to better oneself and, simultaneously,
prove oneself suited for advancement in the Front. Even with this positive drive,
however, the Vietnamese tendency of disassociating behavior from belief had
to be overcome.

The deliberate use of the primary group in criticism and self-criticism
allowed the application of punishments (to break down resistance) and rewards
(to facilitate acceptance) in concrete, immediate ways particularly appropriate to
Vietnamese characteristics. In theory, the primary group's norms were those of
commitment and the members of the group were eager for an individual to adopt
these norms; insofar as he showed signs of "correct thought," the immediate
rewards of group acceptance so crucial in the Vietnamese's sense of self were
granted and insofar as insincerity were detected and criticism provoked, a "loss-
of-face" from one's potential identity group followed.[26] The following
remarks of a former PLAF member suggests the profound depth of loss-of-face
for Vietnamese:

> When the Province Party Committee was aware of the fact [that he had
> planned to marry without the Party's permission], I would be severely
> criticized for cheating, and demoted. I would lose face. My comrades
> would look down upon me and laugh at me, and it would be impossible
> for me to carry on my task.

Chapter 3 categorized loss-of-face into two types. There is a *situational shame* in
which one suffers a loss-of-face from the exposure of an improper act to the
immediate group. The shame engendered in this case evokes strong emotions for
a Vietnamese and can serve as an effective means of changing his behavior to
avoid such punishment. However, another type of loss-of-face is even more
threatening. This shame, *identification shame*, arises when an individual violates
a norm of his identity group. Insofar as the norm violated is itself basic to the
group's solidarity, then such violation challenges the group. Being shamed in this
context evokes the possibility of isolation from the group with a consequent loss

of identity. The fear of being cut off from the group, perhaps raising similar anxieties from childhood rearing experiences common in Vietnam, could be a powerful force for conformity in the group and for penetrating into the individual's innermost thoughts. By thus breaking down the protection afforded by the disassociation of thought from action, the complete submission of the self so essential to the channeling of filialism to the organization might be achieved. Reinforcing these pressures were the inherent sensitivity of group members to dissimulation; this sensitivity could enable one's comrades to penetrate a mask of formality used by an insincere member. Moreover, the individual could never allow his mask to drop—he had no "offstage" [27] —for the members of his primary group were always with him and they were obliged, for his own good, to report insincerity in the *kiem thao* sessions.

### Politization and Ideologized Beliefs

A politicized belief system served as the cognitive framework for an identity of ideological commitment. Identification with the Front-imposed primary group, complete obedience to the authority structure, and politization all reinforced and complemented each other. On the one hand, by learning and internalizing the language of PLAF ideology, the soldier perceived, thought of, and evaluated himself, others, and his environment in ways that cemented solidarity and furthered submission.[28] On the other hand, identification with the group and obedience fostered politization. This section investigates the latter relationship by examining how and why politization could have occurred assuming, for the sake of analysis, the soldier's positive motivations towards the group and the organization.

Why do individual's adopt a set of beliefs? Smith, Bruner, and White suggest that holding opinions serve three functions for the individual—object appraisal, social adjustment, and externalization.[29] We use these three functions to organize the discussion.

#### Object Appraisal and Consonance

The need of the new recruit for object appraisal—for testing the "reality" of his new situation—was very great. He had to assimilate into an unusual and often alien environment. Moreover, the Front's indoctrination immediately impinged upon him. A basic characteristic of PLAF indoctrination techniques was the attempt to establish milieu control. Three aspects of milieu control are relevant to the present discussion: (1) there was *saturation* of the individual with ideology in basic training, in indoctrination sessions, in study sessions, in criticism sessions, etc.; (2) there was *monopolization* in that, on the one hand, all sources of information—from mass media to group discussions—were controlled and, on the other hand, possibly discordant sources were prohibited; (3) there was insistence upon *intrapersonal penetration* into the soldier's inner thoughts, especially by means of the confession. These techniques could lead to uncertainty and overload, thus creating a severe need for the recruit to organize, evaluate, and define his new environment.

A number of characteristics of the peasant's pre-Front belief system facilitated object appraisal along the lines prescribed by the NLF. Recruits were politically unsophisticated. Due to their youth and upbringing in the traditional environment, they had, Chapter 3 postulated, little knowledge of and probably few specific attitudes towards the affairs of politics beyond their village. More generalized orientations towards authority existed, but to a large extent their belief system in regard to specific political themes was ripe for indoctrination— their "political consciousness" had, literally, not been developed. Moreover, many of those who accepted membership had a desire to learn. In short, internalization of much of Front indoctrination was primarily attitude formation rather than attitude change, incrementing and enlarging beliefs rather than replacing them.

Though the recruit's political beliefs might have been unformed, his belief system was far from a *tabula rasa*; the culture had imprinted primary beliefs, orientations, and premises. Insofar as Front ideology was consonant with these Vietnamese predispositions, acceptance would be facilitated.[30] The new information impinging upon the recruit could be evaluated in terms of existing attitudes and orientations; being consonant they could be filtered-through, fitted-in, and added-onto the soldier's belief system. "Once thus categorized," Smith et al. note "[the information] becomes the focus of an already established repertory of reactions and feelings, and the person is saved the energy-consuming and sometimes painful process of figuring out *de novo* how he shall relate himself to it."[31] Monopolization helped the assimilation of the Front's ideology into the individual's belief system by minimizing contrary ideas which might have led to confusion. The apparent clarity of the ideology also contributed because of its simplicity and aura of certainty. Thus, the significance of consonance of ideology with cultural beliefs was that—given, on the one hand, the saturated and controlled environment and, on the other hand, the recruit's motivation to learn coupled with an anxiety about uncertainty—consonancy facilitated object appraisal in the prescribed manner.

Major elements of consonance in the Front's ideology revolved around sentiments of nationalism and patriotism. "Nationalism" in Front propaganda has less to do with governmental institutions than with a national identity of being Vietnamese. Though the Party (of the NLF as well as the North Vietnamese) proclaimed its brotherhood with international communism, it did not do so at the expense of a separate and distinct Vietnamese identity. The sense of nationalism—bordering on xenophobia—is deeply rooted in Vietnamese cultural tradition, as most scholars on Vietnamese history and culture note.[c] Associated with nationalism is a cultural heritage of rebellion against foreigners and of heroism which were based, according to Vietnamese mythology, upon loyalty and righteousness of cause; the similarity of these themes to PLAF ideology is clear. Even key elements in the internal norms of the organization—unity, harmony, hierarchy, propriety, consensus in decision-making (democratic centralism), virtue, heroic death, and the emphasis on education as a means of achievement—find their counterparts in the cultural metaphysics, ethics, and life styles of Vietnamese.

Of course, many elements of the specific content of the Front's ideological language were new, being neither consonant nor dissonant. This was particularly true for abstract elements of Communist theory. Yet, even in this case, the *language* could be learned for it was perceived by Vietnamese not in a literal sense but in the symbolic way so characteristic of the culture's style of cognitive structuring. Pye observed a similar reliance on symbolism among the Chinese Communist guerrillas in Malaya:

> [T]he new words and the jargon which the SEP's learned assumed the quality of symbols, representing in some respects the commonplace realities and ideas with which they were already acquainted. They had only acquired a new way of saying things they already knew. However, the very uniqueness of the words also made them feel that the symbols represented something more. An element of the uncommon had been added that bordered on the mysterious.[32]

In addition to symbolism, other similarities between cultural thought processes and the ideology existed. Mysticism permeated the ideology in its claims of omnipotence and omniscience, in its alignment with historical forces, in the aura of secretness of the Party, in its Utopianism, in its righteousness. Similar mysticism characterizes Vietnamese traditional culture, as noted earlier.[33] The Front's total belief in the inevitability of the revolution contained the ingredient of Vietnamese fatalism. Moreover, in the Vietnamese sense of pragmatic fatalism, once one is aligned with the correct forces—once the "Mandate of Heaven" has been reached—the individual is free to, and is obliged to, expend his resource in accordance with the proper forces.[34] Of course, decisions should be justified in rational terms; again illustrating the fit between cultural tendencies and the analytical mode of reasoning characteristic of the politicized revolutionary.

### Social Adjustment and Ideologized Beliefs

The greatest pressure on the soldier towards expressing himself in the specific ideological language of the Front—its slogans, its cliches, its highly simplified

---

[c]Chapter 3 discusses nationalism and the various cultural themes mentioned in this paragraph.

goals—was a need for social adjustment, a need for security. This was particularly the case in the criticism and self-criticism sessions where the full weight of the group could be brought to bear. Assuming that the group was committed, intense pressures were placed on the soldier to be sincere. In short, one had to say and *think* in terms of the ideological language.

Insofar as the committed thus internalized the ideological language because of the need to conform to the group's and the authority's expectations, other sources for reality testing were driven out. That is, the committed soldier's "identity beliefs"—his innermost thoughts—became "ideologized." [35]

### Externalization and Emotionality

The committed soldier was supposed to be enthusiastic. This characteristic runs counter to the cultural norms of repressed emotions. However, externalization—the expression of inner needs and anxieties—may account, in part, for the committed soldier's acceptance of this usually inviolate cultural restriction. According to Slote, a central problem in Vietnamese culture is the need to repress emotionality and, more particularly, hostility towards the parents arising from the demands of filial obedience (see our discussion in Chapter 3). Pent-up hostility may have accompanied the committed soldier's transference of his obedience from the family to the Front. However, the Front strictly forbid expressions of hostility towards cadres, comrades, and villagers, e.g., cursing or unauthorized physical punishment were prohibited, and instead provided a channel for releasing frustration in the expressions of hatred towards the enemy.

Hostility towards foreigners was sanctioned in the culture. Therefore, the expression of hate need not have involved a serious personality transformation. However, the intensity and pervasiveness of the committed's hatred suggests a profound change. By expressing hatred, the soldier may have externalized deeply repressed, inner hostility towards the traditional authorities; by so doing, they may have broken their dependency on these authorities and thus became susceptible to replacing their old loyalties with the authority of the Front. Indeed, the Front itself declared that hate could make fighters "understand" why they fight, could give them "inner determination" to overcome "outside difficulties," and could prevent them from resigning themselves to "fate." [36] Externalizing hate thus may have resulted in the changed orientation suggested by Fitzgerald: "The enemy was no longer inside, but outside in the world of objective phenomena; the world moved not according to blind, transcendent forces, but according to the will of the people." [37]

### Tactical Manipulation and Status Drives

Another characteristic of revolutionary politization was an orientation towards the use of power in interpersonal relations. The committed were tacti-

cally oriented emphasizing manipulation of people and symbols in order to
achieve objectives that were set by the authorities. This orientation has a marked
similarity to the cultural orientation of pragmatic fatalism. Pragmatic fatalism
implies that once one accepts the basic situation, the means used should be based
upon "rational" consideration; the effect is an emphasis on short-run tactical
maneuvering. Moreover, the finely differentiated status structure and the Vietnamese concern for status reinforced this tendency of maneuvering in interpersonal relations as a way of gaining power over others.

Many features of the PLAF's socialization techniques and rewards system
fostered the development of a "power tactician." Discussions of "policy" in
group meetings followed democratic centralism; yet, the focus was not on
strategic objectives but on tactical implementation. Assignment to agit-prop
work was highly valued among ambitious soldiers for in such a situation they
could gain a sense of status and superiority over others within the secure framework of a supportive organization. In trying to persuade others of the strength
and righteousness of the Front, the agit-prop worker helped convince himself.
Moreover, as Pool observes, he "learned the power of propaganda. He became
skilled in the management of meetings and demonstrations, and in general he
acquired a view of the world in which politics is the driving and dominant
force."[38]

Thus, manipulation of others and a tactical orientation towards power were
perceived as legitimate. Indeed, they were perceived as a prerequisite for
advancement. Moreover, a major reward of advancement itself was precisely in
achieving power over others, as a former Party member unashamedly recalled:

> How did you feel about the Party membership?
> I felt very proud. As a Party member I had new powers; power to
> admit someone to the Group since a Group member could only
> recommend one for membership. It meant power to recommend
> someone for Party membership; power to solve problems arising
> among my comrades; power to speak for the people. Every military
> position was based on Party membership. Every important mission
> was also based on Party membership. Those who were not Party mem-
> bers did not have enough virtue to be trusted with high positions or
> important missions. I was pleased to see that my progress was not
> hindered by my superiors, I was proud of my achievements compared
> to those of my comrades who had joined the Front before me and
> who were not rewarded with Party membership. This was a secret
> feeling and I did not abandon my comrades. On the contrary I had to
> show them how to improve their situation and how to be admitted
> into the Party.

All these politization processes—object appraisal, social adjustment, externalization—occurred simultaneously with each other and with the other identification mechanisms of solidarity with the group and submission to the organization.

Moreover, the elaborateness yet clarity of the ideology and its demands provided the soldier with a cognitive framework that was anchored in a prescribed self-image. As the self-image became increasingly incorporated, he had a consistent way of viewing himself in relationship to his comrades, to his organizational role, to fate. In short, the various aspects of socialization reinforced each other in instilling commitment.


### Conclusion

Though the characteristics of the committed revolutionary were different from those of the peasant in certain critical ways, the development of a revolutionary identity did not involve a total transformation of the peasant into a radically different person, a "brain-washing" destroying all vestiges of traditional needs, drives, and beliefs and substituting completely new, perhaps alien, cognitions and motivations. Instead, commitment developed from the recruit's adaptation to an organizational environment that confronted him with a mixture of consonant and dissonant demands relative to his traditional experience. Thus, many institutional characteristics of the PLAF corresponded to the peasant's traditional notions of what was natural and what was right and proper: the need to conform to a code of proper behavior, the obedience to authority, the integration into a collective ordered life. By accepting this order, the soldier could find a secure role. Such a sense of security opened the recruit to the internalization of new ideas and loyalties. Identification with the organization rather than the family, enthusiasm and hatred rather than repressed emotions, and a sense of power over events rather than acceptance of fate were dissonant with tradition and required transformation.

Assuming perfect socialization, the Front's techniques for promoting this transformation rested upon a principle of contingent gratification, i.e., rewards and penalties depended upon the individual's following the prescribed norms of commitment. The PLAF's institutional structure allowed the application of sanctions to be immediate, appropriate, pervasive, and sustained. In particular, the individual was embedded in a Front-imposed primary group; given the Vietnamese group orientation and the situational uncertainty of new life circumstances, the recruit's need for acceptance from this group was acute; he could gain acceptance and prevent rejection by adopting the group's norms; but the Front so controlled the group that its norms became (in the ideal) those of the organization; therefore, by following prescribed behavior—including "confession" in criticism and self-criticism sessions—the recruit simultaneously satisfied his need for security and internalized the new beliefs and loyalties.

# 8 Realities of Life in the Front: Adaptation and Integration

The PLAF's ideal of organizational compliance—that is, the norms, doctrines, structure, and processes intended by its designers—can be summarized simply. The soldier was to be totally committed to the organization and its goals. The norms of commitment—obedience, unity, and politization—were to guarantee voluntary compliance to the cadre who was to be firmly rooted in a hierarchical authority structure that was controlled by, and interpenetrated with, a highly centralized political command system. Such commitment could not be assumed of new recruits; therefore, the Front's socialization processes—the control structure, the imposed and politicized primary group, the system of rewards and sanctions, and the controlled environment—sought to instill and maintain the soldier's level of commitment.

But this was the theory of revolutionary compliance. Was it the reality of life in the PLAF? This chapter contends that many soldiers failed to develop total commitment. The Front's socialization processes did indeed establish a framework of demands and structures. Yet, peasants adapted to these mechanisms in a variety of ways according to their own motivations and experiences. Thus, as in most organizations, alternative modes of adaptation were possible and a mix of different patterns of compliance resulted. This chapter investigates, employing qualitative and quantitative analysis, the patterns of authority that empirically emerged and hypothesizes why they emerged.

Since the PLAF's mechanisms of compliance failed to produce total commitment in many soldiers, it becomes essential to investigate how, and to what extent, these mechanisms integrated and controlled soldiers possessing diverse patterns of motivations. This chapter presents evidence that the PLAF indeed had the potential for a high degree of integration. Not only did a consonance exist between organizational values and essential cultural values but basic needs, drives, motivations of most soldiers were satisfied. Furthermore, the organizational structure established the parameters within which all behavior took place; by filling positions of leadership with committed and able soldiers, the PLAF could thereby control and channel behavior of individual's who did not attain the ideal of commitment.

In short, turning from norms to empirical adaptation, we will now examine how the system worked in reality rather than just in its designers' intentions.

### Conformity and Why Commitment Failed

Transforming the recruit into a committed revolutionary was a primary objective of the socialization processes of the Front. The preceding chapter argued that, in the ideal, some Vietnamese could have satisfied their needs and gratified their drives by accepting this molding, by becoming committed. Yet this process was far from automatic and far from assured. When all necessary conditions—well-executed socialization and exaggerated susceptibilities—combined perfectly, commitment could occur; when a critical condition was lacking, commitment failed. To analyze why the development of commitment might be blocked, the obvious characteristics and circumstances to turn to are those Front norms and socialization processes dissonant with traditional Vietnamese personality structure. In particular, resistance was likely to arise in the *kiem thao* sessions.

In the criticism and self-criticism sessions described in Chapter 7, the soldier was subjected to criticism from comrades and cadre and was expected to criticize not only his own behavior but to confess to his "incorrect" thinking; in this way, the soldier's defenses to total commitment might be penetrated. The efficacy of this technique for the internalization of revolutionary norms depended upon whether the soldier's confession was "sincere," i.e., whether he believed his confession. But consider the following recollection of a former Viet Cong:

> What did you dislike the most about life in the Front?
> I disliked most the auto-criticism meeting held each morning, especially after a hard night's work. Instead of letting us relax to recover our strength, the cadres would force us to attend self-criticism meetings, wherein everybody pretended to be sincere and loyal, although this was very hypocritical.
> What would you do in these meetings?
> Soldiers of a squad or a platoon met every morning to discuss what they did the previous day. The meeting was always guided by the political commissar of the unit. If someone made a mistake, violated discipline, or wrongly executed an order, he had to confess it before everybody, listen to the criticisms of the political commissar and his friends, show that he regretted it very much and promise not to repeat the same mistake again. As my friends did, sometimes I had to fabricate little mistakes to show that I was sincere and loyal.

Some soldiers feigned confession. To protect oneself against severe criticism and the consequent shame and insecurity this would bring, a soldier could confess to a minor transgression; in doing so, he avoided criticism about loyalty and thus built a protective mechanism against internalization itself. In short, some soldiers ritualized their confession.[1]

Though the relative number of soldiers who actually ritualized their confession cannot be estimated, there was, it is hypothesized, an intrinsic tendency to do so. Ritualization of behavior is consonant with Vietnamese cultural values. Saying what is proper rather than what one "feels" does not lead to a guilt aroused anxiety. On the contrary, to do otherwise in a given group situation might lead to a loss-of-face. Thus, ritualization could have been widespread unless the leadership of the PLAF, who were well aware of this cultural tendency, could counter it.[2]

The critical elements of the PLAF's structure designed to counter dissimulation of behavior from belief were the sanctions, rewards, and cognitive pressures of the Front-imposed group life. In the theory described in Chapter 7, the primary group's norms were those of ideological commitment and the members of the group were eager for an individual to adopt these norms; insofar as the soldier showed signs of "correct thought," the immediate rewards of group acceptance so crucial in the Vietnamese's sense of self were granted and insofar as insincerity was detected and criticism provoked, a loss-of-face from one's potential identity group followed. The preceding quotation suggests how this mechanism could fail to produce the intended results: "[E]verybody pretended to be sincere and loyal. . . . As my friends did, sometimes I had to fabricate little mistakes to show I was sincere and loyal." There were, at least in some units, informal norms adopted by the primary group that served to nullify the reward-punishment mechanism central to ideological commitment. Thus, group acceptance—and rejection—did not necessarily hinge on the soldier internalizing the norms of commitment. On the contrary, insofar as group acceptance was important to the individual, he was motivated, in these *noncommitted* groups, to ritualize his confessions—just "as my friends did"—to gain acceptance. Hence, an "unintended" consequence [3] of the Front's reliance on group pressures was the possibility that the individual could resist commitment to the organization; indeed, the group itself could resist commitment.[4]

Since the demands for sincerity rather than the proper responses dictated by the situation, for emotionality rather than repression of feelings, for filial piety to the organization rather than to the family all ran counter to traditional peasant characteristics, the development of ritualization, informal group norms, and the consequent failure of full commitment was probable. However, primary group life did not function autonomously in the PLAF; it was embedded in an organizational structure and led by a cadre who himself was tied to the organization. Therefore, the extent to which commitment did indeed develop is an empirical issue that must be examined in the larger context. The remainder of the chapter undertakes such an examination. At this point, we can offer several key hypotheses that will guide the subsequent analysis.

The existence of ritualization and informal group norms could imply a wide-scale dissatisfaction and alienation within the PLAF. Though there was dissatisfaction and alienation which will be examined in detail subsequently, it was within bounds under normal conditions and it arose in a way differentiated from the effects associated with the informal norms discussed above. Rather this chapter contends that these informal norms reflected a form of satisfaction with Front life derived from a sense of primary group solidarity within units. Moreover, though the socialization processes were not successful in creating total commitment among those soldiers who adapted by ritualization, such adaptation occurred in the context of the organizational demands and structures implied by revolutionary commitment. It will be shown that the soldier who dissimulated still complied with proper behavior, at least in most areas of vital concern to the effective operation of the PLAF; that the group which maintained informal standards was complying with the letter of proper group behavior though not with the intended spirit. In short, this pattern of adaptation was an alternative pattern of compliance to an authority perceived as legitimate; a pattern to be called *conformity without commitment*.

Assuming the existence of conformity, this chapter investigates more fully the nature of this pattern of compliance, the ways and the degree to which it differed from commitment, and its relative frequency in the PLAF compared to commitment or, indeed, compared to dissatisfaction and alienation. Furthermore, though adapting by conforming was an "unintended" consequence of the demands and structures of the Front, the extent to which it was dysfunctional in the sense of retarding organizational effectiveness is not obvious and must be subjected to further empirical analysis. In short, there was variability in patterns of adaptation, in norms in the unit, in the commitment of soldiers. To deal with such variability implies a need for quantitative analysis.

### Patterns of Adaptation

To examine the inquiries posed above, the quantitative analysis described in this section is guided by two related objectives. First of all, commitment and conformity were, at least to some extent, matters of degree; hence, the analysis ought to measure each soldier's degree of commitment and degree of conformity. Secondly, commitment and conformity were also distinctively different modes of adaptation; consequently, the quantitative analysis ought to discriminate between them and explicate their particular features.

To measure and discriminate the patterns of adaptation, we conducted a content analysis of the intensive interviews followed by a factor analysis. The complexity of these techniques warrants a methodological Appendix at the end of this chapter. At this point, the nature of the procedures can be briefly sketched.

### *Measuring Satisfactions and Dissatisfactions*

A majority of the interviewees in the quantitative sample were directly asked—often approximately mid-way through the interview when a measure of confidence in the interview situation might have been established—questions of the form, "How did you feel about life in the Front?" of "What did you like about life in the Front?" followed by such probes as, "What did you like most?", "Like least?", "Dislike most?", etc. The respondents had complete freedom to answer as they wished (thus, mitigating some of the potentially distorting effects of variation in the form of the questioning). Their responses frequently consisted of relatively long statements. Using these statements, major substantive themes (or categories) that focused on the interviewee's stated satisfactions and dissatisfactions with life in the PLAF were developed by content analysis. (In approximately a third of the interviews the line of questioning described above was not broached but, in many of these cases, the subject of satisfaction arose somewhat spontaneously allowing relevant passages to be similarly coded.) For the sake of reliability—but at the sacrifice of sample size—coders were instructed to ignore testimony that did not specifically discuss satisfactions and dissatisfactions and to code only concrete statements, in contrast to "reading between the lines." The resulting themes are presented by table 8-1.

In addition to sources of error implicit in the content analysis, several analytical assumptions that necessarily risk distortions were required. The Appendix to this chapter discusses these assumptions. However, the following two assumptions are particularly important. Since the themes shown in table 8-1 arose in the interviews in a relatively unprompted manner, they reflect, more or less faithfully it is assumed, the belief systems of the subjects both in terms of substance and structure. Moreover, the themes are assumed equivalent to a measurement model wherein each soldier would have been asked to respond to

Table 8-1
**Stated Satisfactions and Dissatisfaction with Life in the PLAF**
**(Themes Generated by Content Analysis of Interviews)**

*Satisfaction with*
   feeling of solidarity with comrades
   sense of equality
   immediate cadre
   code of proper behavior in relations with Front members
   code of proper behavior in relations towards villagers
   nationalism
   social-political (ideological) goals

*Dissatisfaction with*
   hardships of military life
   lack of, or displeasure with, food
   danger
   close control, surveillance, discipline
   criticism sessions
   immediate cadre
   treatment of self by Front; personal grievances; alienation
   NLF's tactics and policy towards villagers
   ideology

each category of the entire list of satisfactions-dissatisfactions with either a yes or a no.

### Discriminating Complex Patterns

Table 8-1 lists those satisfactions and dissatisfactions cited by the soldiers. Since the working sample of 344 is not a random sample, the frequency of response associated with each category is not displayed. Even if the sample were statistically representative, such a display would be only marginally useful. Thus, consider the attitude listed first in table 8-1, a feeling of satisfaction due to a sense of solidarity, of friendship, of camaraderie with fellow soldiers in one's unit. In light of the possibility of the emergence of informal group norms, it is not obvious whether such sentiments indicate a pattern of commitment or of conformity or indeed of other forms of gratification. Therefore, estimating the actual frequency of the attitude is not as meaningful as is determining the relationship of solidarity to the other feelings of satisfactions and dissatisfactions.

To investigate the complex interrelationships among the various attitudes, the joint relationships between the items of table 8-1 could be calculated. For example, solidarity based upon identification with one's primary group implied relationships of mutual trust among soldiers, relationships characterized by the absence of concern and anxiety over status differentials, i.e., a sense of equality. Therefore, it is expected that satisfaction with solidarity would correlate highly with equality (item 2 of table 8-1). Such was the case: the Pearson's product-moment correlation coefficient between the two themes was .73. Table 8-2 displays the pair-wise correlation coefficients for all the themes. Extending this bivariate analysis, one might expect that identification with the primary group required (or, at least, implied) identification with the leader of the unit, the cadre. The quantitative evidence supports this proposition: the correlation between satisfaction with the cadre and solidarity was .71 and with equality was .76.

The pair-wise correlations among the various satisfaction-dissatisfaction items could be further examined and various qualitative hypotheses could be tested. However, this procedure is both inefficient—there are a very large number of combinations (120!)—and can lead to spurious findings. Moreover, though these specific hypotheses are of interest, the primary concern is in testing the more general systemic patterns of adaptation. That is, a glance at table 8-2 reveals that the items tend to cluster; since these measurements are of satisfactions-dissatisfactions, one would expect that the clustering reflects patterns of adaptation to life in the Front. Therefore, to test these more general patterns (as well as to scale them), the various clusters were identified and discriminated by means of factor analysis.

Using the matrix of correlation coefficients displayed by table 8-2, a Principal Components factor analysis was performed.[5] Those familiar with factor

**Table 8–2**
Interrelationships Among Satisfaction-Dissatisfaction Variables, Matrix of Correlation Coefficients

| Variable | 1 | 2 | 3 | 4 | 5 | 6 | 7 | 8 | 9 | 10 | 11 | 12 | 13 | 14 | 15 | 16 |
|---|---|---|---|---|---|---|---|---|---|---|---|---|---|---|---|---|
| *Satisfactions with* | | | | | | | | | | | | | | | | |
| Solidarity | 1.000 | .731 | .713 | .487 | .640 | .627 | .525 | -.391 | -.362 | -.261 | -.374 | -.306 | -.336 | -.320 | -.358 | -.352 |
| Equality | | 1.000 | .755 | .673 | .583 | .774 | .635 | -.340 | -.552 | -.338 | -.416 | -.372 | -.283 | -.229 | -.366 | -.305 |
| Cadre | | | 1.000 | .679 | .687 | .692 | .470 | -.441 | -.429 | -.360 | -.674 | -.287 | -.358 | -.220 | -.293 | -.319 |
| Id. Aims | | | | 1.000 | .628 | .855 | .656 | -.440 | -.404 | -.670 | -.608 | -.440 | -.374 | -.339 | -.380 | -.509 |
| Relations in PLAF | | | | | 1.000 | .558 | .625 | -.515 | -.341 | -.323 | -.440 | -.454 | -.307 | -.294 | -.472 | -.533 |
| Nationalism | | | | | | 1.000 | .692 | -.539 | -.374 | -.572 | -.470 | -.308 | -.299 | -.209 | -.305 | -.502 |
| Relations with Vil | | | | | | | 1.000 | -.556 | -.393 | -.480 | -.364 | -.525 | -.413 | -.405 | -.591 | -.796 |
| *Dissatisfactions with* | | | | | | | | | | | | | | | | |
| Close Control | | | | | | | | 1.000 | .774 | .512 | .628 | .566 | .460 | .475 | .547 | .520 |
| Criticism | | | | | | | | | 1.000 | .344 | .566 | .440 | .490 | .440 | .490 | .373 |
| Ideology | | | | | | | | | | 1.000 | .575 | .313 | .412 | .336 | .324 | .665 |
| Cadre | | | | | | | | | | | 1.000 | .306 | .280 | .192 | .441 | .347 |
| Hard Life | | | | | | | | | | | | 1.000 | .700 | .555 | .555 | .434 |
| Food | | | | | | | | | | | | | 1.000 | .654 | .554 | .533 |
| Danger | | | | | | | | | | | | | | 1.000 | .521 | .404 |
| Treatment of Self | | | | | | | | | | | | | | | 1.000 | .652 |
| Village Policy | | | | | | | | | | | | | | | | 1.000 |

analysis will recognize the Principal Components results as a preliminary step in the effort to determine meaningful factors. To uncover the underlying patterns in terms of identifiable factors, the results of the Principal Components analysis, i.e., the factor loadings, were rotated in an orthogonal way using a varimax criterion. [6] In other words, the results of this rotation are a number of factors that are uncorrelated with each other and that have substantive meaning, it will be shown, whether considered separately or together. Table 8-3 shows the factor loadings, and other relevant information, from this procedure.

Four factors of mathematical significance were extracted from the linkages among the various satisfactions and dissatisfactions measurements. For ease of sight, those measurements that correlate highly with (load on) each factor are boxed.

Before discussing the details of the composition of the factors, several comments about the overall structuring of attitudes revealed by table 8-3 and the method for interpreting them are appropriate. The purposes of the factor analysis (including the rotation) were to measure, discriminate, and reveal the systemic interrelationships within the patterns of adaptation previously identified by qualitative means. Inspection of table 8-3 reveals two factors of satisfaction and two of dissatisfaction. The process of identifying these factors involves consideration of the ways in which the various measurements correlate with (load on) each factor; thus it will be argued that Factors I and III represent conformity and commitment, respectively, and that Factors II and IV represent, respectively, demoralization and non-integration. Simultaneously—and this is both a strength and a weakness of factor analysis—the systemic character of a factor will be described by assuming the factor does indeed represent a particular pattern of adaptation. This "circular" procedure is reasonably valid insofar as it is supported by qualitative evidence of the type that will be adduced in the following analysis.

## Conformity

Table 8-3 shows that satisfaction with solidarity, with equality, and liking for the soldier's immediate cadre correlate most highly with the factor labelled Factor I.[a] These sentiments reflect the soldier's identification with his unit, that is with his primary group. However, on a priori grounds such identification is consistent either with commitment or with conformity. The factor analysis helps discriminate between these patterns for, as will be discussed in detail, the measurements associated with commitment correlate highly *not* on Factor I but on Factor III and measurements that reflect the dynamics of conformity correlate highly *not* on the other factors but on Factor I.

---

[a]It is customary to label the factors in order of the highest sum of squares. If table 8-3 had followed that custom, column 1 would be labeled Factor II. However, additions will be made to the measurements which reverses the order of the sums of squares.

Table 8-3
Patterns of Satisfactions-Dissatisfactions with Life in Front, Results of Factor Analysis, Varimax Rotated Orthogonal Factor Loadings

| | Factor I Conformity | Factor II Demoralization | Factor III Commitment | Factor IV Non-integration | Communality |
|---|---|---|---|---|---|
| *Satisfactions with* | | | | | |
| Solidarity | .783 | -.209 | .003 | .057 | .660 |
| Equality | .768 | -.109 | .051 | -.134 | .622 |
| Cadre | .684 | -.046 | -.010 | -.450 | .672 |
| Nationalism | .682 | .021 | -.426 | -.212 | .692 |
| Ideol. Aims | .549 | -.008 | .541 | -.290 | .679 |
| Relations in PLAF | .578 | -.276 | .305 | .059 | .509 |
| Relations with Vil | .328 | -.261 | .614 | .211 | .598 |
| *Dissatisfactions with* | | | | | |
| Hard Life | -.168 | .757 | -.140 | .082 | .627 |
| Danger | -.084 | .744 | -.045 | .055 | .565 |
| Food | -.093 | .730 | -.144 | .084 | .562 |
| Cadre | -.182 | .193 | -.088 | .776 | .680 |
| Criticism | -.132 | .517 | .011 | .512 | .548 |
| Close Control | -.086 | .575 | -.182 | .460 | .583 |
| Treatment of Self | -.093 | .671 | -.287 | .129 | .558 |
| Village Policy | -.087 | .422 | -.713 | -.018 | .694 |
| Ideology | -.003 | -.082 | -.697 | .439 | .679 |
| Sum of Squares | 2.996 | 3.133 | 2.100 | 1.705 | 9.934 |

Given the imposed group structure of Front life, the Vietnamese cultural predisposition towards group identity, and the establishment of informal norms by the group as a defense against exceptional demands for commitment, strong sentiments of group solidarity and equality among comrades could be expected to be central to the dynamics of conformity. However, why is satisfaction with one's immediate cadre so strongly related to these sentiments?

The cadre occupied a crucial role in the compliance system of the PLAF. In the ideal described by Chapter 6, he was not only committed and "talented"—i.e., displayed the type of leadership ability that combined the instrumental function of being a task specialist with the expressive function of the maintenance specialist [7] —but he also was responsible for preventing the development of ritualization and informal norms characteristic of conformity. However, the following testimony of a cadre suggests that certain behavior was countenanced:

> Did the men in your unit come to talk to you about their personal problems?
>   Yes. If they missed their families, for example, they would come to tell me about it, and ask for permission to go home.
> Did the Front prohibit meeting with women?
>   Yes. No one was allowed to meet women in private. If a person wanted to get married, he would have to present the matter to his superiors. They would take care of arranging a marriage for him. But "free relations" with women were strictly forbidden.
> This is the theory. Was it in fact adhered to?
>   No, the fighters rarely obeyed that order. They still had relations with women in secret. Many of them were caught and criticized during self-criticism sessions. In the case of the cadres however, it was impossible to catch them in the act since they were the leaders in the unit and could go wherever they pleased.

Thus, in conforming units, a subtle and selective failure on the part of the cadre to execute Front doctrine occurred. Some cadre not being totally "sincere" themselves and often concerned more with group solidarity than with strict implementation of Front doctrine permitted the ritualization of confession that became the group norm. This tacit arrangement, which protected both cadre and men, reinforced the Vietnamese tendency to dissimulate. Pye's conclusion about similar ritualized behavior among guerrillas in the Malayan Communist party also seems applicable to many PLAF units: "Thus, for all concerned, it was desirable to treat the problem of self-criticism as an elaborate game in which each member went through the appropriate confession of some minor sin, promised to do better in the future, and in this way set the stage for the leader to reprove and exhort one and all."[8] In short, some cadres participated in—and helped establish—informal norms of the group that mitigated against the total incorporation of organizational norms; in doing so, they promoted the integration of "primary relationships" and satisfactions afforded by solidarity of the group with "secondary relationships" required by the Front.[9] (The frequency of these supportive cadre relative to more committed cadre will be discussed subsequently.)

The above argument suggests that conformity involved neither a total internalization of organizational values nor an absolute rejection but rather a *selective incorporation*. The quantitative evidence supports this view as a careful examination of the theme labeled satisfaction with nationalism shows.

Satisfaction with the nationalism expressed in the Front is highly correlated (.682) with Factor I. Since the indication of satisfaction with the spirit of nationalism in the PLAF was a voluntary response in the interview, it is reasonable to assume that nationalism was internalized into the belief system of those soldiers who thus responded. Yet, it was previously hypothesized that for conformers the Front's attempts to instill ideological beliefs were frustrated by dissimulation. It would therefore seem either that nationalism is not associated with conformity, in which case Factor I does not represent conformity, or that dissimulation and internalization were selective processes; the latter was the case. The PLAF's socialization processes involved integration into a group life whose structures and activities were defined, and pervaded by, an ideological milieu, as Chapter 7 detailed. Some of the Front's ideological themes were consonant with Vietnamese cultural ideas; others were not. The former were more likely to be internalized; the latter more likely to be subject to dissimulation. The consonant beliefs, seeming both correct and clear to the recruit, allowed him to appraise reality in a way that was reinforced by his new environment. Moreover, the expression of beliefs that were consonant, and thus commonly held, served a social adjustment function of helping to relate to others in the group, of establishing one's sense of identity with the primary group. Among the ideological themes proclaimed by the Front, nationalism was most consonant—though neither salient nor articulated by most peasants before entry—with the Vietnamese's self-identity as a Vietnamese. Therefore, it was likely to become internalized into a soldier's cognitive structure as part of the process of identifying with the primary group. Many of the other objectives and interpretations of the NLF—particularly those derived from Marxism—were neither natural nor easily understood by the soldier and, hence, were more likely to be dissimulated.

Patterns in the factor analysis afford further support for this hypothesis of selective cognitive incorporation. The correlation between satisfaction with ideology other than nationalism and Factor I is .549, a figure high enough that internalization with at least some of the ideological aims of the Front apparently occurred. For example, the assertions of aspirations for peace in NLF ideology might well have been internalized. On the other hand, the correlation is significantly lower than the loading of nationalistic sentiments. Furthermore, indications of satisfactions with ideological aims other than nationalism loads higher —i.e., forms a key part of the interpretation—of another factor orthogonally related to Factor I, which will be analyzed shortly. The evidence, therefore, supports the conclusion that the soldier who *conforms without commitment internalizes Front indoctrination selectively, choosing those beliefs which avoid conflict and reinforce conformity and identification with his primary group.*

The integration of secondary identification of nationalism with primary identification in the immediate group supports a finding derived from the study of armies, one which does not always receive the attention it deserves. As Shils articulates it, "primary group solidarity functions in the corporate body to strengthen the motivation for the fulfillment of the substantive prescriptions and commands issued by the official agents of the corporate body, within the context of *a set of generalized moral predispositions or sense of obligation.*"[10] The sentiment that the Front was, in a generalized sense, right, proper, justified endowed the PLAF with a sense of legitimacy. Recalling the earlier discussion of pragmatic fatalism, such sentiments of legitimacy played a significant part in the soldier's compliance behavior and especially in the pattern of conformity: it fostered the soldier's assimilation into the group, facilitated the integration of the group into the organizational structure, and reinforced his sense of belonging to the PLAF even though he did not fully internalize the Front's ideology and become totally committed. An assessment of the ultimate significance of these sentiments must be deferred until the effects of stress are analyzed in Part III.

One can anticipate that the sense of legitimacy extended also to the soldier's attitude towards the authority structure as embodied in the Front's code of proper behavior. The data confirm this expectation. Satisfaction with the propriety of the PLAF's internal codes of behavior correlates somewhat more highly (.578) than does satisfaction with ideological aims, as table 8-3 shows. Concern with, and exercise of, proper behavior is a principal theme in Vietnamese culture. In the PLAF, proper behavior prescribed discipline to the authority hierarchy, on the one hand, and protection, particularly against the arbitrary use of power by those in authority. The soldier's primary group was structured in accord with these principles and his acceptance of the authority structure formed an intrinsic aspect of his attachment to the group.

The relatively high loading of satisfaction with the internal codes of behavior also suggests the important proposition that identification with the primary group did not necessarily conflict with acceptance of the formal structure. As observed earlier, conforming units adopted some norms which relaxed the formal standards of the organization; such informal standards could seriously retard organizational effectiveness. However, consider the coded theme of satisfaction with the NLF's norms of behavior towards villagers (the last item of satisfaction listed by table 8-3). The items of "proper behavior" included in this coding ranged from the strict prohibition on fraternization with villagers (particularly with women) to NLF policies in the recruitment and control of the population. These restrictions and regulations on behavior towards those outside the primary group—the villagers—seemed to have caused the Front a great deal of difficulty.

The low correlation (.328) of this measurement with Factor I contrasts with the relatively high loading on Factor I of satisfaction with the formal norms regulating relations *within* the Front. The formal rules of behavior towards others outside the group did not enter strongly into identification with the primary group. Hence, the incentive to conform to the rules of the Front was weakened for outside relations; violations of these rules were unlikely to cause the type of criticism that implied a threat of being cut-off from the security of the group. In short, *identification with the informal structure was largely consistent with conformity to the formal structure; insofar as a discrepancy existed, it was in areas not dependent upon group identification.* (The high loading of this measurement on Factor III provides additional evidence of these interpretations, as will be discussed shortly.)

The above evidence suggests that, in these conforming groups, an "area of acceptance" of Front authority and an area of nonacceptance, perhaps of noncompliance, developed. The boundary between acceptance and nonacceptance was defined by the desire to avoid trouble and minimize conflict within the primary group. Therefore, the assessment Pye reached in his study of the Malayan guerrillas also held for conforming units in the PLAF: "These informal standards to which the SEP's sought to conform were not necessarily in direct conflict with the formal ones; indeed this was rarely the case. They were, however, apt to be less exacting, more casual, and more concerned with the avoidance of trouble than with positive action."[11]

The low and negative loadings of all the dissatisfaction measures on Factor I further supports the proposition that those who conformed had a positive orientation towards life in the Front. These loadings suggest that identification with the primary group was, in a quantitative sense, not importantly related to dissatisfactions with Front life. It could be argued that difficulties might have strengthened, or helped develop, group ties, as the following testimony of a soldier suggests:

> Did you like the atmosphere of friendship in the Front?
> We loved each other very much because we were all in the same difficult situation, we shared the same hardships, and we were compatriots.

Yet, such recollections were few in number in the sample, and the low loading (–.168) of dissatisfactions with hard life in the PLAF does not confirm this relationship as being quantitatively strong in the sample. Similar remarks can be made about the whole range of stated dissatisfactions. In short, the orthogonality of the factors and the evidence that dissatisfactions load on factors other than Factor I (the Conformity factor) argue that conformity represents positive sentiments that develop both in the face and in the absence of dissatisfactions.

We can now summarize the essential components of conformity as compared to commitment. Many features of PLAF norms and socialization processes were congruent with Vietnamese characteristics and needs. The Vietnamese—or, at least some Vietnamese—could satisfy their security needs, gratify their status drives, and find their self-identity by developing a feeling of solidarity with the Front-imposed primary group, by submitting to the strong and legitimate authority structure, and by learning and conforming to the proper code of behavior. In the ideal, the norms of the organization would ultimately be internalized so that the individual would fully identify with the organization and would be fully committed; however, the completion of this final step clashed with cultural patterns. The demands for sincerity rather than the proper responses dictated by the situation, for emotionality rather than repression of feelings, for filial piety to the organization rather than to the family all ran counter to the traditional characteristics. The PLAF's success in attaining *commitment* thus hinged on whether the soldier was transformed in these characteristics. Yet, if due to the operation of informal norms, he were not, he would still be able to satisfy basic needs by *conforming*. That is, those soldiers who conformed could realize satisfactions that, for many, were greater than they had known as peasants.

### Commitment

Factor III, like Factor I and unlike Factors II and IV, represents positive sentiments towards life in the Front; satisfactions load positively, dissatisfactions negatively. The two themes (village policy and ideology) that load most heavily (and negatively) on Factor III reflect adamant ideological positions on the part of the interviewees. The high negative value of dissatisfaction with the NLF's village policy arises from soldiers who vehemently denied—usually in highly politicized terms—that they disliked policies involving manipulation, coercion, or terrorism. [12] Similar remarks apply to the last coded item in table 8–3, dissatisfaction with ideology. In addition to these themes, satisfaction with ideological aims and with Front policy towards relations with villagers load strongly and positively. Thus, Factor III might represent commitment. However, the loadings are not sufficiently distinct to advance such an interpretation with much confidence. Therefore, considering the significance of the issue of commitment in the PLAF, this interpretation was fortified by using additional measurements.

One way to validate the interpretation of Factor III would be to check the factor scores against independent measurements of commitment. Independent measurement means, in this context, themes of ideological commitment that appeared in the interviews but in subjects divorced from the satisfaction-dissatisfaction discussion. Since commitment is a complex pattern of motivation, many indicators could be defined for coding purposes and, indeed, they were. Unfortunately, most of these a priori indicators did not prove to be sufficiently frequent or adequately reliable to be of quantitative value. Five themes having prima facie validity—i.e., a reasonable a priori judgment could be made for each

on whether they indicated ideological commitment—were, after coding, frequent
and reliable: statements of anti-Americanism, of belief in NLF propaganda, of
political awareness, of identification with the NLF, and of identification with the
GVN. Correlating these codings, whose content will be discussed shortly, with
the scores of Factor III would provide some validation of the interpretation of
this factor as representing ideological commitment, though a number of technical
problems limit the value of this approach.[b] However, in addition to validation,
it is important to strengthen the measuring and discriminating ability of Factor
III. To do the latter, the measurements of the commitment indicators were
directly incorporated into the factor analysis. The results after appropriate rotation, shown by table 8–4, reveal the same patterns already discussed; this
stability reinforces confidence in the technical aspects of the factor analysis and
increases trust in the interpretation of the factors. In addition, the commitment
indicators load as a priori expected, with one significant exception.

The new indicators will be considered in detail beginning with anti-Americanism. This theme has a prima facie validity as an indicator of commitment
because, on the one hand, it is part of the NLF's ideology, and, on the other hand,
few Vietnamese peasants upon entry had salient anti-American orientation. In
short, it became incorporated into the soldier's belief system as part of becoming
committed. Though no single type of question dealt consistently (across interviews) with anti-Americanism per se, the subject was covered in some depth
in most interviews. Nonetheless, coding this subject in a valid manner was difficult for it was improper—in the interview situation—for Vietnamese to say "bad"
things about Americans, at least in a direct way. Interviewees did let their
feelings be known in the subtle, indirect way so characteristic of Vietnamese
(and, hence, at times contradicted more direct pro or neutral statements). Fortu-
nately, the interviewers frequently asked the respondent to distinguish between
his feelings at the time of the interview from those while he was still in the Front
(e.g., "Those are your feelings now, how did you feel while you were in the
Front?"). Before and after attitudes were coded; the results show that the
respondents indicated significantly more anti-Americanism before. Though this
result may be interpreted in several ways, part of the discrepancy can be
accounted for by the supposition that Vietnamese respondents felt it proper to
indicate their true feelings only as part of their past, when they were under the
influence of the NLF, and thus not accountable for their feelings. The before
attitudes, which in any event are more relevant, were used in the present analysis.

---

[b]The high pair-wise correlation between aims and nationalism counterindicates this
approach because correlations between other commitment measurements and the factor
may be largely a result of the loading of nationalism on the factor; but nationalism loads
highly on identification with the group! To avoid such spuriously high correlations (from
the standpoint of our conceptual problem), a multivariate approach sorting out these various
measurements is indicated. However, such techniques require the solution to a number of
severe technical problems, not the least of which is multicollinearity.

## Table 8–4

**Patterns of Satisfactions and Dissatisfactions with Life in the Front, Results of Factor Analysis Including Separate Measurements of Commitment**

| | Factor I Conformity | Factor II Demoralization | Factor III Commitment | Factor IV Non-integration | Communality |
|---|---|---|---|---|---|
| *Satisfactions with* | | | | | |
| Solidarity | .736 | -.166 | .081 | -.006 | .575 |
| Equality | .764 | -.095 | .070 | -.127 | .618 |
| Cadre | .671 | -.001 | .095 | -.459 | .670 |
| Nationalism | .664 | -.005 | .487 | -.095 | .687 |
| Ideol. Aims | .542 | -.055 | .590 | -.138 | .665 |
| Relations in Front | .548 | -.283 | .222 | -.059 | .433 |
| Relations with Vil | .291 | -.315 | .340 | -.291 | .300 |
| *Commitment Measures* | | | | | |
| Anti-Americanism | .210 | -.063 | .606 | .180 | .448 |
| Belief in Propaganda | .471 | -.230 | .475 | .077 | .507 |
| Political Awareness | .422 | -.124 | -.064 | .421 | .375 |
| Id. with Viet Cong | .324 | -.231 | .518 | .063 | .431 |
| Id. with GVN | .051 | .105 | -.516 | .145 | .301 |
| *Dissatisfactions with* | | | | | |
| Hard Life | -.184 | .768 | -.134 | .040 | .643 |
| Danger | -.106 | .749 | -.075 | -.026 | .579 |
| Food | -.085 | .732 | -.151 | .020 | .566 |
| Cadre | -.220 | .168 | -.132 | .761 | .673 |
| Criticism | -.155 | .480 | -.052 | .516 | .523 |
| Close Control | -.188 | .571 | -.141 | .476 | .586 |
| Treatment of Self | -.077 | .669 | -.212 | .238 | .555 |
| Village Policy | -.055 | .474 | -.531 | .092 | .518 |
| Ideology | -.008 | .140 | -.749 | .248 | .641 |
| Sum of Squares | 3.400 | 3.319 | 2.877 | 1.699 | 11.295 |

To assure sufficient reliability, a three-category coding scheme (plus uncodable) was adopted: anti-Americanism, neutral, or pro-Americanism. In making their judgments, coders were instructed to be conservative towards the neutral position—i.e., if an interviewee expressed mild statements one way or the other or seemed ambivalent, he would be coded neutral. In short, the coding was highly reliable in distinguishing extreme positions. For the purposes of the factor analysis, we assumed this gross categorization constituted a three-point equal interval scale of anti-Americanism.[13]

As anticipated, the anti-Americanism measure loads highly (.606) on Factor III, thus supporting the interpretation of this factor as representing commit-ment.[c] Significantly, the loading of anti-Americanism on Factor I is consistent with previous interpretations—viz., the low but positive loading on Factor I suggests that anti-Americanism, in contrast to nationalism, is not basic to con-formity though it is consistent with conformity.

Another important aspect of commitment was the degree of belief in the Front's propaganda. One might expect that the committed would indicate a total belief in all aspects of the Front's internal propaganda. In coding this subject, the following three broadly-defined categories (plus uncodable) proved reliable: strong belief with no reservation, general belief with specific reservations, and disbelief. Again coders were instructed to be conservative towards the middle category, thus tending to increase reliability. In other words, these measurements were more accurate at the extremes.

Degree of belief in Front propaganda loads relatively highly (.475) on the commitment factor as anticipated (see table 8-4). However, it also loads just as highly on Factor I as well as negatively and higher than might be expected on Factor II. Several possible a priori explanations exist for this dispersion. To check which explanation empirically applied, individual interviews were investigated; it was found that generalized belief with some reservations tended to be associated with high scores on conformity, strong belief with commitment, and disbelief with demoralization. Conformers seemed to accept the basic premises of Front indoctrination; yet they had reservations about specific statements. The most prevalent reservation was in the area of combat reports. The Front never reported defeats and exaggerated victories; many soldiers were aware of this. Most of those soldiers who were recorded as indicating strong belief as well as scoring high on Factor III indicated a total belief (even when confronted by the interviewer with clear examples of Front lies). This was due, in part, to the interview situation where the "hard core" soldier wanted to show to the interviewer how fully dedicated he was. But it also reflected an "ideologized" belief system.

The measurements "identification with the NLF" and "identification with the GVN" represent overall judgments made by the coders. It was obvious to all

---

[c]The loading is somewhat depressed perhaps due to the conservative nature of the coding. The relatively low commonality of the measurement also may be due, in part, to this coding.

the analysts who read the interviews that some respondents were "hard core" revolutionaries. Their answers were not only given in typical Communist jargon—many who did not seem to be hard core also answered in terms of slogans—but they also often said they would return to their units if they were freed. Even among ralliers, some showed signs of total belief. It was found that coders could make a reasonably reliable judgment in grossly classifying interviews into those manifesting strong indications of identifying with the NLF from those who did not.[d] Similarly, a judgment could be made separating the interviewees into those who showed strong inclinations towards the GVN—wanting to join the ARVN, wanting to help increase rallying, etc.—from those who did not. It would have been preferable to combine these measurements into a single scale for, although they are conceptually distinct, their measurements were not made independently. However, for convenience, they entered the factor analysis separately.

The loadings of these measurements of identification with the NLF and with the GVN on Factor III supports the interpretation of this factor as commitment.[e] Checking back upon individual interviews, it was found that all those respondents who were judged as "hard core" received high scores on Factor III. The loadings of these measurements on Factor I also supports its interpretation as conformity without commitment. There is a positive and low loading (.324) of identification with the NLF; it surely should be positive, for conformity does not conflict with positive sentiments and low because full internalization of ideology is not fundamental to conformity. That identification with the GVN does not load on Factor I is expected because conformity represents a positive orientation towards the PLAF.

The measurement of political awareness also required an overall judgment by the coders. A priori it was reasoned that since peasants entered the Front with low levels of political awareness and since an aim of PLAF socialization was to raise the "level of political awareness," a measure of the degree to which soldiers became indoctrinated would be their current level of political awareness. A gross three level classification proved reasonably reliable (75 percent): higher than average awareness, average awareness, lower than average awareness. Knowledge of even crude Communist theory and of "esoteric" doctrine defined those in the higher than average category. Coders were instructed to be conservative towards the "average" category to the extent that those interviews lacking sufficient depth of coverage for an adequate judgment of political awareness were allocated to this category.

Degree of political awareness showed virtually no loading on Factor III. This result was unexpected on a priori grounds. However, investigation of individual

-----

[d]The coders were asked to make a judgment on a four-point scale. However, these results prove unreliable. Collapsing into two categories improved the reliability to approximately 85 percent.

[e]A higher loading might have resulted if the two measurements had been combined into a single scale and if the coding were not so gross.

interviews explains the "unexpected" quantitative result. Soldiers who were judged average awareness tended to score above average on the conformity factor, which is reflected by the fairly strong loading of political awareness (.422) on conformity; this is reasonable for it suggests that successful adaptation does raise political awareness in the areas of nationalism and such social goals as land reform. Soldiers who were judged below average political awareness tended to score above average on the demoralization factor. Soldiers who were judged above average political awareness did not score significantly different from average on Factor III but did score above average on Factor IV. It seems to be the case that, on the one hand, many of those who became committed did not learn even crude Communist theory or esoteric doctrine, and, on the other hand, some of those who did become politically astute did not become committed (or their commitment diminished). The last point will be clarified when Factor IV is discussed.

In summary, Factor III measures a positive pattern of adaptation to Front life that is distinguishable from the alternative pattern of conformity and that is defined by many of those norms of commitment described in Chapter 5. Thus, soldiers who scored high on Factor III were highly politicized, manifested "unshakeable" belief in the organization and in its ultimate victory, and indicated a marked spirit of self-sacrifice. They exhibited primary identification with organizational and political values—in contrast to conforming soldiers for whom such values were secondary sources of identification—and did not manifest strong primary group solidarity. (Subsequent analysis will analyze the later finding in more detail.) Hence, this pattern represents commitment.

A number of issues need further consideration. Did commitment, as it was realized in the PLAF, represent the full internalization of Front norms described by Chapter 5? Or did it represent an ideologized belief system? In the latter event, the Front indoctrination processes would have been only partially successful: the soldier spoke and thought as a dedicated revolutionary, but these cognitions required the continuing support and pressure of the structure and environment of the PLAF. In short, this level of incorporation of Front norms would not imply a fundamental, stable identity transformation: it was fragile and could be eroded. On the other hand, if a total identity-transformation—implying penetration to the core of the soldier's innermost thoughts—occurred, then a "true believer" would indeed have evolved.[14] Neither the quantitative analysis nor the interview material allow us to decide this issue with full confidence, though the analysis of stress in Part III provides indirect evidence. In either event, this pattern of adaptation will be continued to be referred to as commitment.

### Demoralization

The themes defining Factors II and IV were dissatisfactions. The preceding analysis dealt primarily with cases in which the organization offered, and the soldier obtained, positive satisfactions from life in the Front. Now evidence of soldiers whose net sentiments were negative will be treated. These negative sentiments do not necessarily constitute a lack of compliance in the sense of a regular refusal to accept demands of the PLAF. On the contrary, even those soldiers who were dissatisfied complied with most Front demands most of the time. But clearly their predisposition to comply and the reasons for their compliance were distinct from those of soldiers with positive sentiments. Before investigating the reasons for their compliance, the nature of their dissatisfactions will be examined. Though dissatisfactions can arise in a number of ways, the factor analysis, as well as the qualitative evidence, distinguishes two types of dissatisfactions, which for reasons to be detailed shortly, will be called *demoralization* and *non-integration*.

The measurements that load most highly on Factor II (see tables 8-3 and 8-4) are the three concerning deprivations of life as a soldier in the PLAF. Hardships of military life (including homesickness, living in jungle conditions, illnesses, frequent and difficult marches, constant alerts, etc.), the dangers and uncertainties of combat, and the lack and poor quality of food were prevalent conditions of a guerrilla's existence. One, of course, would expect dissatisfactions with these conditions and indeed many soldiers complained of them even to the point of exaggeration.[15] Yet the interview data indicate that a large number of soldiers also did *not* complain; moreover, these soldiers were similarly exposed to dangers and deprivations. Hence, the statement of dissatisfactions in the interview situation reflected the soldier's sentiments towards his experience and these sentiments reflected more than the objective fact of dangers and deprivations. The quantitative and qualitative evidence provides insight into other psychological mechanisms involved.

The following testimony of a former soldier suggests that complaints about dangers and deprivations were closely associated with feelings of demoralization:

> Life in the Front was hard . . . I had seen that the Front troops had suffered heavy losses . . . the dead and wounded were left behind . . . wounded were badly treated . . . I hated the harsh discipline . . . [T]here were so many *kiem thao* sessions and *sinh hoat* sessions that we never had a moment of rest. At night, there were so many alerts that all of us were exhausted, especially after a tiring day. The alerts were part of our training. All this demoralized the fighters.

Factor II can be interpreted and most conveniently identified as demoralization, as the following discussion argues.

Demoralization is a complex phenomenon because it occurs in an organizational context. Thus, one would expect that feelings of demoralization affected, and were affected by, interpersonal relationships and attitudes towards the authority, its demands, structures, and processes. So it was in the PLAF. The above quotation suggests that feelings of deprivation, discouragement, fear, and the like were linked with sentiments of resentment towards organizational demands and structural principles. At a time when the need for security was greatest—when stressful conditions caused anxiety over one's personal security as well as threatened destruction of the individual's primary group with consequent fears of psychological isolation—the Front's demands on the individual tended to increase. The soldier's battlefield mistakes, his gripes over hardships, food, danger, etc., were reviewed in criticism sessions where they were attributed to poor morale; poor morale, in turn, was considered to be a result of poor ideology and a lack of revolutionary commitment.[16] The loadings on Factor II of dissatisfaction with criticism sessions (.48) and with close control, surveillance, and discipline (.57) support this interpretation. For many of those soldiers who became demoralized and were subjected to increased organizational demands, a feeling of alienation against the organization developed. This is reflected in the high loading (.67) on Factor II of the theme labelled dissatisfaction with treatment of self by the Front, which consists of a variety of specific personal grievances (e.g., failure of the Front to fulfill promises, to approve a transfer, to allow a visit home, to permit a marriage) directed against the organization.

The theme of belief in propaganda supplies further reinforcement of the systemic nature of demoralization. As noted earlier, high scorers on demoralization tended to voice disbelief of Front propaganda, particularly concerning combat reports. The demoralized not only realized Front deception on battlefield reports but many also felt that they were being more generally deceived; they tended to generalize their personal grievances into a feeling that the Front lied to them. This was particularly the case for promises of land, or help to their family.

Tables 8-3 and 8-4 show a low loading on Factor II of dissatisfaction with cadre. The quantitative evidence thus separates dissatisfaction with cadre from demoralization and suggests that demoralization, and associated feelings of alienation, were directed towards the organizational system but *not* towards the primary group and its cadre. Though some soldiers blamed their cadres, the following testimony reflects the more common attitude:

> After each defeat, were the fighters still confident in the leadership of the cadres?
> Yes, they were still confident in the leadership of their cadres but they were demoralized . . .

The low loading on Factor II of satisfactions with those themes associated with group life supports this interpretation.[17] Furthermore, the consistent low loadings on Factor II (see table 8-4) of the various ideological and commitment measures—particularly dissatisfaction with ideology +.14, identification with NLF -.23, and identification with GVN +.11—suggest that although some rejection of ideology may play a part, demoralization involved more basic concerns

(Part III argues that these concerns were the soldier's perception of the organization's failure to provide security).

Demoralization should not be interpreted as a pattern of noncompliance. It represents the attitudes of soldiers who by the time they left the Front (either voluntarily or involuntarily) were dissatisfied; the extent to which they obeyed commands of the Front is not being measured by this factor. The nature of this type of negative orientation suggests that these dissatisfactions must be viewed in the context of a soldier's career in the PLAF. Examination of the interviews of soldiers who "scored" high on demoralization reveals that many of them had at first adapted according to either of the two major patterns of compliance and then became dissatisfied, demoralized, and frequently rejected the system. In short, there existed in the PLAF a dynamics of discontentment; the causes of demoralization and its dysfunctional effects will be treated extensively as part of the analysis of stress in Part III.

### Nonintegration

Factor IV discriminates another type of negative orientation towards the Front which involved, it will be argued, nonintegration—i.e., the failure of soldiers to "fit in" with the social structure of the organization either from the outset or later in their career. The themes defining this factor are dissatisfaction with one's immediate cadre (as well as negative loading on satisfaction with cadre), with criticism sessions, and with close control and discipline. Aside from indicating dissatisfaction with the system, its most distinctive feature when compared with demoralization is dissatisfaction with the cadre. Considering the crucial role played by the cadre in the soldier's integration into group life and assimilation into the authority structure, complaints about the cadre suggest a failure to integrate. Checking individual interviews of those with a high score on this factor tends to confirm this suspicion.

Factor IV is a conglomerate measure grouping together a variety of maladapted soldiers. There were a sizable number of recruits who never did psychologically "accept membership" in the PLAF even after the critical initial period (see Chapter 4). These *non-accepters* found little satisfaction with their cadre or with their unit (it was not unusual for them to form friendships with one of their similarly uncommitted comrades particularly from the same hamlet or village), seemed to be criticized more than usual about laziness, generally complied with those commands that they had to but otherwise showed no enthusiasm.

Another group of soldiers were similar to the non-accepters except that they were more extreme in their rejection of Front life. Whereas non-accepters were able to form friendships, although not of the prescribed type, these soldiers were unable to assimilate either into group life or into the authority structure. Consider the following response of a former PLAF member:

> Did you like the atmosphere of solidarity and friendship between the
> Front members?
>> We were always busy with one mission or another. We ate and then we
>> stood guard or did something else. We never had any free time to
>> make friends.

In the usual circumstances, informal standards of the group relaxed the PLAF's demands enough for group relationships to develop. Why was this respondent unable to assimilate into the group? Perhaps this was due to a lack of trust. Distrust did occur in the Front, as the following remarks of a soldier suggests:

> The fighters were distrustful of each other, and everybody kept his
> thoughts to himself. Unless they were close friends and trusted each
> other, they would not confide in each other.

In such cases, a sense of isolation could set in.[18] Though lack of trust is, as Chapter 3 argued, common in Vietnam, its manifestation can be suppressed, in many situations, by means of either of two cultural solutions: (1) acceptance of a status structure including its associated formalistic code of behavior or (2) extension of the identity group on the basis of solidarity. For the *unassimilated*, these solutions failed to become operative. He felt isolated by the system, did not get along with the cadre, formed few close relations with comrades; he resented criticisms, particularly of uncooperative behavior; he tended to be involved in interpersonal conflicts which he attributed to personality clashes.

Another type of soldier accepted the authority structure and rules of proper behavior with considerable enthusiasm but did not become integrated into group life. This pattern of compliance was based upon inducements—primarily status rewards—not identification with the organization nor gratification of security needs. Indeed, such soldiers were quite capable of switching sides if the inducements were right, as Part III discusses in detail. For these reasons, they will be called *pragmatists*. Most of the pragmatists who scored high on Factor IV complained about conflict with cadres; however, these disagreements usually resulted from alleged discrimination or inequities in privileges (which should be interpreted in terms of concern over status). The relatively high loading on Factor IV of political awareness (.421) comes from the pragmatists, most of whom were cadre and were politically skilled as well as politically aware.

Again, we caution against interpreting the various types of nonintegration as being synonymous with noncompliance. Surely, needs, drives, motivations, were not fully met; surely, a predisposition towards noncompliance existed. But, though nonintegrated soldiers limited their participation in Front life, the extent to which they did, the areas of noncompliance involved, and the dysfunctional effects of such behavior require additional analysis.

### Structural Integration

The variability, just described, in motivations, in group norms, in the commitment of soldiers posed potential problems of control for the PLAF. Though conformity represented a positive orientation towards life in the Front, the ritualization, informal norms, and limited areas of acceptance intrinsic to conformity suggests that the activities of conforming soldiers had to be channeled, checked, and controlled. This control was even more necessary for demoralized and nonintegrated soldiers. Therefore, the analysis now examines the extent to which the PLAF was able to integrate soldiers with diverse patterns of motivations into a coherent system. In theory, integration was achieved by staffing the leadership positions of the hierarchical, politically controlled command structure with committed and able cadre. We will thus analyze how fully this theory obtained in reality.

#### Distribution of Commitment Within the Command Structure

The selection process for advancement in the Front was designed to promote the committed into cadre positions. Was the PLAF successful in producing and distributing committed soldiers to positions of command? Using the rough measurements of the various motivational patterns for each soldier in the sample, the approximate extent of commitment, conformity, nonintegration, and demoralization in the PLAF could be estimated. However, these estimates require a number of assumptions, judgments, and qualifications about the nature of the sample that render them speculative.[19] Nonetheless, considerable confidence can be placed on conditional estimates of the distribution of the various motivations *within* the command structure. A limited statistical approach suffices: the average values (and their variations) of the patterns of adaptation for different levels of rank in the military structure will be compared.[f]

Table 8-5 displays the results of a one-way analysis of variance comparing the various factors (measured by their factor scores) for middle-level cadres, low-level cadres, and non-cadres.[g] The table shows that cadres, and especially middle-level cadres, were more likely to be committed. More formally stated, a significant difference exists in the degree of ideological commitment among the three ranks.

---

[f]A major bias in the sample was due to rank. By making the comparisons with rank, we control many of the biases. See Part III for a more thorough discussion of this point.

[g]The distributions of the factor scores are standardized normal distributions. Details of the coding of rank were discussed in Chapter 6.

**Table 8–5**
**Distribution of Satisfactions-Dissatisfactions Factors over Ranks,**
**Total Sample**

| | Commitment | | |
|---|---|---|---|
| | *Mean* | *SD* | *N* |
| Middle-Level Cadres | 0.204 | 1.002 | 91 |
| Low-Level Cadres | 0.076 | 1.048 | 64 |
| Non-Cadres | −0.124 | 0.972 | 189 |
| Total | 0.000 | 1.001 | 344 |
| *Analysis of Variance* | *Mean Square* | *D.F.* | *F-Test* |
| Between Groups | 3.524 | 2 | 3.566* |
| Within Groups | 0.988 | 341 | (*P* = .029) |

| | Conformity | | |
|---|---|---|---|
| | *Mean* | *SD* | *N* |
| Middle-Level Cadres | −0.474 | 0.992 | 91 |
| Low-Level Cadres | 0.082 | 1.015 | 64 |
| Non-Cadres | 0.201 | 0.928 | 189 |
| Total | −0.000 | 1.001 | 344 |
| *Analysis of Variance* | *Mean Square* | *D.F.* | *F-Test* |
| Between Groups | 14.254 | 2 | 15.406*** |
| Within Groups | 0.925 | 341 | (*P* = .0001) |

| | Demoralization | | |
|---|---|---|---|
| | *Mean* | *SD* | *N* |
| Middle-Level Cadres | −0.045 | 1.060 | 91 |
| Low-Level Cadres | −0.085 | 1.003 | 64 |
| Non-Cadres | 0.051 | 0.974 | 189 |
| Total | −0.000 | 1.001 | 344 |
| *Analysis of Variance* | *Mean Square* | *D.F.* | *F-Test* |
| Between Groups | 0.568 | 2 | 0.565 |
| Within Groups | 1.005 | 341 | (*P* = .569) |

| | Nonintegration | | |
|---|---|---|---|
| | *Mean* | *SD* | *N* |
| Middle-Level Cadres | −0.260 | 0.917 | 91 |
| Low-Level Cadres | −0.152 | 1.104 | 64 |
| Non-Cadres | 0.176 | 0.973 | 189 |
| Total | 0.000 | 1.001 | 344 |
| *Analysis of Variance* | *Mean Square* | *D.F.* | *F-Test* |
| Between Groups | 6.754 | 2 | 6.969** |
| Within Groups | 0.969 | 341 | (*P* = .001) |

*Significant below .05 level
**Significant below .01 level
***Significant below .001 level

143

Before analyzing this finding in detail, a few words of methodological caution are in order. Sampling bias may be distorting these results. In particular, the sample contains both defectors and prisoners and it is the case (as we shall see in Part III) that defection is related to commitment. Therefore, for present purposes, the prisoner subsample may provide a less biased sample of the relationship between rank and commitment in the PLAF. Table 8-6 displays the results of an analysis of variance using only the prisoner subsample. The pattern of results in the two tables are similar, though the latter provides stronger evidence.

Cadres were more likely to be committed than non-cadres. This result is especially strong as the level of rank increases. Thus, middle-level cadres have a significantly higher average value of commitment than both lower-level cadres and non-cadres whereas the contrast between the latter two is not great. Table 8-7 provides finer evidence of this point by displaying the results of pair-wide comparisons of the difference-of-the-means of the various levels of rank.

Returning to table 8-6, the data showing the comparative distribution of degree of conformity complements the above finding. Again a significant difference exists among the levels of rank but the direction of the relationship is reversed: non-cadres and low-level cadres were more likely to have adapted by conformity than were middle-level cadres. (Almost the entire difference here is due to the contrast between middle-level cadres and other soldiers. See table 8-7.) This result does not imply that an increase in rank means less compliance. Rather these data reinforce the qualitative impression that the conformity and commitment distributions are complementary with regard to the command structure.

In terms of average values, low-level cadres were significantly less committed than middle-level cadres but had the same level of conformity as non-cadre (see tables 8-6 and 8-7). This statistical result could have been generated in two ways. If commitment and conformity are conceived of in absolute terms, then conforming low-level cadre were more frequent than committed low-level cadre; if these patterns of adaptation are conceptualized as questions of degree, then the "average" low-level cadre was less committed than the "average" middle-level cadre. Probably some mix of these situations obtained in the PLAF. In any event, this finding contrasting low-level cadre to middle-level cadre suggests three hypotheses about the nature of the leadership structure.

First of all, the finding implies that the commitment criteria for advancement were not as rigorously applied in selecting low-level cadre and that more strenuous filtering in terms of one's commitment occurred as the level of rank increased.

Secondly, the data suggest that the process of advancement itself fostered commitment. When the soldier was first selected out from among his comrades for advancement, he felt a great deal of satisfaction. He had had to work hard for

**Table 8-6**
**Distributions of Patterns of Satisfactions-Dissatisfactions over Ranks, Prisoners Only**

| | Commitment | | |
| --- | --- | --- | --- |
| | Mean | SD | N |
| Middle-Level Cadres | 0.757 | 0.778 | 31 |
| Low-Level Cadres | 0.202 | 1.152 | 24 |
| Non-Cadres | −0.016 | 0.853 | 80 |
| Total | 0.200 | 0.944 | 135 |
| Analysis of Variance | Mean Square | D.F. | F-Test |
| Between Groups | 6.678 | 2 | 8.303*** |
| Within Groups | 0.804 | 132 | (P = .000) |

| | Conformity | | |
| --- | --- | --- | --- |
| | Mean | SD | N |
| Middle-Level Cadres | −0.654 | 1.116 | 31 |
| Low-Level Cadres | 0.177 | 0.974 | 24 |
| Non-Cadres | 0.174 | 0.867 | 80 |
| Total | −0.015 | 1.004 | 135 |
| Analysis of Variance | Mean Square | D.F. | F-Test |
| Between Groups | 8.199 | 2 | 9.124*** |
| Within Groups | 0.899 | 132 | (P = .000) |

| | Demoralization | | |
| --- | --- | --- | --- |
| | Mean | SD | N |
| Middle-Level Cadres | −0.375 | 1.475 | 31 |
| Low-Level Cadres | −0.452 | 1.216 | 24 |
| Non-Cadres | −0.100 | 1.225 | 80 |
| Total | −0.226 | 1.284 | 135 |
| Analysis of Variance | Mean Square | D.F. | F-Test |
| Between Groups | 1.591 | 2 | 0.965 |
| Within Groups | 1.650 | 132 | (P = .384) |

| | Nonintegration | | |
| --- | --- | --- | --- |
| | Mean | SD | N |
| Middle-Level Cadres | −0.137 | 0.747 | 31 |
| Low-Level Cadres | 0.040 | 1.080 | 24 |
| Non-Cadres | 0.337 | 0.836 | 80 |
| Total | 0.175 | 0.832 | 135 |
| Analysis of Variance | Mean Square | D.F. | F-Test |
| Between Groups | 2.767 | 2 | 3.700* |
| Within Groups | 0.748 | 132 | (P = .027) |

*Significant below .05 level
***Significant below .001 level

**Table 8-7**
**Pairwise Comparisons of Levels of Rank for Satisfaction-Dissatisfaction Factors, Prisoners Only**

**A. Middle-Level Cadres vs Low-Level Cadres**

| | | Mid-Cadre | Low-Cadre | Difference | S.E. | D.F. | t-Test |
|---|---|---|---|---|---|---|---|
| Commitment | Mean | 0.757 | 0.202 | 0.555 | 0.261 | 53 | 2.132* (P = 0.038) |
| | SD | 0.778 | -1.152 | | | | |
| | N | 31.000 | 24.000 | | | | |
| Demoralization | Mean | -0.375 | -0.452 | 0.077 | 0.372 | 53 | 0.208 (P = 1.000) Approx. |
| | SD | 1.475 | 1.216 | | | | |
| | N | 31.000 | 24.000 | | | | |
| Conformity | Mean | -0.654 | 0.177 | -0.830 | 0.287 | 53 | -2.889** (P = 0.006) |
| | SD | 1.116 | 0.974 | | | | |
| | N | 31.000 | 24.000 | | | | |
| Nonintegration | Mean | -0.137 | 0.040 | 0.177 | 0.246 | 53 | -0.717 (P = 0.477) |
| | SD | 0.747 | 1.080 | | | | |
| | N | 31.000 | 24.000 | | | | |

**B. Middle-Level Cadres vs Non-Cadres**

| | | Mid-Cadre | Non-Cadre | Difference | S.E. | D.F. | t-Test |
|---|---|---|---|---|---|---|---|
| Commitment | Mean | 0.757 | -0.016 | 0.773 | 0.176 | 109 | 4.387*** (P = 0.000) |
| | SD | 0.778 | 0.853 | | | | |
| | N | 31.000 | 80.000 | | | | |
| Demoralization | Mean | -0.375 | -0.100 | -0.275 | 0.275 | 109 | -1.000 (P = 0.320) |
| | SD | 1.475 | 1.225 | | | | |
| | N | 31.000 | 80.000 | | | | |
| Conformity | Mean | -0.654 | 0.174 | -0.828 | 0.199 | 109 | -4.154*** (P = 0.000) |
| | SD | 1.116 | 0.867 | | | | |
| | N | 31.000 | 80.000 | | | | |

| | | Low-Cadre | Non-Cadre | Difference | S.E. | D.F. | t-Test |
|---|---|---|---|---|---|---|---|
| Nonintegration | Mean | 0.137 | -0.337 | 0.473 | 0.172 | 109 | 2.753** |
| | SD | 0.747 | 0.836 | | | | (P = 0.007) |
| | N | 31.000 | 80.000 | | | | |

## C. Low-Level Cadres vs Non-Cadres

| | | Low-Cadre | Non-Cadre | Difference | S.E. | D.F. | t-Test |
|---|---|---|---|---|---|---|---|
| Commitment | Mean | 0.202 | -0.016 | 0.218 | 0.216 | 102 | 1.007 |
| | SD | 1.152 | 0.853 | | | | (P = 0.316) |
| | N | 24.000 | 80.000 | | | | |
| Demoralization | Mean | -0.452 | -0.100 | -0.352 | 0.285 | 102 | -1.237 |
| | SD | 1.216 | 1.225 | | | | (P = 0.219) |
| | N | 24.000 | 80.000 | | | | |
| Conformity | Mean | 0.177 | 0.174 | 0.002 | 0.208 | 102 | 0.011 |
| | SD | 0.974 | 0.867 | | | | (P = 0.219) |
| | N | 24.000 | 80.000 | | | | |
| Nonintegration | Mean | -0.040 | -0.337 | 0.296 | 0.209 | 102 | 1.421 |
| | SD | 1.080 | 0.836 | | | | (P = 0.158) |
| | N | 24.000 | 80.000 | | | | |

*Significant below .05 level
**Significant below .01 level
***Significant below .001 level

this reward which set him apart from—and above—his colleagues. This point can
be illustrated by the comment of a middle-level cadre about his feelings when he
achieved Party membership:

> I felt very proud . . . I had new powers; . . . power to recommend some-
> one for Party membership; power to solve problems arising among my
> comrades; power to speak for the people. . . . Those who were not
> Party members did not have enough virtue to be trusted with high posi-
> tions or important missions. I was pleased to see that my progress was
> not hindered by my superiors. . . .

Not only did the soldier feel an increased sense of status and self-esteem but also
an increased sense of security at being accepted by the Front. According to the
ideal of the Front doctrine of unity, this new relationship to the organization
should not subvert his solidarity with his unit. Again the reality often deviated
from the ideal. Continuing the quotation above, notice how this middle-level
cadre reveals the conflict between his inner feelings and his prescribed (proper
according to the Front) behavior:

> . . . I was proud of my achievements compared to those of my
> comrades who had joined the Front before me and who were not
> rewarded. . . . This was a secret feeling and I did not abandon my com-
> rades. On the contrary I had to show them how to improve their
> situation . . .

Thus, attendant to the new position of higher authority was a tendency to become
psychically separated from one's previous source of identification. Moreover,
the role of the middle-level cadre, which involved a larger scope of responsibility,
tended to divorce the promoted soldier from the intimate interactions on a continuous basis that characterized the low-level cadre's relationship to his primary
group. This separation (combined with the more manipulative and tactical tasks
of a middle-level cadre, especially of a political officer in running the Party
apparatus, in preparing indoctrination and information, in controlling criticism
and morale sessions, in dispensing rewards and sanctions, etc.) may have aided
the transference of the new cadre's identification with his immediate unit to
a total identification with the organization. This hypothesis is consistent with the
factor analysis results which indicated that statements of primary group solidarity did not serve as a defining quality of commitment.

   A third related implication of the evidence of a lower level of commitment
among low-level cadre is the suggestion that the role of the low-level cadre
represented a difficult and pivotal position from the standpoint of both the
individual and the organization. Commitment was an extended process with different levels of expectations and demands placed on the individual as he
advanced. Some soldiers who were promoted to low-level cadre failed to meet
the exacting requirements of leadership and commitment (and, hence, were

ineffective in developing commitment in others); for these cadres, the selection and filtering process had been faulty. Even those cadres who showed signs of commitment and were effective leaders continued to be tested by the Front with increasing responsibilities. As discussed in detail later, these cadres often faced the dilemma of sacrificing their identity in the group for increased status in—and identification with—the organization. Some low-level cadres resolved this crisis on the side of solidarity with the group. By doing so, however, they lessened the prospects of becoming fully committed and thus increased the chance of their unit conforming without commitment. The next section will consider these dynamics in more detail.

### Leadership in Practice

The data of tables 8-5, 8-6, and 8-7 indicate that non-cadre were likely to be conformers; moreover, nonintegration primarily occurred among non-cadre and demoralization occurred throughout all ranks. It is this less than ideal situation that the PLAF's compliance system had to integrate into an effective whole. The way integration was accomplished in practice will be analyzed by examining the role of the cadre.

The cadre could integrate the soldier and his unit into the structure of the PLAF in each, and all, of the following related ways: (1) by serving as a concrete model of a committed revolutionary in a position of authority with which the soldier could identify and emulate, (2) by functioning as the nucleus around which the primary group formed and became solidified, and (3) by monitoring and, thus, preventing or channeling the development of informal group norms. [20] Since particularly the first two mechanisms involved the type of face-to-face interactions of a relatively smaller unit, the *initial* burden of fulfilling these tasks fell on the low-level cadre.

The low-level cadre often did serve as a concrete model of identification for the rank-and-file soldier, particularly the new recruit. Due to a variety of factors operating in Front life (e.g., the situational uncertainties, the higher status position of the cadre vis-à-vis the recruit, the importance for the peasant of the model to be a personal one, the Front doctrine of unity which stressed persuasion and a compassionate leadership approach, and the common knowledge that the cadre position had to be earned by being "virtuous") such identification was quite likely in the PLAF. However, considerable variability existed among low-level cadre in their leadership ability and, as the quantitative analysis showed, in their commitment. Therefore, identification with the low-level cadre could produce undesirable effects from the standpoint of the organization. In the extreme the following situation occurred:

> Before being arrested by the VC, I felt life normal, however hard it
> might be sometimes, but I was satisfied because I liked to stay home to

till my land. When I was sent uphill to live with the VC, I felt homesick. . . . [I]t was very cold and it rained very much. I did not like this
sort of life and I wanted to go down to the delta.

[T]he leader of my cell . . . was comrade Kiem whom I liked very much
since he was kind and gentle to me. He gave me medicine when I was
sick. He himself prepared rice soup and often inquired about my stom-
ach ache. He spent his spare time to teach me arithmetic and singing. I
sometimes followed him downhill to go fishing.

Undoubtedly the identification of this peasant for his cadre was strong;[21] yet,
since the cadre himself was not ideologically committed (as is apparent from
this selection as well as the context of the entire interview), the soldier in turn
did not form a loyalty to the organization. This type of situation will be called
dysfunctional gratification.

Quantitatively speaking, the above case was rather rare and was more likely
to occur in guerrilla units where the organizational structure might not be
imposing. In the usual situation (consideration of demoralized cadre will be
deferred until Part III), low-level cadre appeared to demonstrate adequate
loyalty, enthusiasm and ability so that conformity was not hindered; yet, identification with such cadre was not sufficient to induce commitment.

Due to the organizational structure, the low-level cadre occupied a key
position for influencing what informal norms of the primary group developed
and the extent to which they were dysfunctional.[h] However, the position of the
low-level cadre intrinsically implied a role conflict. On the one hand, he was
supposed to be compassionate and to use persuasion to win the confidence and
respect of his men. Many did, as the following quote suggests:

I was a squad leader. The fighters in my squad and I used to sit around
and talk. They liked me and they told me of their feelings.

On the other hand, the cadre had formal responsibilities to the organization. Thus,
he had to maintain a balance between fulfilling the demands of the organization,
which included serving as a model of proper organizational behavior, and being a
"maintenance expert." This balance was a delicate one. If, due to over-zealous-
ness or a lack of leadership ability, he totally prevented informal mechanisms, he
could lose the confidence of his men and disrupt their integration as a unit; if,
due to insufficient commitment, he allowed the informal practices of his men to
deviate substantially from Front norms, the unit would lack adequate integration into the command system. In practice, the average low-level cadre did not
have a high level of commitment, as the preceding section suggests. Therefore,

---

[h]The factor analysis presented evidence that the immediate cadre was the nucleus of
primary group solidarity. Given the organizational structure as well as Vietnamese attitudes
towards authority, the existence of an informal leader who did not occupy a status position
was quite unlikely.

low-level cadres were likely to permit the ritualization, relaxed informal norms, and limited areas of acceptance of authority that characterizes conformity.

Two clarifications are necessary to place the above argument in perspective. First of all, it may be that conforming, or less than fully committed, low-level cadre fostered the integration of primary and secondary relationships by tempering unrealistic demands for commitment and, hence, prevented severe dysfunctional effects. Under minimal stressful conditions, a high degree of integration could be obtained. The following quotation indicates one way it occurred:

> What were your relations with your cadre?
> After working hours, we could joke with them and considered them as our equals. But things were different during working hours.
> Did you have confidence in them?
> Yes, I was confident that they could lead the unit in combat and protect my life. If the fighters didn't have confidence in them, how could they lead their unit?

Under conditions of severe stress, "after working hours" did not exist. Hence, the role of the low-level cadre in fostering integration must be reexamined when the effects of stress are considered in Part III.

Secondly, even though low-level cadre normally permitted a degree of laxity, the extent to which the unit could vary from compliance was severely limited since the low-level cadre and his unit were embedded in the control system that regularly monitored them. That is, the structure—command, monitoring, and sanctions—tended to check any essential deviation of units from their mission. Operationally it fell to the middle-level cadre to enforce this control function.

A strong impression gained from the interviews is that, in comparison to cadre below them, middle-level cadre were, with little variation, very able; moreover, the data indicate that there was a high level of commitment, in both absolute and relative terms, among the middle-level cadre. This suggests the integrative and control functions served by the middle-level cadre were executed effectively. Nonetheless, these functions were complex. As Chapter 6 describes, units of company size had political officers (frequently assistant company commanders) in addition to the usual military commander.[i] They served as a major channel to and from higher political command in the Party apparatus and, as such, were responsible for indoctrination and information, for surveillance and criticism sessions, for settling lower-level disputes, for the distribution of re-

---

[i]Though the data are not as conclusive as we should like, it appears that political officers were more committed than their military counterparts. Indeed, the data indicate that few middle-level cadre were nonintegrated (see table 8–6) and those who were nonintegrated tended to be the military commanders as contrasted to the political officers. Moreover, these nonintegrated military cadre tended to be the pragmatists whose main motivation came from status inducements rather than from internalization of organizational values or gratification of security needs.

wards and sanctions. In short, the burden of control and of monitoring and preventing noncompliant behavior rested, in many units, with the political officer. In implementing their tasks, they were supposed to set an example and use persuasion in fostering unity, politization, and obedience on a voluntary basis. Though their success in directly inducing commitment appeared limited, they were effective, under normal conditions, in checking noncompliant behavior and keeping informal group norms within tolerable limits. The structure of the PLAF enabled them to do so. Perhaps this is most evident in the use of sanctions against noncompliant behavior.

Punishment in the PLAF was administered by the formal discipline system and in the criticism sessions. Humiliation by public shaming was the most frequent punishment. As noted earlier, this humiliation evoked a situational loss-of-face even for those soldiers who did not strongly identify with their group; hence, it served as an effective means of "control and mobilization."[22] There was no ambiguity that overt noncompliance would be punished, even though persuasion was the goal. In short, a coercive framework underscored all demands.

The significance of this implied coercive framework was not limited to controlling and mobilizing recalcitrant soldiers. The potential use of force was essential to all forms of compliance: it gave the aura—and the reality—of strength to the command structure which, considering Vietnamese concern with security and the peasant's tendency to pragmatically accept his situation, was so necessary for individual Vietnamese obedience; it provided a framework for embedding the primary group and set the boundaries within which informal standards would be tolerated; it invested the cadre with the status and power without which personal identification and control would be unlikely. Thus, the perception of a strong organizational structure helped integrate peasants of different persuasions at all levels in the PLAF.


### Summary

The reality of institutionalization in the Front deviated from the ideal. Rather than the total commitment of all soldiers, various patterns of adaptation to the PLAF's structure, processes, and environment existed. The major alternative pattern to commitment, and the most frequent mode of adaptation, was conformity. Conformity represented a positive orientation towards Front life: basic needs of realizing security and status were satisfied due to identification with one's primary group and due to the feeling of belonging to and accepting the authority of a strong and legitimate organization whose characteristics were consonant with many commonly-held beliefs of the peasant culture.

Conformity, and all adaptation, occurred within the parameters set by the organizational structure. The soldier fitted into, and was psychologically dependent upon, his primary group which was embedded into the command and control structure by means of norms of obedience and unity, of constant surveillance and of criticism sessions, of rewards and sanctions, and of a controlled milieu. The cadre, who in turn was embedded in the political-military command system, provided a prime link in this integrative framework for he had to prevent, channel, and keep within tolerable limits tendencies towards non-compliant behavior. The Front's advancement process promoted soldiers who were more fully identified with organizational values and who manifested leadership ability into those pivotal positions of authority. Consequently, the PLAF attained a high level of integration.

The above description, though accurate we believe, is incomplete. Our analysis purposely "holds constant" stresses on the PLAF caused by the war, i.e., we dealt with a minimal stressful environment. This approach is warranted for we wanted to describe the basic compliance system of the PLAF. The evidence on demoralization, which reflects dissatisfaction under stress, suggests the need for further analysis. Table 8-6 shows no significant comparative difference among ranks on the demoralization measurement, nor does table 8-8 which presents

**Table 8-8**
**Distribution of Satisfaction-Dissatisfaction over Ranks, Defectors Only**

|  | Commitment | | |
| --- | --- | --- | --- |
|  | Mean | SD | N |
| Middle-Level Cadres | -0.082 | 0.989 | 60 |
| Low-Level Cadres | 0.001 | 0.989 | 40 |
| Non-Cadres | -0.209 | 1.066 | 105 |
| Total | 0.131 | 1.028 | 205 |
| Analysis of Variance | Mean Square | D.F. | F-Test |
| Between Groups | 0.743 | 2 | 0.701 |
| Within Groups | 1.060 | 202 | (P = .497) |

|  | Conformity | | |
| --- | --- | --- | --- |
|  | Mean | SD | N |
| Middle-Level Cadres | -0.382 | 0.917 | 60 |
| Low-Level Cadres | 0.025 | 1.047 | 40 |
| Non-Cadres | 0.226 | 0.992 | 105 |
| Total | 0.009 | 1.012 | 205 |
| Analysis of Variance | Mean Square | D.F. | F-Test |
| Between Groups | 7.049 | 2 | 7.311*** |
| Within Groups | 0.964 | 202 | (P = .001) |

|  | Demoralization | | |
| --- | --- | --- | --- |
|  | Mean | SD | N |
| Middle-Level Cadres | 0.125 | 0.723 | 60 |

(continued)

**Table 8–8** (continued)

|  | Demoralization | | |
|---|---|---|---|
|  | *Mean* | *SD* | *N* |
| Low-Level Cadres | 0.135 | 0.789 | 40 |
| Non-Cadres | 0.162 | 0.736 | 105 |
| Total | 0.146 | 0.739 | 205 |
| *Analysis of Variance* | *Mean Square* | *D.F.* | *F-Test* |
| Between Groups | 0.029 | 2 | 0.052 |
| Within Groups | 0.552 | 202 | (*P* = .950) |

|  | Nonintegration | | |
|---|---|---|---|
|  | *Mean* | *SD* | *N* |
| Middle-Level Cadres | −0.324 | 0.994 | 60 |
| Low-Level Cadres | −0.266 | 1.115 | 40 |
| Non-Cadres | 0.061 | 1.071 | 105 |
| Total | 0.115 | 1.068 | 205 |
| *Analysis of Variance* | *Mean Square* | *D.F.* | *F-Test* |
| Between Groups | 3.401 | 2 | 3.039 |
| Within Groups | 1.119 | 202 | (*P* = .050) |

***Significance below .001 level.

similar results for the defector subsample. (Low-level cadres indicate more demoralization than the other levels; however, the differences fail to be significant.)[j] Since demoralization occurred at all levels in the authority structure, the PLAF's ability to deal with it was not simply a question of controlling reluctant rank-and-file soldiers; the integrative structure of the revolutionary organization was threatened. In short, we need to examine the capacity of the PLAF's compliance mechanisms for coping with a war environment; this is the task of Part III.

----

[j]Lest this finding be misinterpreted, four caveats ought to be stated. First of all, the causes of demoralization may have differed at different levels of rank—indeed, they did as Part III argues. Secondly, the effects of demoralization on organizational behavior and, in particular, on cohesion may differ for the different ranks—Part III shows they did. Thirdly, this finding does not imply wide-spread demoralization. Indeed, the average feeling of demoralization for the prisoner subsample of table 8–6 is negative indicating limited demoralization. Fourthly, by dealing only with the prisoner subsample, a sampling bias may be introduced since defectors, who might have felt more demoralized, were not included. To check this possibility, an analysis of variance was run on the defector subsample. The results shown in table 8–8 confirm the homogeneity of demoralization in the authority structure; however, as anticipated, the average level of demoralization being significantly positive indicates more demoralization among defectors than prisoners.

## Appendix 8A
## Measurement Assumptions


*Content Analysis*

The success of analysis depends more upon the data base than upon the analyst's ingenuity. In the ideal, one might hope for direct observational opportunities, or one might devise, administer, revise, readminister a series of carefully concocted questions to PLAF members. Such luxuries did not exist for this study. Rather the intensive interviews with former NLF members provided the basic data upon which content analysis was performed. The interviews as well as the content analysis imply a number of major validity problems. Since Chapter 2 discussed many of the general issues involved with the interviewing, we will deal here more specifically with problems arising from the details of the content analysis.

In addition to general validity problems, the severest obstacle to adequate quantitative analysis in this study was cross-interview inconsistency: not all areas of concern for measuring and discriminating different patterns of compliance were covered in sufficient and uniform depth from interview to interview to permit a wholly satisfactory content analysis. In short, some interviews were better than others for our purposes. Yet, to select just the few exceptionally "revealing" interviews would reduce the sample size and, consequently, nullify the possibility of drawing reasonably reliable inferences about patterns in the PLAF itself. Hence, the analysis had to operate within the significant constraints of generating a statistically sufficient data base. Within this limitation, various measurement and discrimination techniques were feasible and, indeed, were attempted. However instructive methodologically a chronicle of these attempts would be, it would certainly be boring—and inefficient substantively. Rather we presented only that technique in the text, which after trial and much error, seemed most fruitful. Those readers familiar with the frustrations of data analysis are well aware of the many compromises necessary in balancing methodological and substantive concerns; others should realize that the approach adopted was neither unique nor perfect. It, nonetheless, did provide a useful, productive means for accomplishing the important tasks of quantitative analysis.

A desirable rule of empirical analysis is to avoid measuring a complex phenomenon with a single measurement. Where possible, one should measure the way a particular soldier adapted by defining a series of "indicators" of commitment, conformity, and the like and should use these definitions as criteria for categories of content analysis. Though this procedure was followed and found useful in preliminary analysis, the technique used in the text employed a variant of this approach: the responses to a single "question" were used to generate a multiple-item series of indicators.

As indicated in the text, we focused on a single-line of questioning on the soldier's feeling about life in the Front (How did you feel about life in the Front?, etc.). This choice for content analysis, rather than more direct questioning about commitment or conformity, seemed appropriate for the following reasons: (a) this questioning did not provide prominent cues that might allow Vietnamese to answer in the way demanded by the situation, (b) more specifically, this line of inquiry did not pertain either directly to commitment and conformity or directly to associated indicators of the same—e.g., did you obey orders?, would you have been willing to sacrifice your life?, did you respect your cadre?, how often were you criticized?, and the like, (c) this line of questioning occurred mid-way in many of the interviews after rapport had set in but before fatigue had, (d) the responses to this line of questioning tended to be long, free of slogans, and spontaneous (perhaps due to the conditions mentioned above, to the low likelihood of similar questions having been asked in previous military interrogations, and to the opportunity for the ex-soldiers to speak out on subjects about which they felt proud, knowledgeable, etc., and hence could "show off"), (e) the frequency of this line of questioning being asked and of answers (valid enough to be coded) being given was sufficiently high (between 70–85 percent) to provide cross-interview consistency and a reasonable sample size (344), and (f) the fairly complex coding of the responses turned out to have adequate inter-coder reliability.[23] Though we believe the coded themes listed in table 8–1 reasonably reflect the belief systems of the subjects both in terms of substance and structure, they do not do so without qualification. Moreover, the coding itself dictated a number of analytical steps and assumptions that introduce necessary distortions of the testimony's reality. Let us review the major operational decisions involved.

There was a tendency for statements of a given individual to indicate either satisfaction or dissatisfaction but not both; thus, the major division in table 8–1. This tendency may have been partly due to the form of the questioning and partly due to Vietnamese cognitive functioning and response habits; on the other hand, it may reflect the individual's beliefs. The dissatisfactions were not a mirror image of satisfactions, though it would have been more orderly if they were. For example, some soldiers said they were pleased with the spirit of nationalism in the PLAF, but none indicated displeasure with nationalism. Or some soldiers complained about the hardships of military life; no one welcomed them.

Responses were not highly differentiated, reflecting both a tendency to reply in terms of slogans learned in the Front and a characteristic of peasants. For example, though nationalistic aspirations were clearly distinguished and expressed in language relatively free from Communist jargon, ideological social-political aims of the Front—reunification, socialism, etc.—tended to be spoken about by many soldiers in slogans. The categorization of themes shown in table 8-1 reflects these dispositions towards a lack and uneveness of differentiation— e.g., satisfaction with nationalism could be distinguished reliably from attitudes towards other NLF objectives, but attitudes towards all other goals had to be lumped together.

Such "lumping together" is one example of a necessary aggregation of highly specific themes (words, phrases, etc.) into the final categories shown in table 8-1. The coding procedure called for both a transcription of key phrases and a check-off of aggregated categories similar to those shown in the table. This procedure allowed a reliability check and subsequent adjustment of the aggregation. The resulting categories, reflecting the empirical responses, are neither logical nor of the same level of aggregation. For example, complaints about food could reliably be separated (due to its high frequency and unambiguity) from other hardships of military life even though the latter is a catch-all theme that could logically include dissatisfaction with food. The category of dissatisfaction with the treatment of self by the Front includes a number of specific personal grievances that were not mentioned frequently enough to warrant separate categories; the justification for placing them under a single heading was that, on the one hand, they related on prima facie grounds, and, on the other hand, this aggregation could be accomplished with high intercoder reliability. In short, the uneven, unlogical aggregation of themes indicated in table 8-1 gained reliability at a minimal cost to empirical validity.

No attempt was made to judge the intensity of feeling towards a given theme. Only the presence of an attitude was recorded. This technique implies a challengeable yet reasonable series of assumptions. If a soldier did not mention a theme, it is assumed the theme was not salient for him. For example, the absence of a comment about a feeling of solidarity was taken to mean that this attitude was of a relatively low saliency. Such an assumption is vulnerable to two crucial criticisms. Some major themes may have been omitted not because of saliency but because of lying, suppression, repression, etc. Of course, this could— and undoubtedly did—happen in a more or less random manner across respondents. The extent of this random error does not seem significant enough in this case to warrant dismissing the procedure employed. On the other hand, some themes may have been excluded in a systematic way. The only major theme (recognized by the author) where systematic exclusion seemed to have occurred was in concern over status. A cultural constraint exists on the overt expression of such sentiments. Since the coding rules restricted "reading-between-the-lines," the expressions of status concern were too subtle for reliable coding. The effects of this invalidity are serious but not fatal.

A second important criticism of the saliency assumption deals with the allocation of comments among the themes listed in table 8-1. For example a subject may have indicated, for conscious or unconscious reasons, satisfaction with his immediate cadre but no dissatisfaction with the rigors of military life, even though the latter were salient to him at least while he was serving in the PLAF. General difficulties of this type pertaining to response bias are discussed in Chapter 2 and further comment here on the serious problems of inference involved would be redundant. Insofar as the respondent's comments reflected what was most salient to him, then the effect of not commenting on other satisfactions and dissatisfactions would be to exaggerate the most salient. Such exaggeration is not unusual in the cultural context.

The net effect of these assumptions is a measurement model equivalent to a situation wherein each soldier would have been asked to respond to each of the items listed by table 8-1 with a yes or no. The dichotomous coding allowed us to correlate the themes over the interviewees and produce a correlation matrix suitable for factor analysis.

### Validity of Factor Analysis Discrimination and Measurement

The factor analysis produced a series of orthogonal dimensions. These distinct factors corresponded to patterns that were discerned and discriminated independently by qualitative procedures. We went on to apply statistical techniques using the factor scores as measurements of the various patterns of adaptation. How valid are these procedures? The answer depends upon one's purposes. Our measurements were gross but they may have been sufficient, for, as Mosteller and Tukey have put it, "we all desire an adequate assessment both of the indications and their uncertainties, but we shouldn't refuse good cake only because we can't have frosting too."[24] That we have baked an edible cake can be seen in two respects. First of all, the main patterns of adaptation were identified by qualitative evidence and the factor analysis (including rotation) was designed to discriminate and measure them rather than to "discover" them; that the statistical discrimination agreed with the *prior* qualitative indications lends credence to the procedure. Secondly, the quantitative interrelationships among the variables for each factor were interpreted a posteriori in terms of the microlevel details of life in the Front; though such agreement in detail does not fully confirm the factors or the factor scores, it does strengthen our confidence in the findings.

The factor scores were used as scale scores in the analysis of the distribution of the patterns of compliance over the command structure (and will be so used in the regression of Chapter 9). (The scores are standardized and normally distributed.) Thus, we conceive of a *degree* of commitment, a *degree* of conformity, a *degree* of demoralization, and a *degree* of nonintegration. Though each soldier was therefore rated on each pattern of adaptation, the factor analysis would not have been fruitful if soldiers were not discriminated as to their qualitatively distinct patterns. That is, those soldiers who scored high on commitment (e.g., at least one standard deviation above the mean) did not score high on conformity nor did they score low; they did tend to score low on nonintegration and somewhat lower than average on demoralization. Similar comparative remarks hold for all the factors. Therefore, there is reasonable justification for referring to high scorers on, for example, commitment as being the "committed." (We recognize that since these "scales" are not anchored, high scores represent relative, not absolute, values.) The discriminating ability of the factors across soldiers was far from complete. Though high scorers on conformity and on commitment tend to be different soldiers, as the scores become lower discrimination becomes fuzzier. Demoralization and nonintegration differentiate respondents in much the same manner. To some extent, such discrimination reflects the crudity of the measurements. But it also reflects the fact that these patterns ought to be questions of degree. Those who conformed were to some degree committed. In the analysis, the four scales were employed to judge either difference of degree or of kind depending upon which interpretation was more valid or appropriate in context.

# Part III
# Maintenance

## Introduction to Part III

Mobilizing peasants and integrating them into a new order are not sufficient for a successful revolution. The new patterns of authority and the evolving institutional bonds should be capable of withstanding stresses inherent in revolutionary change: in a word, the revolutionary organization must maintain itself.

Maintenance depends upon several complex elements. First of all, the individual's basis for compliance should be stable over time and not susceptible to intrinsic decay. The satisfactions and rewards, the commitment and conformity, the feeling of identity and legitimacy ought to possess a durability to withstand strains and frustrations arising from the internal dynamics of the organization. If career frustrations, conditions of prolonged life as a revolutionary, demands of the organization, requirements of adapting to a prescribed role outweigh positive sentiments, then the links binding the individual to the organization might weaken and he might choose to end his participation. Secondly, the system as a *whole* ought to be able to withstand external stress. That is, given individual susceptibilities, the structural mechanisms that integrate individuals into a coherent institution needs to be maintained. The following chapter investigates the inherent strength of the bonds tying the individual to the NLF—to be called cohesion—and the vulnerability of the integrative structure to external stress and to internal disintegrative tendencies.

Implicitly, the analysis views maintenance as a criterion of the revolutionary organization's institutional development. Many analysts of political development argue that traditional political systems are less able to endure strains and crises than modern systems. "The ultimate test of development," according to Lucian Pye, "is the capacity of a people to establish and maintain large, complex, but flexible organizational forms."[1] We shall argue that the Front's ability to maintain itself depended upon the extent to which it transformed peasant parochialism into sentiments of commitment towards the organization.

161

# 9 Cohesion, Disintegration, and Maintenance

The PLAF's system of compliance produced a highly integrated organization. Yet it may have been vulnerable to stress. Adaptation by conformity and, indeed, by commitment implied strong dependency relationships in a highly centralized, hierarchical structure. A number of analysts of organizations believe that, at least in the context of Western cultures, such systems are fragile. For example, Chris Argyris argues that

> [u]nder conditions of crisis, the bottom will look to the top. If the top withholds its rewards, it will be perceived as a traitor even though, rationally, no one could expect the top to increase its rewards under crisis conditions. Individuals who are highly dependent upon the top *and* who have little internal confidence will tend to panic and take extreme measures.[1]

How vulnerable was the PLAF to the stresses of war? One approach to examining this question would be to analyze aggregate data involving such measures as combat effectiveness, rates of capturing prisoners, and rates of defection. For the time period under consideration, the results of such analyses—when the changing levels of United States involvement are taken into account—are mixed. On the one hand, defection rates increased and, on the other hand, the NLF continued to demonstrate amazing resilience in the face of intensified combat activity. Though this information provides a backdrop for the analysis, the basic concern here is not with establishing how much, if any, disintegration occurred in a particular time period. Rather this study attempts to assess the potential of the revolutionary organization for maintaining itself, its ability to survive and retain its revolutionary character. The sheer survival of the revolutionary organization clearly depends upon the military force used against it. In addition, however, maintenance depends upon the internal dynamics of the organization. This chapter examines the PLAF's potential for maintenance by analyzing the effects of sustained war conditions on three critical aspects of its internal dynamics—the strength of the bonds linking the individual to the organization, the susceptibility of organizational structure and processes to disintegration, and the effectiveness of organizational response to stress.

### Approach to the Analysis of Cohesion

*Decision to Stay or Leave*

To assess the strength of the bonds tying the individual to the Front, we assume that each soldier continually faced a "decision to participate" in the PLAF, a decision in which two alternatives existed—to remain in the organization or to leave it. The probability of the soldier remaining in the PLAF will be called his cohesion (or, more precisely, his degree of cohesion). The explanation of a soldier's cohesion, i.e., why he remained in or left the Front, ultimately rests upon how the various forces impinging upon him affected his sense of security, his status needs, and the dictates of pragmatic fatalism. This chapter's approach to understanding cohesion in the PLAF is to examine and estimate the various cohesive and disintegrative forces operating on the soldier and to explain their effects in terms of Vietnamese basic personality characteristics.

Various factors affecting the soldier can be identified by making several a priori distinctions. A basic distinction for present purposes is the following: cohesion is assumed to be a function of the individual's perceived desirability of staying in (or leaving) the PLAF and his perceived costs of leaving.[2] The remainder of this section outlines the way these two components of the cohesion decision will be analyzed.

The perceived desirability of staying in or leaving the Front is assumed to result from an implicit, subjective weighing by the soldier of the forces impinging upon him. All such forces cannot be considered in detail. However, we can analyze the major forces quantitatively by assuming that the patterns of adaptation to Front life (as measured in Part II) represent predispositions toward staying in or leaving the Front. For example, commitment and conformity can be expected to be cohesive. By estimating their relative effects on cohesion, the strength of attachment to the PLAF provided by these patterns of compliance will be assessed.

The above estimates would be meaningless unless they were made in the light of and balanced by negative forces resulting from stresses on the soldier. Stress may be analytically separated into two related aspects—viz., stress arising from the environment external to the organization and stress arising from internal pressures. Experience in combat, the major external stress, could directly affect the soldier's perception of the security he derived from being in the PLAF. But, in addition, the exigencies of combat could exacerbate internal pressures. The quantitative measure of demoralization reflects these dynamics, as this chapter details. In addition, the nonintegration factor incorporates dissatisfactions arising from pressures due to assimilation into Front life, to acceptance of authority and the required norms of behavior, and to advancement or the lack of advancement; such internal pressures will be seen to vary according to the stage in one's career in the PLAF. To help separate external from internal pressures, we will

**Table 9–1**
**Stated Reasons for Defection**

1. hardships, dissatisfaction with the rigors of military life
2. demoralization, pessimism, war weariness
3. feelings of alienation from, or non-acceptance of,
    i. PLAF's social system
    ii. NLF's external methods
4. feelings of disillusionment, disenchantment, duplicity
    i. "unintentional" discrepancy between norms and practices
    ii. "intentional" discrepancy between words and deeds
    iii. discrepancy between overt and "real" aims
5. feelings of personal frustration, anxiety, and rejection
    i. towards advancement in the Front and prospects for the future
    ii. futility of remaining
    iii. inadequacy and difficulty in assimilating
    iv. family pressures
6. rational calculations
    i. GVN incentives
    ii. Front disincentives
7. specific difficulties and grievances

measure each soldier's combat experience and length of stay in the PLAF and estimate their impacts on cohesion in light of internal negative forces of demoralization and nonintegration.

This quantitative analysis of the perceived desirability of staying will be interpreted using qualitative evidence from the interview material. Virtually all the interviews with defectors discussed the individual's reasons for defecting in a reasonably detailed way. These reasons were coded by the team of analysts; the resulting major themes after aggregation are listed in table 9–1. Though these themes represent a fairly complete range of reasons for defection, their validity for quantitative purposes must be questioned. Defection was, in many cases, the culmination of a process. Asking the defector to recall the chain of events and sentiments involved is bound—as Chapter 2 details—to result in contradictions, ambiguities, and distortions. For the interview material used here, these difficulties arose too often to assure reliable quantitative analysis. Nonetheless, when treated with due caution and in conjunction with independent quantitative evidence, the stated reasons for defection can provide insight into the negative stresses of life in the PLAF. Therefore, the themes of table 9–1 will be used to supplement the statistical analysis at which time their content will be discussed.

The perceived costs of leaving played a significant role in cohesion. Though a quantitative measure of the costs of leaving would have been desirable, the interview data did not enable a usable coding. Consequently, the quantitative analysis generally omits this variable and, hence, cohesion will be estimated only as a function of perceived desirability of staying. This omission biases the effects of the various forces causing an underestimation of negative forces and an overestimation of positive factors. However, the nature of the costs of leaving the PLAF will be discussed subsequently in qualitative terms.

The next three sections discuss an operational measurement of cohesion, the measurement of external stress, and the basic statistical model used for estimation purposes.

### Operationalizing Cohesion

An operational definition of individual cohesion may be derived from the following model. First, the soldier's cohesion is defined as the probability that he stayed in (or one minus the probability that he left the PLAF). Second, it is assumed a judgment can be made as to whether the soldier, in fact, stayed or left; in the former case, he cohered to the organization and his cohesion was 1.0; in the latter case, his cohesion was 0. In particular, the sample contains prisoners and defectors; the former were assigned a cohesion of 1.0 and the latter of 0.

The fruitfulness of this dichotomous measurement of cohesion should be weighed on pragmatic grounds. It surely has clarity, unambiguity, and prima facie validity—all significant attributes for a dependent variable. Moreover, our concern is not in estimating the cohesion of any particular soldier—in which case a finer measurement might be in order—but rather in explaining why some soldiers left and others stayed. In other words, the use of this measurement of cohesion is equivalent to comparing prisoners and defectors on a series of factors for which they might systematically differ. If they do differ on a factor (e.g., degree of combat experience), then the extent of the factor's impact on cohesion can be estimated.

Nonetheless, the measurement is not free of difficulties. First of all, prisoners are not identical to soldiers who stayed and, therefore, the assignment of 1.0 (perfect cohesion) to prisoners needs to be justified. As discussed in Chapter 2, the sample of prisoners used here may be considered as having been generated by a two-stage selection procedure; in the first stage, the population was "sampled from" by the process of being captured; in the second stage, the prisoner subpopulation was sampled from by the selection of interviewees. The first stage sample was biased since it systematically excluded members of the PLAF whose probability of being captured was low. In particular, the military elite (the high commanders) were unlikely to be caught and thus were not in the sample. In addition, soldiers who refused to surrender and fought until their "last drop of blood"—as the Front required—were, of course, not included. Since these members may have been the most thoroughly committed, their exclusion is not unimportant; they merit, according to our criteria of cohesion, a rating of 1.0. Even among those soldiers who did surrender (and thus were in the prisoner subpopulation) gradations could be made in how they were captured—some were wounded, bound, and forcibly captured; others surrendered voluntarily. It could be argued that these gradations reflect meaningful differences in cohesion. [3] However, for quantitative purposes, these distinctions would introduce severe problems in validity, reliability, and sampling.[a] Instead we assume that, with the exception of systematically excluded groups, the subpopulation of prisoners resulted from a sufficiently random process of capture and that these prisoners represent the relevant characteristics of stayers all of whom are assigned a cohesion of 1.0. A second difficulty with the measure of cohesion involves the assignment of zero cohesion to all members of the "defector" sample. Not all leavers were ralliers. Indeed, probably the bulk of leavers were deserters who just returned home and did not rally. Some deserters are in the sample either because they decided to rally subsequent to their desertion or because they were captured by the GVN after their desertion; in both cases, they were classified as having zero cohesion. For ease of discussion, both ralliers and deserters are called defectors.[b]

The second stage selection process, for both prisoners and defectors, introduced severe biases. The subsample of defectors is not a representative sample of all defectors; nor is the subsample of prisoners a representative sample of all prisoners. Therefore, inferences about the impact of combat severity (or defectors and prisoners may reflect sample bias. In particular, the sample fails to be representative in terms of the rank of the respondents. To compensate for this sample bias, rank will be used as a control variable. By doing so, the issue of sample bias is shifted to that of comparing conditional distributions. This constraint is not severe because the most fruitful hypotheses deal with within rank and across rank comparisons of cohesion.

### Measuring Combat Experience

War's harshness produces stressful conditions; however, the way these stresses affect soldiers is far from obvious. According to Front norms, the committed revolutionary's reaction to combat danger ought to increase resolve. The interviews offer evidence that for at least some highly committed individual's resolve strengthened, as the remark of a former soldier indicates: "The greater the difficulties facing the Front the greater the spirit of its members." Of course, this was a slogan, but one which, nonetheless, might reflect a true sentiment. Stress also may have increased cohesion by promoting a feeling of unity within

---

[a]We were able to make a distinction among prisoners using the concept of potential defecting prisoners; we will make further use of this distinction subsequently. However, given the validity problems associated with such a distinction and given our limited sample size, this classification will not be used in the statistical model.

[b]Deserters are underestimated in the sample of defectors. However, since their number was too small for statistical comparison, they were lumped together with ralliers. By doing so, at least one important mechanism in PLAF cohesion will be slighted—viz., the fear of treatment by the GVN.

the primary group.[4] The interviews offer evidence that stress did increase
solidarity. For example, a conforming soldier said: "We love each other very
much because we were all in the same difficult situation, we shared the same hardships, and we were compatriots." On the other hand, the factor analysis of
Chapter 8 suggested that this effect was quantitatively important in the PLAF.
Moreover, it is quite evident from the interviews that stress also produced highly
negative forces. Stress was perhaps the most frequently cited reason given by
ralliers as their reason for defection (see table 9-1). For example, a former Party
member said:

> When I joined the Front I had expected to endure many hardships but
> I did not expect them to be that hard. They made my political con-
> victions waver, and made me think twice of what I had learned in the
> indoctrination documents. This was the cause of my dissatisfaction.

War experiences thus had different impacts on different individuals. Why?
In addition to variability of personality characteristics, the soldier's ultimate reaction to combat depended upon his life circumstances in the organization and
these circumstances varied, as Chapter 8 detailed. Thus, in estimating the net impact of war stresses on cohesion, and ultimately on the PLAF, the individual's
position in the organization, his satisfactions, his feelings of security, his realized
and anticipated status aspirations, his perception of the future need to be taken
into account. Before doing so, the initial task is to generate a quantitative
measurement of the degree of combat experience.

A wide variety of direct war related experiences impinged upon the soldier.
Perhaps the most important of these was combat itself. However, combat involved
more than a unitary experience and, thus, combat experience ought to be
measured by many factors.[5] For example, such aspects of a single battle as the
extent of casualties, the immediacy of casualties to oneself and his unit, and the
perception of defeat, victory, or inconclusiveness all constitute meaningful
dimensions of the overall experience. Moreover, the impact of any single battle
cannot be isolated from the cumulative effects of past actions. Nor can such
hardships of a soldier's life as lack of food and logistical deficiencies fail to interact with direct and cumulative experiences. Ideally, separate measurements of
each of these factors should be made for each soldier in the sample, so that
hypothesis about their separate and simultaneous effects upon cohesion could be
advanced with some degree of confidence. Unfortunately, the interviews (or
other available sources of information) did not permit refined measurements.
Instead, we utilized gross indicators of a variety of war experiences; since these
variables were grossly measured and since they correlate strongly, the separate
variables were combined into a single quantitative scale.[c]

---

[c]Another practical reason for combining the various indicators into a single scale was a
severe problem of missing data. Since the interviewers did not consistently nor comprehen-
sively probe on matters of combat experience, no item had a "response rate" of more than

**Table 9–2**

**Indicators of Combat Experience, Items Coded in the RAND Content Analysis**

**A. Combat Activities in Which Respondent Participated**

---

*Operations Initiated by PLAF*
  total number of operations*
  number of operations during six months prior*

*Relative Number of Operations Against Respondent's Unit*
  offensive air attacks
  defensive air attacks
  ground attacks
  artillery
  ambush

*Relative Casualties from Operations Against Respondent's Unit (during six months prior to leaving)*
  offensive air attacks
  defensive air attacks
  ground attacks
  artillery

*Overall Casualties*
  number of casualties in unit from all operations during six months prior to leaving*

---

**B. Logistical Difficulties (Problems with)**

---

  air surveillance
  food ration
  ammunition
  replacements
  low operating strength
  constant movement

---

*The starred items were coded as interval scales in the natural way. Unstarred items were coded using three-point scales.

Table 9–2 lists various measurements of combat experience coded by Frank Denton of the RAND Corporation from the interviews.[d] One group of experiences measured from the testimony of the respondents consisted of those combat activities in which the respondent was a participant. These measures included the respondent's reports of the number of PLAF initiated operations he was involved in, the relative amount of operations against his unit (subdivided into

---

70 percent. The scaling procedure, by combining the scores for all items, allowed the generation of an overall score for each respondent. Errors were introduced thereby but they are within a tolerable level.

[d]The original RAND coding was used here. Many a priori significant aspects of combat experience were not included in the RAND content analysis. However, subsequent content analysis attempted by the author did not prove more useful. The difficulty arises from the interviews themselves which, since they were intended for other purposes, did not deal consistently or in sufficient depth with combat experience.

Table 9–3
Loadings on Combat Experience Factor, Results of
Principle-Factor Method

| Item | Factor I Loading |
|---|---|
| No. of defensive air attacks | .659 |
| No. of casualties, prior 6 months | .631 |
| Percent casualties artillery | .587 |
| Percent casualties offensive air | .565 |
| No. of artillery attacks | .550 |
| No. of VC initiated operation | .520 |
| No. of offensive air attacks | .512 |
| No. of ground attacks | .483 |
| No. of VC init. oper., prior 6 months | .455 |
| Percent casualties ground attacks | .454 |
| Percent casualties air defense | .428 |
| No. of ambushes | .330 |
| Replacement troubles | .252 |
| Problems with air surveillance | .236 |
| Low operating strength | .203 |
| Inadequate munitions | .037 |
| Inadequate rations | .034 |
| Constant movement | −.007 |

different modes of combat prevalent in Vietnam), the relative extent of casualties to his units from the various operations, and the overall number of casualties from all operations. A second group of experiences deals with logistical type of difficulties common in Vietnam. These included problems with air surveillance, with rations, with shortages of ammunition, with low operating strength of the unit, with replacing soldiers, and with the necessity for frequent movement. In all, 18 relevant items were coded with adequate reliability.[e] Clearly many matters of concern—e.g., the number of defeats suffered by the soldier's unit—are not included for they could not be reliably coded. Nonetheless, the items coded were sufficiently relevant and comprehensive to be combined into a single scale of combat experience.

To combine these various aspects of war experience into a single quantitative scale, a factor analysis using the principle-factor method was executed. Table 9–3 shows the factor loadings obtained for the principle factor.[f] These loadings

[e]An average reliability estimated by RAND was on the order of 90 percent. The various coding scales used are indicated on table 9–2. These conventions were necessitated by the nature of the interview. Though the mix of scales presents a less than ideal situation for data analysis, it is compatible with our intention of producing a single scale.

[f]The other factors are not shown. Since, the first factor, in the principle-factor method without rotation, is that factor which contributes the maximum variance, we would hope that it combines all the measurements into a single general dimension. This was reasonably the case for these items as evidenced by the 3.435 latent root of the first factor, compared

will help interpret the nature of this combined measurement. The most highly correlated item is the "amount of defensive air attacks subjected to" followed closely by the "number of casualties sustained by the soldier's unit in the six months prior to his separation from the Front." All the combat activity items load fairly highly, however. On the other hand, the logistical difficulties items do not correlate highly; hence, they contribute little to the definition of the factor. Thus this factor most heavily measures the extent of direct combat experience especially of large scale battles and casualties therefrom. Considering this mix of casualties and operations, the scale will be referred to as "severity of combat experience" or, more simply, "combat experience."

*Statistical Method*

The model upon which the statistical analysis will be based is the simple one previously intimated—viz., cohesion is the "sum" of the forces impinging upon the soldier to stay or leave the Front.[6] The model actually employed also posits a multiplicative relationship between the various forces and the rank held by soldiers in the PLAF. Three reasons justify such a relationship. First of all, the position occupied by a soldier in the PLAF critically affected his life circumstances and the way he perceived the forces acting on him. It is not unreasonable to presume—indeed, it will be demonstrated—that different dynamics of cohesion operated for soldiers holding different ranks. Secondly, cohesion itself is an aspect of the ability of the organization to maintain integration. Since integration depended upon the leadership structure, estimating cohesion within ranks and comparing across ranks will enable an analysis of the ability of the leadership structure to maintain itself and prevent disintegration. Thirdly, introducing rank multiplicatively permits a statistical control for sampling bias for reasons to be discussed shortly.

The above model will be estimated—i.e., the effects of the various factors on cohesion will be quantitatively explained—by means of a single equation, multiple linear regression using ordinary least squares. To illustrate the statistical procedure, table 9-4 presents the results of regressing cohesion on severity of combat experience where the relationship is controlled for different levels of rank. More specifically, the dependent variable used for cohesion is a dichotomous variable which is 0 for defectors and 1 for prisoners. When the dependent variable is dichotomous in a regression, an appropriate interpretation of the dependent variable is a conditional probability, which in this case would be the probability

---

to 1.745, 1.680, 1.249, etc., for subsequent factors. The logistical difficulties items do emerge as a separate dimension from combat activities; however, they load quite low on the first factor. Likert-type scaling was used in preliminary analysis and correlated .87 with the scale used in the text.

**Table 9-4**

**The Effect of Severity of Combat Experience on Cohesion**

**A. Multiple Regression of Cohesion on Severity of Combat Experience Controlled for Rank**

Prob. of Cohesion = $b_1 R_M + b_2 R_L + b_3 R_N + b_4 (R_M \times C) + b_5 (R_L \times C)$
$$+ b_6 (R_N \times C)$$

| Independent Variable | Coeff. | St. Er. | 338 D.F. t-Ratio |
|---|---|---|---|
| Middle-level Cadre ($R_M$) | .634 | .053 | 12.04 |
| Low-level Cadre ($R_L$) | .621 | .063 | 10.30 |
| Non-Cadre ($R_N$) | .578 | .036 | 16.22 |
| Combat Experience of Mid-Cadre ($R_M \times C$) | -.086 | .052 | -1.66 |
| Combat Experience of Low-Cadre ($R_L \times C$) | -.046 | .050 | -.91 |
| Combat Experience of Non-Cadre ($R_N \times C$) | -.136 | .039 | -3.49* |

$R = .79; F(6/338) = 90.87;$

Standard Error of Residual = .482

**B. Regression of Cohesion on Severity of Combat Experience Stratified for Level of Rank**

| | |
|---|---|
| (1) Middle-level Cadres[†] | P(Cohesion) = .634 - .086C |
| St. Er. | (.053) (.052) |
| t-Ratio | (12.0) (-1.66) |
| (2) Low-level Cadres[††] | P(Cohesion) = .621 - .046C |
| St. Er. | (.060) (.050) |
| t-Ratio | (10.3) (-.91) |
| (3) Non-Cadres[†††] | P(Cohesion) = .578 - .136C |
| St. Er. | (.036) (.039) |
| t-Ratio | (16.2) (-3.49*) |

[†]Sample size is 91.

[††]Sample size is 64.

[†††]Sample size is 189.

*Significant below .05 level.

of cohesion (i.e., one minus the probability of defection). Several technical problems exist for this method of estimation, particularly in light of the "sloppy" nature of the data.[7] However, for the issues at hand, these difficulties do not appear to invalidate the method. Rather due caution must be exercised. In short, weighing the significance of the substantive problems against difficulties inherent in the data, the potential errors involved in this statistical method seem well worth risking.

Turning to the regression shown by table 9–4 (Part A), six regressors were used and, hence six regression coefficients need to be considered. However, three of the variables are dummy variables standing for the three levels of rank—middle-level cadre, low-level cadre, and non-cadre—and three are the products of each level with combat experience. This use of dummy variables allows us to stratify the sample into three subsamples, one for each rank—i.e., the procedure is equivalent to conducting three separate regressions on combat experience and comparing the results. The coefficients of the rank dummy variables can thus be thought of as the intercept terms in separate regressions, as table 9–4 (Part B) illustrates by writing the single-equation as if they were three disjoint equations. The other regression coefficients represent the (linear) effect of combat experience on the probability of cohesion for the various ranks.

The results of this regression show that severity of combat experience had different impacts on cohesion for the different levels of rank. For non-cadres, the greater the severity of combat experience, the greater the probability of defection; for cadres the effect is the same but fails to be significant. Before interpreting the substance of this conclusion, some technical qualifications are appropriate.

Since the multiple regression simultaneously stratifies the sample into separate control subsamples as well as estimates the effect of the independent variable (combat severity) on the dependent variable, some of the criteria for judging the statistical properties of the results are not as relevant as usual. Thus, the multiple correlation coefficient of .79 is not a good measure of goodness of fit for it reflects the dummy rank variables used as controls. Similarly, the $F$-ratio is not a useful indication of the overall statistical significance of the findings. Instead the significance of the regression coefficients must be analyzed either separately or jointly. The intercept terms for rank reflect the proportion of defectors in a given rank strata rather than a substantively meaningful effect. Thus, interpreting the regression revolves primarily around consideration of the three coefficients of combat severity shown in table 9–4 (Part B) along with their standard error and $t$-ratio.

Since the severity of combat experience is standardized, the physical meaning of the coefficients is abstract. Thus, for non-cadres table 9–4 shows that an increase of one standard deviation above average severity of combat experience results in a decrease of .136 in the probability of cohesion. The standard error of this estimate is .039, which indicates a fairly reliable estimate. Given this estimate and error, the chances of severity of combat experience having no effect on cohesion is quite low. Indeed, the $t$-ratio of –3.49 is highly significant (the asterisk denotes this significance).

Whereas severity of combat experience had a definite impact on the probability of cohesion for non-cadres, there seems to have been no significant impact for cadres. However, for both low-level cadres and high-level cadres, the direction of effect, indicated by the sign of the coefficient, is consonant with the hypothesis that the more severe the combat experience is the more likely defection is. For high-level cadre the effect is not significant at the .10 level but is significant at the .20 level. Since other variables will be introduced into the formulation, there is no pressing need to reach a decision about whether this impact is significant or not.

Severe combat experience appears to have decreased cohesion in the PLAF, and this effect seems greater for non-cadres than for cadres. However, due caution must be exercised since other variables may affect these results. For example, cohesion may depend upon tenure, i.e., how long a soldier was in the PLAF; yet since combat experience also may be related to tenure, the estimates of the effects of combat experience may be biased. The next step then is to introduce other variables affecting cohesion into the regression. The Appendix to this chapter details some of the preliminary analysis involved in introducing additional variables. The remainder of this chapter analyzes the findings of estimating the full model.

In summary, the strength of the regression method lies in its ability to sort out the effects of various factors on cohesion. In particular, the relative individual impacts of commitment, conformity, and the various stresses can be evaluated. However, the method is fallible. Due to the need for controlling for sampling bias, degrees of freedom and, consequently, accuracy are lost. More importantly, there are errors of measurement in the independent variables. Unless a series of strong assumptions hold, these errors will result—using least squares—in biased and inconsistent estimates. If the biases are severe enough, the analysis will be wrong. Nonetheless, in the light of the importance of evaluating cohesive and disintegrative effects and in lieu of better data, the risks seem worth taking. To minimize these risks, a simple model will be used even though more complicated models would better capture the reality. The value of this approach should be judged in terms of the pattern of results revealed rather than in any specific estimate.

### Cohesion of Non-Cadre

Table 9–5 presents the results of a linear multiple-regression of cohesion in the PLAF on the various patterns of satisfaction-dissatisfaction, combat experience, and tenure controlled for by rank. To facilitate exposition, the findings within each level of rank will be examined in turn, beginning with non-cadre; comparisons across ranks will be considered when appropriate.

The greater the degree of severity of combat experience for the rank-and-file soldier, the more likely he was to defect. Table 9–5 not only supports this hypothesis but also indicates that combat experience had the largest impact (–.136) on cohesion of all the forces included in this model. This finding may

Table 9–5

**Cohesion Regressed on Satisfaction-Dissatisfaction Factors, Combat Experience, and Tenure, Controlled for Rank**

| Rank | Independent Variable | Coeff. | St. Err. | t-ratio (323 d.f.) |
|---|---|---|---|---|
| Non-Cadres | | .529 | .051 | 10.30 |
| | Conformity | .038 | .038 | 1.01 |
| | Demoralization | −.059 | .036 | −1.64 |
| | Commitment | .088 | .036 | 2.42* |
| | Nonintegration | −.071 | .035 | −2.02* |
| | Combat Experience | −.136 | .039 | −3.53* |
| | Log Tenure | −8.627 | 7.210 | −1.20 |
| Low-level Cadres | | .358 | .125 | 2.85 |
| | Conformity | .007 | .059 | .12 |
| | Demoralization | −.148 | .058 | −2.53* |
| | Commitment | .046 | .056 | .82 |
| | Nonintegration | .073 | .053 | −1.37 |
| | Combat Experience | −.053 | .050 | −1.06 |
| | Log Tenure | −34.270 | 14.136 | −2.42* |
| Middle-level Cadres | | .791 | .132 | 6.00 |
| | Conformity | .029 | .052 | .56 |
| | Demoralization | −.089 | .049 | −1.81* |
| | Commitment | .200 | .051 | 3.91* |
| | Nonintegration | .009 | .055 | .17 |
| | Combat Experience | −.105 | .051 | −2.07* |
| | Log Tenure | 11.800 | 14.000 | .84 |

$R = .82$
F-ratio (21/323) = 31.17
St. Err. of Residual = .458
*Significant below .05 level.

seem trivial. Yet it does not hold for cadres, as will be discussed in detail shortly. Hence, discussion of why it holds for non-cadres is in order.

Combat stress threatens one's personal safety and security in the most direct way. Indeed, among those reasons cited by defectors for leaving, the fear and anxieties caused by combat related stresses including death, dismemberment, and the like were most frequently and openly discussed (see table 9–1). [8] However, under the minimal stressful conditions assumed in the last chapter, many rank-and-file soldiers had drawn satisfaction from adapting by conformity; more specifically, they were able to gratify needs for security and self-esteem from solidarity with their primary group and a limited identification with the strong authority structure into which they were embedded. Could such satisfactions outweigh the stress resulting from combat? The statistical analysis suggests an answer. The conformity factor, though having a cohesive force of

.038, fails to be significant. This implies that the *ties to the primary group and the organization* (reflected in the conformity factor) *did not outweigh, for many rank-and-file soldiers,* the *insecurity arising from combat conditions*. Thus, conformity was indeed susceptible to stress.

The above findings can be interpreted in dynamic terms. The bulk of rank-and-file soldiers adapted by conformity which represented net positive attractions to the Front; yet the evidence of their susceptibility to stress implies that some soldiers changed their orientation and decided to leave. In short, they went from accepting the Front's authority to rejecting it. Why? This chapter contends that the answer lies not in alterations of personality but rather in changed perceptions of reality; that peasants continued to act purposively to realize their security and status concerns within psychocultural constraints and, in doing so, they reacted to what they saw as *new* life circumstances. Thus, many of the issues to be investigated in subsequent sections revolve around how and why soldiers changed their perceptions. The analysis begins by examining soldiers' perceptions of the future of the NLF.

## Pessimism

A not uncommon sentiment expressed by numerous defectors (see table 9-1) and, indeed, by some prisoners was a feeling of pessimism towards whether the Front would win the war. In particular, a perception that the NLF would lose the war developed among many of those soldiers who had previously possessed that positive orientation towards life in the Front characteristic of conformity. Thus, an analysis of pessimism and its effects on cohesion would provide pertinent evidence on the relative susceptibility of conformity to stress. Unfortunately, the interview material could not be coded validly enough to introduce a measure of pessimism directly into the statistical model of cohesion. However, a gross coding permitting a simple analysis was possible. In approximately half of the RAND interviews, subjects were asked whether they thought the NLF would win the war. The answers were coded into the categories Front would lose, uncertain or ambivalent answers, and Front would win. This gross classification reflects the care that had to be exercised in interpreting the responses on this line of questioning given the situation the interviewees were in. By instructing coders to place ambivalent, ambiguous, contradictory answers into the middle category, satisfactory reliability at the extremes was assured.[g] This conservative, though necessary, approach reduced the sample size and the

------

[g]The RAND coding used the same classification and our coding was highly correlated with the RAND coding if one excludes the middle category and unknown classification. That is, both codings agreed at the extremes. The reliability for coding of the three substantive categories was approximately 90 percent. Our attempts at refining this scheme were not successful.

**Table 9-6**
**Cohesion and Pessimism**

**A. Comparison of Defectors and Prisoners on Pessimism**

| | Attitude Towards Outcome of War | | | |
| --- | --- | --- | --- | --- |
| | NLF Lose | Uncertain | NLF Win | Total |
| | % | % | % | % |
| Defectors | 63.4 | 58.2 | 36.9 | 54.3 |
| Prisoners | 36.6 | 41.8 | 63.1 | 45.7 |
| Number of Interviews | 40 | 88 | 46 | 174 |

**B. Comparison of Defectors, Potential Defecting Prisoners, and Hard Core Prisoners on Pessimism**

| | Attitude Towards Outcome of War | | | |
| --- | --- | --- | --- | --- |
| | NLF Lose | Uncertain | NLF Win | Total |
| | % | % | % | % |
| Defectors | 63.4 | 58.2 | 36.9 | 54.3 |
| Pot. Def. Pris. | 31.5 | 16.1 | 16.8 | 19.6 |
| Hard Core Pris. | 5.1 | 25.7 | 46.3 | 26.1 |
| Number of Interviews* | 40 | 88 | 46 | 174 |

chi-square = 20.6 (sig. at .001 level); gamma = −.36
*Unknown: Defectors 96 (47%), PDPs 53 (26%), HCP 55 (27%);
Total Unknown 204.

variability so that a refined quantitative analysis could not be undertaken.[h]
Moreover, the very real possibility of distortion necessitated the introduction of a control which further restricted significant statistical analysis. Nonetheless, the data do shed light on the effect of pessimism.

Table 9-6 (Part A) shows the result of comparing defectors and prisoners on their attitude towards the outcome of the war. Those who were pessimistic

---

[h]The *base* sample used for table 9-6 involved 378 as contrasted to 344 for the regression of table 9-5. The discrepancy arises from the necessity of deleting 34 respondents from the regression because of missing data in the dependent variable. Missing data was not a serious problem for the independent variables in the regression since missing data of key variables were simulated in producing factor scores. (These simulations tend to bias the results in the regression towards zero.) However, since the measurement of the independent variable (pessimism) for the cross-tabulation of table 9-6 had an "unknown" total of 204 (54 percent) from the sample of 378, pessimism (of necessity a dummy variable) could not be usefully introduced into the regression. Unfortunately, the size restrictions prohibited the valid introduction of a control for rank in the contingency analysis of table 9-6 (Part B);

were more likely to be defectors. (This result is statistically significant.) Before interpreting these results, a control can be introduced that corrects for a bias. As discussed previously, omitting the perceived costs of leaving tends to underestimate negative effects, in general, and, in this case, the possible negative effects of pessimism. A rough compensation for this bias can be made by the introduction of a subcategorization of the prisoner sample. Some prisoners indicated they wanted to defect if they had the opportunity; indeed, some prisoners apparently had surrendered voluntarily. These prisoners, who will be referred to as Potential Defecting Prisoners, could be expected to respond as defectors did.[9] Incorporating this control in table 9-6 (Part B), the effect of pessimism on cohesion is even more striking: of the pessimistic 5 percent are Hard Core Prisoners whereas of those who said they thought the NLF would win 46 percent are Hard Core Prisoners. (The result is statistically significant.)

These findings may seem obvious. However, they are not in accord with the following conclusion of Shils and Janowitz for the Wehrmacht of World War II: "The statistics regarding German soldier opinion . . . show that pessimism as to final triumph was quite compatible with excellence in fighting behavior. . . . Even pessimism was counterbalanced by the reassurances provided by identification with a strong and benevolent Fuhrer, by identification with good officers, and by the psychological support of a closely integrated primary group."[10] In contrast to the German army, the evidence for the PLAF indicates that (1) the perception that the Front would lose was not compatible with cohesion, and (2) severe combat experience was not "counterbalanced" by the satisfactions of conformity derived from identification with one's unit and cadre and from secondary identification with the organization and its goals. The bulk of non-cadre realized security and status satisfactions by conforming to a role within what they regarded as a strong, proper, and legitimate organization. External stress resulted—in ways that will be analyzed shortly—in altering that perception. If the soldier sensed that he was associated with a losing cause, that ultimate victory was not assured, that the strength of the NLF might be illusionary, then he might come to believe that a minimal acceptable level of security could not be guaranteed, that the organization no longer warranted legitimacy, and that the prudent and indeed proper behavior was to leave.[11] "While the game is being played out," Paul Mus said about Vietnamese peasants "a person can easily withdraw his bet."[12]

## PLAF's Response to Stress

Though combat experience could directly evoke fears, anxieties, and changes in perception of reality leading to pessimism, these difficulties occurred in an

---

insofar as the cell sizes were large enough for interpretation, the partitions for middle-level cadres and non-cadres tended to support the findings of table 9-6 (Part B).

organizational setting. Therefore, the PLAF's response to such stresses could have mitigated their negative effects on cohesion of rank-and-file soldiers and, hence, maintained integration. The analysis of the preceding section indicates that the PLAF's success in counterbalancing or preventing the development of pessimism was limited; this section examines why by analyzing the techniques used by the Front to counter disintegrative tendencies.

In the face of external stress, the Front relied on those same mechanisms that promoted integration but did so even more intensively. In particular, the PLAF employed its structure and processes to manipulate information, to tighten controls and raise the costs of leaving, and to increase rewards and demands for commitment.

**Manipulation of Information.**   A major technique used by the PLAF to abate the development of pessimistic perceptions was the manipulation of the information available to the rank-and-file soldiers: NLF propaganda stressed battlefield victories, never admitted defeats, and constantly emphasized eventual winning (though at times they emphasized short-term victory, at times long term). In short, the PLAF tried to convince the soldier that the organization could remain strong enough to prevail against outside forces and provide for the individual's security. However, the Front's attempt to develop a closed information system were not completely successful, as Chapter 8 pointed out. Skepticism and mild disbelief were engendered, and the net effect of the propaganda was to so cloud the situation that only uncertainty as to the facts was left. In this case, the extent to which pessimism developed depended upon the individual's concrete experiences. (In the time period under consideration, pessimism was not a widespread attitude among the interviewees. In part, this was due to the not unfavorable military situation for the Front while many of the interviewees were in the PLAF.) When confronted directly with the reality of severe combat experiences, the conforming soldier's faith could be profoundly shaken.

**Perceived Costs of Leaving.**   Manipulation of information also played a significant part in the Front's attempts to increase the costs of leaving as they were perceived by the soldier. Though a quantitative measurement of the perceived costs of leaving for each soldier was not possible, the decision situation faced by the soldier and the control mechanisms used by the PLAF can be sketched.

The soldier's perceived costs-benefits of leaving may be conceived of as dependent upon his subjective probability of escape, the penalties if captured initially or later, the evoked alternatives to the Front, and the perceived consequences of one alternative compared to another. More specifically, in order to leave the PLAF, the soldier had to escape (or, at least, be captured "voluntarily," which violated Front doctrine). The information system and constant surveillance, especially the requirement that cell-members had to be together at all times, made escape risky. Indeed, the subterfuges engaged in by some of the ralliers were quite ingenious. If the soldier were caught, he faced punishment. The penalties varied from a reprimand and reeducation for simple desertion to execution when spying activities or "traitorous" behavior were suspected.[13]

Even if he were not caught, the soldier faced severe difficulties. In many cases, he was in a remote area, far away from home, often in the jungle; the prospect of getting lost under these conditions was terrifying for many superstitious peasants. Were he able to reach home, he stood the chance of being captured by local NLF units who would return him to his unit or by GVN forces who would treat him as a POW. Moreover, the PLAF threatened retribution against the families of ralliers. Considering Vietnamese filial devotion, such threats could be quite effective. Due to the fear of retribution against the family, it was not unusual for defectors to make provision for their family to leave their native village.

Even successful rallying involved risks and uncertainties as seen by the soldier. PLAF propaganda emphasized that prisoners and defectors would receive harsh treatment in the hands of the ARVN or GVN. This propaganda was widely accepted because it had the ring, and too often the reality, of truth. An important element in the risk of defecting was sheer uncertainty, which as we have argued, is anxiety-arousing for Vietnamese:

> . . . I didn't know how to go about surrendering to the ARVN, because I didn't know my way around in the lowlands. In fact, I wouldn't have wanted to rally because I didn't understand the [GVN] policy—how could I trust it? I wouldn't have known how I might be treated.

In many instances, the soldier who was considering defecting tried to make personal contact, usually through family relations, with a *Chieu Hoi* official so that some of the uncertainty might be reduced.

Thus, the PLAF attempted by means of constant surveillance, of controlled information, and of sanctions to so raise the perceived costs of leaving that the soldier would "not think of leaving"—i.e., that he would fatalistically accept his situation and feel he had no other choice. Without an adequate measurement of the perceived costs of leaving, a quantitative estimate of how effective these means were in deterring potential defectors was not possible. Nonetheless, indirect evidence provides a rough assessment. Consider the nonintegrated rank-and-file soldiers, most of whom were either unassimilated or non-accepters. Since the perceived desirability of staying was always low for these soldiers, it can be assumed that the costs of leaving largely determined whether they stayed. Table 9-5 shows the nonintegration factor has a significant negative impact (-.071) on cohesion. (Omission of the costs of leaving tends to underestimate this effect as well as underestimating the impact of demoralization and overestimating those of conformity and commitment.) We surmise that for those soldiers *who thought of leaving*, i.e., perceived of leaving as a feasible alternative to life in the Front, it was a question of time until war conditions loosened controls (decreased the costs of leaving) sufficiently for them to escape. On the other hand, control measures may have been effective in two related ways: first of all, in reinforcing that aura of strength and omnipresence which fortified conformity and commitment; secondly, in so controlling the situation that demoralized soldiers resigned themselves to their "fate" and did not perceive of any real alternative to life in the Front.

**Increased Demands for Commitment.** In addition to the general manipulation of information and the increased control measures to raise the costs of leaving, the Front employed a range of techniques to cope with specific disintegrative effects of combat experience. A common reaction of the rank-and-file soldier to combat experiences, particularly of defeats, was the development of a "loss of fighting spirit"—i.e., a feeling of demoralization—that could lead, in ways to be discussed subsequently, to pessimism. To counter this, frequent morale building sessions were held in the group context of the unit. These sessions not only downgraded the strength and morale of the enemy and offered optimistic assessments of the ultimate outcome of the struggle, but particularly emphasized those political-social-revolutionary themes that formed the ideological basis of commitment. Moreover, rewards (in the form of promotions, commendations, medals, ceremonies, material privileges, etc.) were often awarded after combat, and combat-related, activities. In short, attempts were made to fortify those gratifications and values that gave the soldier a feeling of security and of self-esteem in belonging to the Front. However, the attempts to combat demoralization simultaneously led to increased demands for commitment. As Chapter 8 discusses, a repercussion of these increased demands for commitment was a tendency on the part of committed cadre to interpret low morale in ideological terms and, hence, to accuse soldiers of having "bad" thoughts; rather than alleviate demoralization, this increased internal stress could exacerbate it. Therefore, *the PLAF's response to severe stress resulted in an unintended consequence producing internal strain on the integrative mechanisms.*

How effective were increased demands for commitment in light of their unintended consequences? Though this question cannot be answered directly, the quantitative analysis provides some suggestive indications. The demoralization factor reflects internal strains on the soldier arising from increased demands and increased controls. The quantitative evidence shows that feelings of demoralization did decrease cohesion for rank-and-file soldiers (see table 9–5). However, its impact (-.059) was on the borderline of significance and, more importantly, was not as great as the negative effect of severity of combat experience. This suggests that, for the range of variation of combat variables considered in these data, the direct effects of combat were more devastating for the rank-and-file soldier than additional difficulties caused by internal stress. Therefore, it appears that the increased reliance on control mechanisms and the increased demands for commitment were neither strongly dysfunctional nor markedly effective.

### Committed Non-Cadre

The area in which the Front was most successful in preventing the disintegrative effects of stress was less in specific responses than in the continued maintenance of its command structure, as will be shown in the course of examining the cohesion of cadres. The following analysis suggests that an important aspect of this resilience depended upon the cohesion of committed non-cadre.

Adaptation by conformity was vulnerable to stress. Was this the case for commitment? The commitment factor has a significant impact (.088) on cohesion; that is, the more committed the non-cadre was, the less likely he was to defect. The most important aspect of this quantitative result, however, is the impact of commitment relative to conformity: commitment is more strongly cohesive than conformity. The finding is subject to error.[i] Assuming the order of the estimates is accurate, the implication is that, for non-cadres, committed are less vulnerable to stress than conformers. The committed non-cadres responded to the interview situation in terms indicating full belief in the revolution, though they displayed little knowledge of the theoretical doctrine or, indeed, of the inner workings of the Front; when probed they showed no signs of pessimism.

Most rank-and-file soldiers did not develop high levels of commitment; nonetheless, the finding that commitment was strongly cohesive is important since the committed soldier could help abate demoralization, prevent pessimism, and deter defection in several ways. Due to the cell and group structure, committed soldiers were likely to be in close contact with conforming soldiers. Consequently, committed rank-and-file soldiers—many of whom were Party members or prospective Party members—were in a position to help enforce the surveillance

---

[i]A serious error might be causing "commitment" to have an artificially high relationship with cohesion. Recall that cohesion is a dichotomous variable essentially comparing prisoners to defectors. It could be that prisoners were more likely to respond in the interview situation in terms of commitment than was truly the case while they were members of the PLAF. (One cause of this particular response bias might arise from the structure of POW camps which frequently retained the authority hierarchy as it existed in the NLF. Chapter 2 discusses these response biases more fully.) If such were the case, then commitment would have an artifically high impact. Though this bias undoubtedly was present, we do not believe it could have reversed the order of the impacts of commitment and conformity. To check on this bias, the *prisoner subsample* was subjected to analysis by regressing the dichotomous variable Prisoner (1.0)/Potential Defecting Prisoner (0.0) on the explanatory variables of table 9–5; in short, the prisoner versus defector bias was removed. Unfortunately, the resulting small sample size (170) did not permit useful analysis for either low-level cadre or middle-level cadre. For non-cadre, the results (in terms of the direction, rank order, and significance of the coefficients) were in accord with table 9–5.

system that both made escape difficult and impressed the soldier with the omni-presence of a strong organizational structure. Moreover, the development of demoralization and pessimism depended not only upon the soldier's experiences, but also, given the uncertain informational environment, upon reality testing in the group context (see Chapter 7). Hence, the committed soldier's confidence, persistent belief, and, most importantly, his compliant behavior could provide a constant cognitive anchor and model. In short, insofar as rank-and-file soldiers were committed, the framework of command could penetrate to the lowest level and help maintain integration.

### Cohesion of Low-Level Cadres

Under minimal stressful conditions, the integration of conforming soldiers required that their primary groups be embedded in the organizational structure. Since conforming soldiers were susceptible to severe combat experiences, the maintenance of integration under conditions of stress was extremely sensitive to the cohesiveness of the Front's leadership structure. This section analyzes the cohesion of low-level cadres and examines the manner in which they implemented the PLAF's response to stress.

Table 9–5 shows a pattern of effects on cohesion for low-level cadres that is quite distinct from either non-cadres or middle-level cadres. The main effects are negative indicating both the susceptibility of low-level cadre and the extreme difficulties faced by PLAF soldiers in this position. Moreover, the limited—indeed, not statistically significant—effect of severity of combat experience (–.053) compared to the main effect of demoralization (–.148) suggests that the pressures on the low-level cadre were due more to the internal dynamics of relationships in the PLAF than to direct outside stresses. This is not to claim that combat did not produce stress; rather that the lower-level cadre experienced combat stress both directly and, more importantly, indirectly in the form of demands made by the organization. In short, the position of low-level cadre contained intrinsic disintegrative tendencies. We shall examine these tendencies and assess the degree to which they might weaken organizational controls.

### Role Conflict

As Chapter 8 discusses, the low-level cadre was faced with pressures from the organization to meet formal norms and pressures from below to relax these standards. Under garrison conditions, the formal and informal standards were not necessarily in conflict, but demands for commitment and control sharply increased under conditions of external stress. The cadre then had the responsi-bility of enforcing these demands. In particular, he had to monitor and implement the constant surveillance and questioning of his unit's morale. Therefore he was faced with a role-conflict dilemma: [14] should he relax the demands of the organization and thus risk future advancement and the security provided by identifying with the organization, or should he enforce them and consequently rupture the close personal associations fundamental to his identification with the primary group?

Cadres could resolve this crisis in one of three ways. Perhaps the most usual way was for the cadre to side with the group and thus reduce his own anxieties and fears. Yet, by doing so, the PLAF's response to stress of increased demands for commitment and increased reliance on controls were not implemented effectively. This dynamic helps to explain the lack of major dysfunctional effects on non-cadre resulting from internal pressures.

Some cadres resolved their dilemma of increased pressures from above and from below by fully executing the demands of the PLAF. By doing so, the cadre might cut his ties to the group, perhaps irrevocably, and pave the way for total commitment to the organization. In return, he could hope for further advancement. Thus, one result of combat experience and stress was to further commitment among some soldiers. Commitment was undoubtedly cohesive for low-level cadre. Table 9–5 shows that, quantitatively, it tended to be cohesive (though given the small sample size and the finding of Chapter 8 that commitment among low-level cadre was no more prevalent than among non-cadre, commitment fails to be significant). Insofar as low-level cadre were thus committed, integration could be maintained despite some increase in dysfunctional internal pressures.

Other low-level cadre could not resolve the dilemma of pressures above and below. Neither willing to lose status nor the security of the group, they tried to walk the tightrope and satisfy both pressures. This behavior usually intensified the stresses on the cadre to the point that he felt isolated from both his men and from his leaders. Such isolation often manifested itself in personal conflicts and feelings of frustration. Many of these cadres became nonintegrated and defected. Table 9–5 supports this assertion by showing that the nonintegration factor has a negative effect (-.073) on cohesion (though it is on the borderline of significance).[j] The units led by such cadres were subject to severe disintegrative effects of the type illustrated by the comment of a low-level cadre:

> How many casualties did your reconnaissance unit suffer during the last six months of your service?
> [None.] By that time, I was confused about a lot of questions, and refused to go on missions or execute the orders of my superiors. My unit was all confused, and as a result we did nothing at all . . .

---

[j]In preliminary probit analysis, nonintegration had a clearly significant negative impact.

*Other Disintegrative Tendencies*

The fully nonintegrated low-level cadre represented an extreme case leading to disintegrative effects whereas the committed cadre, at the opposite end, maintained the leadership structure. The extent to which conforming low-level cadre, who stood between these cases, actually contributed to disintegrative tendencies (rather than simply being neither effective nor dysfunctional) depended upon their susceptibility to demoralization. The role-conflict dilemma of the low-level cadre could lead, under minimal stressful conditions, to discontentment and demoralization; stressful conditions exacerbated the conflict. In addition to this difficulty, a number of other sources of discontent could arise.

The discrepancy between a soldier's expectation for advancement and the status level he achieved could cause discontent. The Front provided strong incentives for the soldier who, wishing to maximize his status, sought advancement. Promotion to the low-level cadre position (and, similarly, to prospective Party membership) raised expectations of future advancement. Since many of those who had risen to a cadre position had a high personal ambition, not to advance—or not to advance as rapidly as expected—could cause the soldier to reassess his belief that the Front would satisfy his ambitions. Moreover, considering the ties of loyalty and devotion to the organization that had developed, not to be promoted as expected was often interpreted by the soldier as rejection. In particular, this effect occurred in the case of a discrepancy between a man's position in the military hierarchy as compared to his status in the Party. For those who had been advanced in the military but not in the Party, the feeling and reality of rejection and loss in stature could be intense. Another situation often cited by ralliers was discrimination due to "class:"

> I joined the Front in order to erase all my family's mistakes and bring back honor to my family [the family had been classified in the "land-lord" class]. People looked down on me again just because of the class discrimination. After three years of fighting and hardships, my family and I didn't get any better. I was very dissatisfied and decided to rally.

Such discrimination usually arose when the issue of Party membership was at stake.

The quantitative evidence is consistent with this career-related source of discontent. Table 9-5 shows that (log) tenure has a significant negative impact on cohesion. Tenure is a surrogate for processes that occurred as the soldier's length of service in the PLAF increased. One way to ferret out the underlying processes is to examine the pattern of tenure for defectors. The previously presented figure 4-2 showed that there were, after an initial acceptance period, two peak periods of frequent defection. In the period of roughly a year and a half of service, defections were relatively frequent; this mode may represent the time when many soldiers reached an advancement crisis of the type described above.[15] (Role conflicts for low-level cadre also would be most likely during this period.)

The data on defection as a function of length of service revealed a secondary mode in the period of three to five years.[k] This mode can be explained by two types of disaffection. In examining middle-level cadres, it will be argued that disillusionment occurred for some soldiers as they advanced to higher positions and became more exposed to the esoteric policies of the Front. In addition, and particularly for the low-level cadre, discouragement—a feeling of personal sacrifice, of not being adequately rewarded, of opportunities foregone—was often expressed and usually related to a weariness both of war and of a prolonged career as a soldier. The following recollection of a former squad leader illustrates these feelings of discouragement:

> I decided to rally because I saw that even though I had been fighting for the Front for five years, my family hadn't gained anything from my efforts. Besides I had to live far from my family and sacrifice my personal happiness. When I die, my family will be worse off because they won't get anything from the Front.

In many situations, discouragement and a not-worth-it feeling developed into pessimism:

> Why did you rally?
> I joined the VC because I had been taken in by their propaganda. I believed what they told me. They told me that the war would end soon. I had been with them for two years, and I found that the war became fiercer every day; there was no let up of any kind. I was discouraged and I thought to myself I couldn't go on fighting. So I rallied.

Such sentiments usually involved a feeling of alienation with the Front for not keeping its promises, as is revealed by continuing with the above respondent's testimony:

> [I decided to rally] when I realized that the VC's promise of the end of the war in 1965 would not materialize . . . I didn't think I could trust the Front's policy any longer.

These quotations suggest that low-level cadre were subject to those dynamics which rendered conforming non-cadre susceptible to stress: when the low-level

---

[k]This mode may be a result of the "artificially" constrained range of length of service as compared to the length of the war. Thus, we should be particularly careful that this presumed mode is not merely an artifact. Were the point pivotal we would find it necessary to do a cohort analysis. However, the sample size limits how far such an analysis could be carried.

cadre, under conditions of stress, sensed that the PLAF was vulnerable and that the personal rewards tying him to the organization were uncertain, the organization lost its legitimacy and the proper behavior was to leave.

Thus, the limited identification with the organization of conforming low-level cadre left them susceptible: in addition to direct effects of combat stress, the dilemma of role conflict, the career crises, and the disaffection arising from prolonged combat conditions could cause defection. Though we have no reliable way to estimate how widespread these difficulties were, the PLAF's structure and processes seemed intrinsically vulnerable to these problems.

## Cohesion of Middle-Level Cadres

To counter the susceptibilities of both non-cadre and low-level cadre, the Front had to maintain the aura of strength which convinced soldiers that their security and status interests would continue to be served in the PLAF. This task ultimately depended upon the cohesion of middle-level cadre and their implementation of the Front's mechanisms of compliance.

The results of the statistical analysis of the cohesion of middle-level cadre, presented in table 9-5, contrasts sharply with those for non-cadre and low-level cadre. Commitment is the factor with the greatest effect (.200) and, of course, it is cohesive. This suggests that commitment could provide a strong psychic shield against the stress of combat experience. Insofar as the level of commitment was high among middle-level cadre, the leadership structure could remain intact. Yet, table 9-5 also shows that severe combat experience had a significant negative impact on cohesion (-.105), though of only half the cohesive force of commitment. Moreover, demoralization also significantly weakened cohesion (-.089). Thus, the evidence of cohesion among middle-level cadre is somewhat mixed: the single strongest force was commitment, but disintegrative tendencies also operated that might erode the leadership structure.

The above statistical results suggest that some middle-level cadre had high levels of commitment and correspondingly high cohesion whereas other cadre not being highly committed were susceptible to disintegrative pressures. This section examines the disintegrative forces reducing cohesion among middle-level cadre.

### Internal Sources of Stress

The role of the middle-level cadre separated them, psychologically and physically, from their former primary group relationships. Upon advancement, middle-level cadres had increased power, were made aware of the political command and control apparatus that heretofore had been shrouded, and assumed fuller responsibilities in executing Front policies. All this could be deeply gratifying and could promote the transference of identification from the primary group to the organization itself. However, complete transference was far from automatic and variability existed in the extent to which it developed.

It is convenient to postulate three degrees of transference: complete, none, and partial. First, insofar as transference of identification to the organization was complete, commitment occurred. Second, some middle-level cadres did not transfer their loyalties and basically retained their orientation towards the primary group and consequently were susceptible to stress similar to conforming soldiers at lower levels; thus, table 9–5 shows that severe combat experience has a direct strongly negative impact on cohesion and conformity fails to be significant (its impact is in the positive direction). Third, for some middle-level cadres, only a partial transference developed. Such cadres were, it is hypothesized, subject to internal pressures that could eventuate in demoralization. Thus, the demoralization factor, which reflects internal pressures, has a disintegrative effect of −.089 (significant at the .05 level for a one-tailed test). The following discussion analyzes salient dynamics leading to demoralization among middle-level cadre and shows that partial transference of identification to the organization left soldiers susceptible to internal pressures.

Demoralization, as measured here, often contained a strong component of alienation. For the higher-ranking cadre who had passed numerous filters testing his commitment, a principal form of this alienation was one of disillusionment (see items 3 and 4 of table 9–1). Consider the following testimony of a former middle-level cadre:

> While I was in the Front, I was praised and commended many times . . .
> [later] I hated them for trying to cheat all of us. Before I studied their
> policy and line, I didn't know about their hypocrisy. But after I
> attended their political and military training course, I saw clearly their
> cunning schemes for cheating the people.

This testimony suggests that increasing exposure to esoteric aspects of Front policy and methods of manipulation could result in disillusionment and a rejection of both the system and its methods.[1] Since commitment to the organization was so closely associated with ideology, disillusionment often was expressed in political terms. Consider the testimony of a former platoon leader and party member who rallied:

> At first I was only indoctrinated on a small scale. Later, after I was
> admitted to the ranks of the Party, the indoctrination documents gave
> more details on the aims of the Front. . . . The Party member was in the
> highest position to know the situation. The documents for indoctrina
> tion were at a higher level than at the Group level. . . . I realized after

---

[1]The policy of terrorism by the NLF was at times mentioned as a source of disillusionment by cadres. See note 12 of Chapter 8.

thorough analysis that the Revolution of the Front was nothing but a class struggle incited by the Soviet Union and Communist China. It was not a real revolution. The more I thought about it the more I became dissatisfied, because in a real revolution, i.e., a popular revolution, the people would not stand up and fight [against] themselves, class against class, but rather would stand up and fight the foreigners to win back their freedom. [This] was the only reason that made me rally to the GVN. I did not rally because of a dispute or demotion.

This disillusionment—not with the nationalistic aims but with the Front's "class struggle"—represents a repudiation of the Front, one which was an often mentioned reason for defection among cadres. The Front had succeeded in politicizing the individual; yet this politization was partial and, hence, dysfunctional for it was not fully linked to commitment to the organization.

Due to the PLAF's insistence upon an ideologically based commitment, the Front was intrinsically vulnerable to disillusionment. However, the most usual situation seemed to be a chain of events in which personal frustrations lead to political doubts.[16] Indeed, for the respondent quoted immediately above, further probing revealed:

When I joined the Front I had expected to endure many hardships but I did not expect them to be that hard. They made my political convictions waver, and made me think twice of what I had learned in the indoctrination documents. . . .

I had lost my faith in the Front about one year before [rallying]. Now that I look back I can see that it was the hardships which made me change my mind. [Lack of food] made me ask myself why I was enduring these hardships. My faith began to be shaken . . .

For the most part this "loss of faith" resulted from the failure of the organization to provide security, at least as the soldier perceived it. The soldier quoted above cited a lack of food and other hardships as the source of his disillusionment. These appear symbolic, however.[17] This respondent's testimony unintentionally reveals a more basic source of alienation. After indicating that his *only* reasons for defecting were political ones, he immediately denied that dispute or demotion played any role in his decision to leave; but his career in the Front, as revealed in the interview, indicates that at about a year before rallying—the time when lack of food made his "political convictions waver"—he had asked for a transfer, was denied his request, and instead sent to a different unit at a position of lower status. Since the rewards of status offered by the PLAF served as a sign of the organization's acceptance of the individual, the denial of rewards was perceived as rejection. The soldier's feeling of being rejected could turn into his rejection of the system.

Thus, some middle-level cadres failed to achieve a complete identification with the organization and hence were susceptible to disillusionment and demoralization. In the time period under consideration, however, commitment was high among middle-level cadres and disillusionment was not widespread. Indeed, it may have been the case that the exigencies of war—by making promotion more rapid and by reinforcing the ideological images of the enemy—increased the likelihood of a complete transference of identification to the organization.

### Costs-Benefits of Leaving

The costs-benefits calculations for middle-level cadre were somewhat different than the calculations of lower-ranking cadres or non-cadres. First of all, the probability of escape was easier for middle-level cadre: they had fewer people watching them and they had better knowledge of the informant system. On the other hand, the PLAF's punishment for defectors was more severe for middle-level cadre. Secondly, the GVN offered in the *Chieu Hoi* program (at least in later years) a variety of inducements, including in some cases specific political posts, to higher-ranking officers. The existence of this viable alternative could be attractive to those middle-level cadres who were not committed. This is reflected among those cadres previously called pragmatists. Recall that they tended to fall in the nonintegrated category. Though the nonintegration factor fails to be significant in table 9–5 (reflecting the low proportion of higher-ranking cadres who scored high on this measurement), qualitative analysis indicates that anticipated incentives offered by the GVN played a crucial role in the defection of pragmatists. They apparently decided that their own status aspirations would be better served by being an officer in the ARVN, an official in the GVN, etc. Among the pragmatists—the numbers were too small in this time period to be statistically significant—most indicated they thought the PLAF could not win; sensing they were involved in a losing cause, they switched sides. These switches could be extremely valuable to the GVN and could represent a serious loss to the PLAF.

The cohesive force of tenure for middle-level cadre shown in table 9–5 suggests another group of soldiers who, in contrast to pragmatists, perceived no alternative to the Front. (Although tenure failed to be significant statistically, its positive impact is opposite to the disintegrative character of tenure for the other rank strata.) This cohesive effect is due to the presence of regroupees in the sample. One reason that regroupees displayed cohesion (due to tenure but separate from the other effects) is that for most of them life in the Front was the only life they knew. We should make the further point that the formation and development of the Front cannot be understood in historical terms without taking into account the "iron framework" provided by the infiltration of regroupees.[18] However, from the ahistorical perspective of this analysis, we are principally concerned with the systematic characteristics of the regroupees, vis-à-vis other cadres of comparable levels, on critical cohesive factors. Many regroupees, particularly those of high rank, were highly dedicated and committed revolutionaries. Being older, having burnt their bridges, and knowing no other life than as a soldier contributed to their cohesion. (On the other hand, a disintegrative element for regroupees was a vulnerability to war weariness.)

## Conclusion

Though the Front produced high levels of mobilization and high levels of integration of peasants into a centralized political system, its potential for maintaining itself was mixed.

Most peasants adapted to Front life by conformity: they accepted the PLAF's authority (on most essential demands), they integrated into the prescribed group life, they accorded legitimacy to the revolutionary organization. Nevertheless, the conformer's cohesion was limited. That is, the bonds tying him to the PLAF could be eroded by severe combat experience. The primary group was a principle source of security and satisfaction to the peasant only if he perceived the group as part of a strong and stable structure. Stress caused peasants to reassess their feelings that the Front could provide this security. Under these conditions, the Front lost its legitimacy and the wise, pragmatic, and moral course was to leave. This susceptibility to stress, when combined with the highly centralized organizational structure in which soldiers were so dependent upon the cadres above them, raises the possibility of rapid disintegration in the face of defeats and severe combat: not simply erosion but virtual collapse. This inherent structural vulnerability is illustrated by the following testimony of a former low-level cadre:

> The Assistant Company Commander . . . was my closest friend in the Front, and we liked each other very much. After he rallied, he sent me a message asking me to do likewise. . . . When we were both still in the Front, we used to confide in each other. We told each other that if the VC regime was unjust, we should find and follow another path. . . . Before I rallied I told the men in my unit that they were like me, they had contributed to the Front but they had not enjoyed any privileges.

A lack of cohesion on the part of middle-level cadres could profoundly influence the low-level cadre; in turn, the very nature of the PLAF's integration mechanisms implied that this disintegrative effect would be transmitted to rank-and-file soldiers. However, the likelihood of such institutional deterioration critically depended upon the extent to which the Front could develop committed, and able, cadre.

Committed soldiers were highly resistant to external stress. Such strong cohesion has two implications. First of all, the defection of soldiers was limited to peasants who were *not* committed. That is, the Front could retain a "hard core" of committed cadre and soldiers under the worst conditions (excluding death and capture). Secondly, since the Front's selection processes tended to promote committed soldiers to cadre positions, the leadership structure could survive stress. Insofar as it did survive, the extent and rate of defection of uncommitted soldiers could be retarded, though by no means eliminated.

In sum, the Front's ability to maintain itself was critically sensitive to the proportion of committed cadres it could produce. It had not achieved a high level of maintenance and, consequently, the institutional development of this revolutionary organization was incomplete.

To develop a more enduring institution, the cohesion of peasants may require institutional bonds based upon more than the pragmatic, structural, and cognitive links of conformists. Sentiments of loyalty to the system itself may be necessary. Imbuing peasants with such loyalty presupposes changes in peasant primary beliefs so that the family, the village, and immediate personal concerns can be subordinated to an allegience to the new order.

## Appendix 9A
## Preliminary Steps in Regression

The following discussion indicates some of the steps involved in generating the multivariate model of table 9–5 and, thus, may be useful to readers unfamiliar with regression techniques. In addition, the results shown in this Appendix can be used for purposes of comparison with table 9–5.

Table 9–7 shows the results of a multiple regression of the probability of defection on (log) tenure and combat experience controlled for the various rank strata. (Log tenure fits the data here better than tenure for reasons described earlier; see figure 4–2. Tenure is measured in months.) Within each rank, estimates of the separate impacts of the two independent variables on cohesion are exhibited by the regression coefficients. Let us briefly review the findings.

For non-cadre, tenure fails to be significantly related to the probability of cohesion whereas severity of combat experience has a strong and significant impact. For low-level cadre, these results are reversed: (linear) changes in combat experience have no significant effect, but increasing (log) tenure increases the probability of defection. These results are interesting particularly in view of the results for middle-level (or higher ranking) cadres: as (log) tenure increases, the probability of cohesion increases but as severity of combat experience increases, the probability of cohesion decreases (both results border on being insignificant).

Table 9–7
**Cohesion Regressed on Combat Experience and Tenure, Controlled for Rank**

| Rank | Independent Variable | Coeff. | St. Err. | t-ratio (335 d.f.) |
|---|---|---|---|---|
| Non-Cadres | | .561 | .049 | 11.41 |
| | Log Tenure | −3.675 | 7.171 | −.51 |
| | Combat Experience | −.131 | .040 | −3.31* |
| Low-level Cadres | | .364 | .128 | 2.83 |
| | Log Tenure | −33.149 | 14.578 | −2.27* |
| | Combat Experience | −.032 | .050 | −.63 |
| Middle-level Cadres | | .824 | .130 | 6.18 |
| | Log Tenure | 22.150 | 14.332 | 1.55 |
| | Combat Experience | −.087 | .052 | −1.69 |

$R = .79$
$F$-ratio (9/335) = 62.31
St. Err. of Res. = .478
*Significant below .05 level.

193

Table 9–8
Cohesion Regressed on Satisfaction-Dissatisfaction Factors, Controlled for Rank

| Rank | Independent Variable | Coeff. | St. Err. | t-ratio (329 d.f.) |
|------|----------------------|--------|----------|--------------------|
| Non-Cadres | | .551 | .037 | 15.03 |
| | Conformity | .026 | .039 | .68 |
| | Demoralization | −.069 | .036 | −1.89* |
| | Commitment | .060 | .036 | 1.66* |
| | Nonintegration | −.065 | .036 | −1.79* |
| Low-level Cadres | | .632 | .060 | 10.45 |
| | Conformity | .025 | .059 | .42 |
| | Demoralization | −.140 | .060 | −2.35* |
| | Commitment | .032 | .057 | .55 |
| | Nonintegration | −.062 | .055 | −1.13 |
| Middle-level Cadres | | .711 | .058 | 12.16 |
| | Conformity | .024 | .054 | .45 |
| | Demoralization | −.100 | .051 | −1.93* |
| | Commitment | .191 | .051 | 3.74* |
| | Nonintegration | −.011 | .056 | −.19 |

$R = .80$
$F$-ratio (15/329) = 38.99
St. Err. of Res. = .478
*Significant below .05 level.

In short, severity of combat experience has a strong negative valence for non-cadres and has a weak negative valence for middle-level cadres and (log) tenure is a negative force for low-level cadres and a positive, though weak force for middle-level cadres. What explains these results? A number of speculative explanations could be offered based on this table. However, the results might be the consequence of the interrelationships of these experience variables with the independently measured satisfaction and dissatisfaction factors.

Table 9–8 displays the results of a multiple regression of the probability of cohesion on the four factors making up the patterns of satisfactions and dissatisfactions with life in the Front: degree of conformity, of demoralization, of commitment, and of nonintegration. As before, the level of rank the soldier had attained in the PLAF is used as a control in order to minimize the effects of sampling bias. The variables extracted from the factor analysis are orthogonal for the entire sample; using uncorrelated variables directly in a multiple linear regression provides the advantage that the effect of each of these independent variables upon cohesion can be determined separately. However, since each variable must be controlled according to the rank strata, the orthogonality of the factors within each strata is no longer guaranteed. Insofar as the variables for a rank strata are correlated, the separation of the independent effects of the variable on the

probability of cohesion can cause problems. For our data, these potential difficulties did not appear to materialize. (Technically speaking, the problem alluded
to here is multicolinearity. Though the pairwise correlation of factors within a
rank strata were no longer zero, they were quite low with the highest correlation
being .38. Examination of the residuals for each factor did not reveal signs of
multicolinearity. Unfortunately, these residuals were not as neat as one would
like.)

For the sake of imparting familiarity with the statistical model, we will
indicate some results suggested by table 9–8. The regression coefficients of the
adaptation factors indicate the separate impacts of the factors on the probability
of cohesion. Since these factors are all standardized, their physical interpretation
is somewhat obscure. However, they all indicate the change in the probability of
cohesion for an increase of 1 standard deviation above the average value of the
independent variable. Thus, for example, the table reports that for non-cadres as
demoralization increases the probability of cohesion decreases, and, more precisely, a linear increase of 1 standard deviation in demoralization results in a decrease
of 6.9 percent in the probability of cohesion (see the first column of numbers).
A glance at these coefficients for non-cadres indicates that the impact of the
variables are in the directions anticipated—namely, conformity and commitment
are cohesive forces whereas demoralization and nonintegration are negative
forces. But the extent of the relative impacts vary (for non-cadre) from a high for
demoralization (-.069) to a low for conformity (.026). However, since these
coefficients are estimates of "true" effects, they are subject to statistical error.
The second column indicates the amount of error in the estimates and the third
column indicates the $t$-ratio to judge whether the estimates differ significantly
from zero in consideration of possible statistical error. Demoralization, nonintegration, and ideological commitment produce significant (at the .05 level for
a 1-tailed test using the Student's $t$-distribution) effects for non-cadres but
conformity does not.

Though significant, the impact of the variables for non-cadres is surprisingly
low. The reason for this is obvious. The patterns of satisfaction and dissatisfaction were quite properly measured without taking into account differences in
experiences among soldiers in the PLAF. As revealed in the preceding analysis,
two clearly important systematic experiences were severity of combat experience
and the length of service. It is reasonable to suspect that the relationships among
the patterns of adaptation are interacting with tenure and combat experience.
To sort out these influences on cohesion, the analysis in the text includes combat
experience and tenure in addition to the other explanatory variables.

# 10 Micro-Conditions of Institutional Development

The revolutionary organization is a means for achieving military goals and replacing existing power holders. But the Communist revolutionary organization cannot be considered solely in these terms; to do so is to overlook its real significance. Revolution remains unfulfilled until social and political patterns of behavior have been restructured and new patterns maintained. That is, the revolution cannot be judged successful until a new order becomes institutionalized. In the Communist model, as represented by the People's Liberation Armed Forces, institutionalization occurs within the revolutionary organization as a result of bonds tying individuals to the organization. The successful revolutionary organization, in short, embodies the new order.

Whereas a successful revolution must ultimately develop stable institutions, institutionalization of a new order need not rely on revolutionary violence. In this sense, revolution is a method by which societies, especially traditional societies, change, and the Communist revolutionary organization represents one model for accomplishing societal change by organizational processes. Broadly speaking, the Communist revolution in Vietnam is a special and extreme type of institution-building by what we shall call a mobilizing organization—a modernizing political system that seeks a new order based upon high levels of mass participation and high levels of integration of people into a centralized organizational structure. In this concluding chapter, we interpret the experience of the PLAF in terms of its success in building a stable system. In so doing, we will generalize away from the revolutionary context and attempt to define the conditions under which mobilizing organizations can develop new institutional patterns.

Though these goals are ambitious, our expectations are modest. Neither this study nor the literature provides a theory of institutional development.[1] Given this pretheoretical state of knowledge, our objective is to propose a research approach and research hypotheses, most quite speculative, that identify critical concepts, assumptions, and relationships. We focus on the microlevel and offer propositions relating peasant cognitions and motivations to the structure and processes of mobilizing organizations. These microlevel propositions do not deal with specific cultures, specific social and historical contexts, specific leaders and ideologies, and specific political organizations and economic conditions; hence, they lack the power to explain the origins and predict the outcome of particular institutional developments. However, we believe that the eventual theoretical understanding of institutional development will necessarily include microlevel propositions of the type discussed below.


### Mobilization and Participation

Recruitment is a basic task in building an army, an organization, or a new order. Recruitment of peasants into the PLAF was neither the spontaneous volunteering often attributed to revolutionary movements nor the conscription of villagers into enforced servitude. Instead, it involved a mixture of coercion and persuasion that sought to overcome the peasant's traditional patterns of behavior and convince him to accept a new authority. By inducting peasants on a large scale, the mobilizing organization created a capability for accomplishing social goals that traditional ways of organizing could seldom match. Moreover, membership in the organization removed peasants from village circumstances and exposed them to processes of social change that prepared them for accepting new patterns of behavior and new institutional bonds. In short, looking beyond the context of military struggle and competing forces, this recruitment of large numbers of ordinary peasants can be seen as the process of mobilization that must precede all institutional development.

Within the limits of the war environment and opposing forces, the NLF mobilized many peasants. The Front's relative success in mobilization suggests several underlying conditions under which mobilizing organizations can gain the acceptance of peasants.

The central problem of mobilization can be stated simply: the organization must overcome the peasant's cognitive and motivational resistances to changing traditional ways. In a word, an *inertia* seems to characterize the peasant's orientation towards action in numerous cultures studied in the literature, including the Vietnamese.

The NLF's experience suggests that overcoming peasant inertia may require a combination of two elements. First, traditional behavior must be rendered insecure and unacceptable. The NLF deliberately attempted to do this by means that involved violence, controlling village life, raising anti-government consciousness, and provoking hatred. However, these revolutionary techniques are not the only means by which traditional allegiances break down. The intrusion of the modern world upon peasant societies can set in motion broad scale processes that disintegrate the social and economic life of the peasantry, destroy old institutionalized means for achievement, and deny the legitimacy of the political order. These processes promote a feeling of insecurity, but they are seldom accompanied by a stable alternative to traditional ways. Thus, the second element needed to mobilize peasants is the provision of an attractive opportunity.

Peasants can be convinced to participate in a mobilizing organization, even though such participation implies change in their traditional behaviors, provided that they perceive the opportunities offered by the organization as leading to improvements in terms of their self-interests, narrowly defined.[2] Rage, intense discontent, altruism, or nationalism have sufficed to mobilize peasants in some situations,[3] but these purely emotional motivations are neither necessary nor likely to provide more than a temporary basis for accepting a new order. It is more fruitful, in many cases, to assume that peasants act purposively in pursuit of personal goals and, consequently, their active participation in mobilizing organizations depends upon the balance of incentives offered.[4]

This emphasis on peasant "rationality" is not intended to deny the significance of underlying needs, drives, and beliefs. On the contrary, the NLF experience clearly shows that psychocultural conditions constrain the peasant's willingness to participate in several ways.

First of all, viewed from the microlevel of individual cognitions, there is a need for cultural continuity. In contrast to traditional life circumstances where the routines of village life establish stable expectations, situations that appear new can raise profound uncertainties in the peasant's mind about the consequences of his behavior for his personal interests. Such uncertainties can evoke deep feelings of insecurities among peasants, more so, we hypothesize, than for Western modern man. The more the mobilizing organization requires peasants to break with tradition, the more likely it is to create uncertainty and, consequently, the less likely peasants are to participate.

Thus, successful mobilizing organizations—including revolutionary ones—are constrained by, and consequently reflect, the psychoculture in which they are embedded and which they seek to change. What specifically can be changed and what cannot be depend upon empirical realities. In the PLAF's revolutionary organization, the institutional structure linking peasants to a centralized authority was new, but the primary social and authority relations were *consonant* with psychocultural beliefs. Even though many of their traditional behaviors would be restructured, Vietnamese peasants could pursue traditional objectives within an organizational framework that served as a surrogate for village relationships.

Another related constraint is a moral one. Drawing upon the Vietnamese case, we hypothesize that peasants would be unlikely to accept membership if the behavior required of them did not conform to their cultural notions of what is right and proper; nor would they participate if the organization did not appear to conform to their sense of propriety. That is, a mobilizing organization must *not be illegitimate* (in the eyes of the peasants). Although acting within the boundaries of proper behavior guarantees neither the legitimacy of a new institution nor its ability to mobilize peasants, improper behavior severely reduces the prospects of institution-building. The nature and constituents of illegitimate as well as legitimate behavior in different cultural settings seems a subject worthy of further research.[5]

In the NLF—and presumably in any mobilizing organization—the "decision to participate" was the culmination of a process of persuasion. The Front's relative success in persuasion suggests several observations about the nature of the mobilizing organization that may be generalizable beyond the violence and coercive features of revolution. A key component of the Front's techniques was direct, personal contact with peasants. Such contact can greatly reduce peasants' uncertainties about confronting new situations. However, to appeal to each peasant on a face-to-face basis, an organization building a mass base must develop a "grass roots" system, one that relies heavily on the decentralized implementation of organizational objectives by local recruitment teams. It is hard to conceive of such a system being effective unless the members of recruitment teams possessed a common set of accepted beliefs about how to treat peasants and how to persuade them to participate—that is, unless the members were imbued with an *organizational ideology*. Whether the situation is revolutionary or not, a coherent organizational ideology seems to be an essential feature of any effective mobilizing organization.

This significant organizational role of ideology—namely, providing members (who themselves are not far removed from peasant attitudes of noninvolvement, village parochialism, and a dominant concern with the family's self-interest) with a coherent cognitive framework, a language, a set of symbols, and guidelines with which they could present a proper face to the villagers—should be distinguished from the direct appeal of ideology to peasants. Ideology in itself was not sufficient to attract the peasants to participate in the NLF. That is, few peasants accepted membership because of ideology alone.[6] However, ideology did affect their decision to participate, in ways that may be generalizable. When articulated by means and in situations suitable to villagers (e.g., in group meetings, personal contact, etc.), ideology increased feelings of dissatisfaction with village life, raised doubts about the legitimacy of the old order, and portrayed an image of a new life in which traditional desires could be satisfied. Thus, ideology fortified and helped create the perception that traditional behavior fell below an acceptable level of security and that the organizational opportunity was worth pursuing. Moreover, it reduced uncertainty about the new opportunity by providing a coherent interpretation of the world, an interpretation consonant with primary beliefs and normative desires latent in the culture (e.g., in nationalistic and heroic sentiments). Finally, ideology was used to justify the violence of the organization and the peasant's proposed role in that violence. Thus, it helped persuade individuals that the organization was not illegitimate and that their activities would be proper and right.

Generalizing, we suspect that though ideology would not be a sufficient incentive in many situations, it may be an essential component in the process of persuading peasants of the correctness and propriety of accepting membership.

## Institutional Development and Change

Our analysis of why peasants accepted membership in the Front suggests that participation is the result of convincing peasants that they face new life situations; it does not presuppose alterations in peasant personality. Indeed, whatever combination of circumstances and motivations result in the mobilization of peasants, it seems likely that, at entry, they retain their limited view of the world (derived from village life), their loyalty to the family, and their concerns for their personal interests. In short, high levels of participation are possible without the peasants having prior fundamental attachments to the organization. Yet, if the mobilizing organization, whether it be revolutionary or not, is to function effectively, individual behavior must be compatible with the needs of the organization. That is, regularized patterns of accepting and obeying the desires of the organization—which we call patterns of compliance—must be established, and diverse individuals have to be integrated into appropriate roles.

The Front achieved a high level of compliance and integration for reasons that we shall review below. Yet, it is a striking paradox that this revolutionary organization was not able to maintain a high level of integration. This problem stems less from the peculiarities of the PLAF and the war environment than from a dilemma intrinsic to institutional development by mobilizing organizations. The key to understanding the dilemma, if not resolving it, lies in the nature of the institutional bonds linking peasants to the organization.

The Front produced two major types of positively oriented individuals, the committed and the conformers. Though the details of commitment and conformity in the PLAF cannot be expected to be generalizable to other mobilizing organizations, it is reasonable to hypothesize that patterns of adaptation analogous to commitment and conformity are likely to arise in any successful mobilizing organization. In the Front, both patterns produced compliance, but commitment was cohesive whereas conformity was susceptible to stress. This difference, which we believe was not unique to the PLAF, reflects basically different institutional bonds linking the individual to the organization. Before analyzing these patterns in general terms, let us review the particulars of commitment and conformity in the PLAF.

Conformity was the predominant pattern of compliance in the PLAF. These soldiers complied for three interrelated reasons. First, they were fulfilling personal needs. Thus, conforming implied "fitting-into," and following the norms of, the Front-imposed primary group, and such behavior provided a feeling of security; conforming implied submitting to a strong authority and hence realizing rewards of self-esteem and of advancement in a hierarchical social-political structure; conforming implied learning an ideological language and accepting a role and, as a consequence, forming a satisfying self-identity.

Second, conforming soldiers learned to perceive the world in ways consistent with the Front's view. They thus agreed with the "correctness" of the PLAF's activities over a wide range of concerns.

Third, conforming soldiers complied because they accepted the Front as a legitimate authority and hence felt it ought to be obeyed. A revolutionary organization does not automatically possess legitimacy, as an organization (including an army) in a stable society would. To be legitimate in the Vietnamese culture, the organization had to be viewed as acting properly, as being strong, and as fulfilling its obligations (while not exceeding its rights). The Front's propriety was established by its consonance with Vietnamese primary beliefs about the way social and political life ought to be organized. That is, the hierarchical command structure, the actual functioning of the prescribed group life, the system of sanctions and rewards, the code of proper behavior, and most of the pedagogical practices were analogous to mores and customs of family and village life. (Those aspects of Front demands that were dissonant were either modified or not followed as sincerely as desired due to the operation of informal norms.) The NLF ideology fostered legitimacy by its themes of nationalism, heroism, and righteousness, which activated latent sentiments commonly held in the culture. Other ideological themes (e.g., historical determinism and omnipotence) were viewed symbolically and fortified the perception that the Front had the strength and the destiny to succeed; this perception is necessary to the according of legitimacy in the Vietnamese culture. Fulfilling obligations, the third element in developing legitimacy, required that the PLAF provide an acceptable level of security. Under conditions of minimal stress, the PLAF did so in the ways suggested above.

In short, the bonds tying the conforming individual to the revolutionary organization in Vietnam were based upon the satisfaction of personal needs within an institutional framework that was accepted as legitimate and correct.

To estimate the strength of these bonds, we examined the cohesion of individuals in the face of severe stress. We found that combat experience could so erode the conformer's cohesion that he left the Front. This loss of cohesion was not primarily the result of deterioration of the soldier's primary group or of changes in political sentiments; it resulted rather from a perception that the group was no longer part of a strong structure, that the Front was no longer able to fulfill its obligations of security and a stable future, that the revolution had lost its legitimacy.

Commitment, like conformity, implied the satisfaction of personal needs and the acceptance of the Front as legitimate. But it went beyond this. The committed soldier internalized the values of the organization so totally that his self-identity became fully defined in terms of his role as a revolutionary. His primary identification was neither to the family nor to the primary group but to the organization. We have hypothesized reasons why commitment developed among some soldiers. But at this juncture, these reasons are of secondary importance; the crucial point is that commitment—involving total belief and devotion, complete submission to the Party and the organization, and the spirit of self-sacrifice—was highly cohesive. Not only did the committed obey voluntarily, they showed little vulnerability to the stresses of severe combat.

To interpret this finding that conformity was vulnerable and commitment not, we shall recast the characteristics of each of these patterns in general terms. Chapter 2 suggested that people comply because of agreement, self-interest, and authority. Insofar as individuals develop generalized agreement with organizational policies, views, and procedures and, in short, perceive the world in ways congruent with the institution, then institutional bonds of agreement (or, alternatively, a cognitive bond) can be said to exist. Similarly, bonds of self-interest arise from a generalized expectation of the satisfaction of personal interests, and bonds of authority imply a generalized acceptance of authority. We can characterize the way members adapt to organizational life by their configuration on these three types of bonds.

The ideal committed individual so fully identifies with the organization that his self-interest is defined solely by organizational interests, his beliefs lead him to a generalized agreement with the organization, and his generalized acceptance of authority has a virtually unlimited area of acceptance. Commitment in the Front often approximated this ideal. Conformers also satisfied their self-interests, accepted authority, and agreed with the PLAF but in critically different ways.

Whereas the committed identified their self-interest with organizational interests, the conformer's personal concerns of security and social advancement were neither synonymous nor in conflict with organizational goals. Conformers satisfied personal interests by identifying with the primary group imposed by the Front. But we have argued that the PLAF was structured so that (a) the groups' norms generally reinforced formal organizational demands, although informal norms developed that protected conforming soldiers from demands for total commitment, and (b) the cadre, who served as the leader around whom primary-group norms were developed and maintained, received rewards and sanctions according to how well he kept the group's behavior consistent with organizational demands. Hence, identification with the primary group implied following the group's norms which, due to the Front's structure, implied compliance with the organization. In short, conforming members were structurally linked to the organization.

Though the specifics of the Front's structure and processes that fostered this two-step integrative link do not seem generalizable to other institutional and cultural settings, structural integration may be among the most significant means of developing institutional ties. In most cultures studied in the literature, the primary group directly motivates a wide range of individual behavior. Insofar as mobilizing organizations can channel the norms and activities of the primary group, the individual's behavior also can be channeled, independent of his degree of identification with, belief in, or even knowledge of the central concerns of the institution. Abstracting away from the particularities of such Communist control techniques as the three-man cell, the interpenetrating Party apparatus, and the informants system, the crucial element in integrating the primary group is its immediate leader. Insofar as low-level leaders comply—even though their reasons for complying may be quite different from those of their subordinates—the primary group and thereby the individual can be integrated.

The importance of this two-step integrative link confirms the practical organizer's awareness of that prosaic task of institution-building, the careful cultivation of low-level leaders. The NLF's techniques of leadership development, which perhaps could be generalized away from the context of armies and wars, involved promotion based primarily upon achievement and loyalty to the organization. These twin principles seem obvious until one realizes that in many traditional and transitional societies, ascribed characteristics and personalistic loyalties are more often the norm.[7]  In short, the development of low-level leadership is an area where the new order becomes anchored.

It is theoretically possible for a member to satisfy his self-interest but accept authority only to a limited extent. For example, the PLAF's pragmatists complied with organizational demands in order to achieve personal goals yet were willing to shift sides for better offers. In contrast, conformers in the Front developed a wide area of acceptance of authority. Though such acceptance was not of the unlimited nature of commitment, conformers by-and-large did their jobs automatically, even when the activities required of them were different from those of their peasant life. The satisfaction of personal interests contributed to the generalized acceptance of authority—indeed, we believe it was necessary for the continued acceptance of authority—but it was not sufficient in itself. The maintenance of authority among conformers required a feeling of legitimacy.

Legitimacy developed in the Front as a result of the member's perception that the PLAF's structure and processes were proper (that is, were consonant with cultural notions of how social and political life ought to be organized), that the organization was strong and stable, and that personal concerns would be satisfied. However, though legitimacy contributed to a broad acceptance of authority and hence fostered integration, it failed to provide a cushion against stress. This negative finding may be attributable to the extreme stress of war as well as the particular orientation towards authority of the Vietnamese peasant psychoculture and thus may not be generalizable. Yet, since stress inevitably accompanies institutional development, the potential of legitimacy for forestalling disintegration is a critical issue.

To explain the failure of legitimacy to provide cohesion in this context, one could argue (a) that legitimacy is a question of degree, not simply a dichotomous concept, and the stronger the feelings of legitimacy, the stronger the cohesion, (b) that the development of legitimacy is similar to a learning process and develops slowly, and (c) that a strong feeling of legitimacy did not develop among conformers because of the short time involved in the revolution.[8]  This explanation may have considerable validity in the context of modern societies, but another interpretation may be applicable in peasant societies similar to the Vietnamese—namely, the traditional orientation towards authority is a pragmatic one in which legitimacy is either accorded to a regime or not, in which the probability of legitimacy being accorded is contingent upon the satisfaction of personal interests, and in which the according of legitimacy does not imply feelings akin to political loyalty or trust towards the state. This second interpretation is consistent with the conformer's susceptibility to stress. Conformers would have been less susceptible only if they had undergone a profound personality change. Perhaps such a personality change occurred in the committed, their total identification with the organization being based upon a transference of filial sentiments from the family to the organization. However, there was little evidence of such a personality change among conformers in the PLAF. Rather they seemed to *transfer the object* of their feelings of legitimacy to the new institution *without transforming* their traditional orientation towards authority.

Legitimacy's lack of cohesive strength can be particularly detrimental to institutions built on structural integration. Structural integration relies upon the low-level leader's channeling of primary-group norms in accordance with organizational desires. But the willingness of group members to accept the authority of the formal leader depends upon members according legitimacy to the institutional framework in which the primary group is embedded. If legitimacy is pragmatically based, then members who perceive the organization as weak and their own future as uncertain might withdraw their acceptance of membership.[a]

Despite the vulnerability of the bond of legitimacy, two features of the Front helped retard disintegration. One was the development of generalized agreement. Conformers had a relatively large area of agreement, mixed with some disbelief. Perhaps because the peasant's cognitive processes place considerable weight on concrete experiences, the direct exposure of NLF members to severe combat conditions led many of them to withdraw, despite their general agreement with the Front. However, members not as directly or severely exposed assessed events either in accord with the Front or, at worst, with a disbelief that engendered uncertainty. Since inertia may be on the side of continuing acceptance of membership, the Front had a cushion which cadres could use to bolster morale and reduce uncertainty. In less stressful situations than war, the cushioning effect of cognitive bonds might be expected to be greater.

How, and how totally, cognitive bonds can be developed are critical questions for research. The relatively extensive area of agreement in the PLAF resulted from an intensive learning process. Given such specific features of the Front as

---

[a]In the analysis of the NLF, we defined the concept of cohesion to be the probability of a member not leaving the organization. Since the alternative of physically leaving the PLAF was possible, this definition made operational sense. However, the option of leaving may not be available in some situations, for example, when the mobilizing organization encompasses the state. To broaden the concept of leaving, we use the term "withdrawal from membership" to refer to the situation in which a member psychically rescinds his acceptance of membership and no longer considers rules of obedience to be binding (though he may still comply, for example, because of sanctions); he becomes, in short, nonintegrated.

pervasive political socialization and milieu control, generalizations must be made cautiously. Nonetheless, a conclusion worth further investigation is that the development of agreement—whether it be called consciousness raising, myth building, or symbol manipulation—requires an ideology that interprets the world in ways *consonant with primary beliefs* in the culture. (We reiterate our earlier warning of the obvious need to conceptualize consonance carefully and to operationalize it in empirical terms.)[9]

This need for consonance in order to develop bonds of agreement does not imply the absence of cognitive change. The easiest changes to effect in peasant beliefs are those that result from incrementing or expanding prior beliefs with elements of the organizational ideology that are not dissonant with the culture. Such changes foster integration into the new order, as the earlier analysis of conformers has shown. However, these limited changes imply limited cohesion. To strengthen cohesion, the exclusive devotion to the family, the identification as a villager, and the pragmatic orientation towards authority need to be transformed into new conceptions of loyalty, identification, and membership. These transformations require a profound break with tradition and thus can be expected to occur, in the short run, only for that minority of peasants that become committed.

The principle feature of the PLAF that prevented severe institutional decay was the commitment of a relatively high proportion of low-level leaders. Insofar as cadres were committed and consequently resistant to stress, they helped assure conformers of the continued functioning of their primary group, of the long-run strength of the Front, of the prospects for security and social advancement, and of the legitimacy of the organization. In short, committed cadre were essential to the maintenance of structural integration in the PLAF. Yet, because the development of commitment involved significant changes in peasant personality, the proportion of committed cadres was limited. Moreover, as the Front began mobilizing more peasants, this proportion decreased and thus the susceptibility of the PLAF to stress increased.

Commitment as total as that demanded by the Front of its cadres may not be necessary for the stability of nascent political systems in situations less traumatic than a revolution. Nonetheless, mobilizing organizations that depend upon structural integration must develop low-level leaders capable of withstanding stress; to do so, the organization must elicit a type of loyalty not usually found in traditional peasant societies.

Our analysis has come full circle to the dilemma inherent in all attempts to institutionalize a new order. Cultural consonance and the satisfaction of personal interests are needed to mobilize large segments of the population and to integrate them into a centralized organizational structure. In the short run, establishing such a new order depends upon psychocultural continuity and, hence, brings modest changes that result less from transforming individuals than from restructuring their life patterns. Yet, if severe stress cannot be avoided in the formative periods of the mobilizing organization, it is unlikely that institutional bonds relying on structure, self-interest, pragmatic conceptions of legitimacy, and partial agreement will be able to sustain a new order. Unless, in Samuel Huntington's words, "loyalty to . . . immediate social groupings is subordinated into loyalty to the state," maintenance of the new order is problematic and institutional development is incomplete.[10] But in order to instill peasants with such loyalty, the organization must bring about significant personality changes. And organizational demands for changes that break sharply with tradition reduce the prospects for mobilization and integration.

The delicate balance between continuity and change confronts all institutional development. The genius of the Communist model in Vietnam was its ability to create a revolutionary organization that reflected the past even as it attempted to reshape the future. The flaw in this model was its dependency upon a total commitment that could be met by relatively few peasants. Its ultimate prospects for success rest upon whether the committed leadership can survive the stresses it generates long enough for the restructured life patterns of peasants to bring about not full commitment but nonetheless basic changes—changes in the ways peasants think about themselves in relation to others, to nature, and to the state.

# Notes

## Notes to Chapter 1
## Revolution and Institutionalization

1. The writings on Western revolutions form a distinguished body of literature. Among the most influential works are Alexis de Tocqueville, *The Old Régime and the French Revolution* (New York: Doubleday Anchor Books, 1955; orig. 1856); Lyford P. Edwards, *The Natural History of Revolution* (Chicago: U. of Chicago Press, 1970; orig. 1927); Leon Trotsky, *The History of the Russian Revolution,* three volumes (New York: Simon and Schuster, 1932); Crane Brinton, *The Anatomy of Revolution* (New York: Vintage, 1958; orig., 1938); George S. Pettee, *The Process of Revolution* (New York: Harper & Bros., 1938); and Hannah Arendt, *On Revolution* (New York: The Viking Press, 1963). More recent writings on the nature of revolution do take into account patterns arising from non-Western revolutions—e.g., Harry Eckstein, "On the Etiology of Internal Wars," *History and Theory,* IV, 2 (1965); Chalmers Johnson, *Revolutionary Change* (Boston: Little, Brown, 1966); and Claude E. Welch, Jr. and Mavis B. Taintor (eds.), *Revolution and Political Change* (North Scituate, Mass.: Duxbury Press, 1972).
2. This conception of revolution follows Samuel P. Huntington's definition in *Political Order in Changing Societies* (New Haven: Yale U. Press, Paper edit., 1968), p. 264. Huntington's discussion of revolution and political order, Chapter 5, sets the stage for the central theoretical inquiries of this study.
3. The next few pages briefly outline relevant, major changes in the political order of Vietnam as it emerged from a traditional society. We make no attempt to anchor this outline in its historical and social context. For readers unaware of this essential background, the following works (taken together) cover much of the relevant material: Joseph Buttinger, *The Smaller Dragon: A Political History of Vietnam* (New York: Frederick A. Praeger, 1958); _____, *Vietnam: A Dragon Embattled,* 2 vols. (New York: Frederick A. Praeger, 1967); John F. Cady, *Southeast Asia: Its Historical Development* (New York: McGraw-Hill, 1964); Bernard B. Fall, *Street Without Joy: Indochina at War, 1946–54* (Harrisburg, Pa.: The Stockpole Co., 1961); _____, *The Two Viet Nams: A Political and Military Analysis* (New York: Frederick A. Praeger, 1963); Frances Fitzgerald, *Fire in the Lake: The Vietnamese and the Americans in Vietnam* (Boston: Little, Brown, and Co., 1972); John T. McAlister, Jr., *Viet Nam: The Origins of Revolution* (New York: Alfred A. Knopf, 1969); Paul Mus, "Viet Nam: A Nation Off Balance," *Yale Review,* vol. 41 (Summer 1952), pp. 524–38; John T. McAlister, Jr. and Paul Mus, *The Vietnamese and Their Revolution* (New York: Harper & Row, Harper

Torchbooks, 1970); Douglas Pike, *Viet Cong: The Organization and Techniques of the National Liberation Front of South Vietnam* (Cambridge: The M.I.T. Press, 1966); Jeffrey Race, *War Comes to Long An: Revolutionary Conflict in a Vietnamese Province* (Berkeley: U. of Calif. Press, 1972); Robert Shaplen, *The Lost Revolution* (New York: Harper & Row, 1965); David Joel Steinberg et al., *In Search of Southeast Asia: A Modern History* (New York: Frederick A. Praeger, 1971); Truong Chinh, *The August Revolution* (Hanoi: Foreign Languages Publishing House, 1958); and Vo Nguyen Giap, *People's War, People's Army* (Hanoi: Foreign Languages Publishing House, 1961).

4. McAlister and Mus, p. 56.
5. This phrase of Paul Mus, "Viet Nam: A Nation Off Balance" seems to catch the essence of a period of imminent change. Mus' writings offer insights into traditional Vietnam (particularly its culture and political life) and its transformation that are truly profound. This study's intellectual debt to him will become evident to those who know his work.
6. See McAlister and Mus, pp. 57–59.
7. McAlister, *Viet Nam: The Origins of Revolution*, p. 140.
8. Huntington, p. 335.
9. Fitzgerald, p. 92.
10. Organizational and guerrilla activities began several years before the "official" beginning of the NLF in December, 1960. Two controversial issues—always raised but never settled—concern the relationship between the Viet Minh and the NLF and between the Democratic Republic of Vietnam (Hanoi) and the NLF. We shall not attempt to deal explicitly with these issues. However, we should note that many writers agree (a) that the Viet Minh War had a strong nationalistic spirit not matched in the Second Indochina War (this study will examine the role played by nationalism in the PLAF) and (b) that the revolutionary organization of the Viet Minh and the NLF were similar. For background on the controversy, see various papers in Marcus G. Raskin and Bernard B. Fall (eds.), *The Viet-Nam Reader: Articles and Documents on American Foreign Policy and the Viet-Nam Crisis* (New York: Random House, Vintage Books, rev. edit. 1960); and Philippe Devillers, "The Struggle for the Unification of Vietnam," *China Quarterly* 9 (January–March, 1962).
11. During the period between 1955 and 1958, the Diem government waged a campaign of repression against former members of the Resistance. This campaign succeeded in destroying much of the Viet Minh organization remaining within the villages but it also convinced many ex-Resistance members that they could not live in peace. These former Resistance fighters in the South were recruited and organized by Communist cadre so that by 1958 a network of organizations had taken root. By 1962 (following the February 1962 congress convened by the Front, the formation of the southern Communist People's Revolutionary Party, and the battle of Ap Bac), the reality of the organization had been established. See Joseph J. Zasloff, *Origins of the Insurgency in South Vietnam 1954–1960: The Role of Southern Viet-*

*minh Cadres* (Santa Monica, Calif.: The RAND Corp. RM-5163, May, 1968) and Douglas Pike, *Viet Cong,* chapters 4–9.

12. The figures quoted in the paragraph are from Douglas Pike, *War, Peace, and the Viet Cong* (Cambridge, Mass.: The M.I.T. Press, 1969).

13. McAlister, p. 9.

14. Pike, *Viet Cong,* p. 377.

15. Pike alludes to an *alien* organization in the following passage: "Revolutionary guerrilla warfare . . . was an imported product, revolution from the outside; its stock in trade, the grievance, was often artificially created; its goal of liberation, a deception." (*Viet Cong,* p. 33.) Pike's discussion of peasants being entrapped is summarized on his p. 376.

16. See S.A. Stouffer et al. *The American Soldier* (Princeton: Princeton U. Press, 1949), Vol. II, Chap. 3; Edward A. Shils, "Primary Groups in the American Army" in R.K. Merton and P.F. Lazarsfeld (eds.), *Continuities in Social Research* (Glencoe, Ill.: The Free Press, 1950), especially p. 22; and Morris Janowitz, *Sociology and the Military Establishment* (New York: Russell Sage Foundation, 1959), Chap. 3.

17. Karl Deutsch, "Social Mobilization and Political Development," *The American Political Science Review* 55, 3 (Sept. 1961), p. 493.

18. Ibid.

19. The literature uses the term "integration" in a wide variety of ways. Since we emphasize institution-building, our definition of integration is most appropriate to those theories that conceive of institution-building as a core process of political development. See Myron Weiner, "Political Integration and Political Development" *The Annals,* vol. 358 (March, 1965), pp. 52–64; Joseph LaPalombara (ed.), *Bureaucracy and Political Development* (Princeton: Princeton U. Press, 1964); Lucian W. Pye, *Aspects of Political Development* (Boston: Little, Brown and Co., 1966) Chap. II; ———, *Politics, Personality, and Nation-Building* (New Haven: Yale U. Press, 1962); S.N. Eisenstadt, "Institutionalization and Change," *American Sociological Review* 24 (April 1964), pp. 235–47; and Samuel P. Huntington, *Political Order in Changing Societies* (New Haven: Yale U. Press, 1968), Chap. 1.

20. *Political Order in Changing Societies,* Chap. 1.


## Notes to Chapter 2
## A Microstructural Approach

1. The term "microstructural analysis" is borrowed from Manning Nash, an anthropologist, who imaginatively applies this approach to the study of social change by examining individual choices in the setting of the village social and political structure: "Microstructural analysis proceeds from the viewpoint of given individuals . . . in the framework of a social system. It tries to say what ends persons pursue, what means are available to them, and what are the consequences of the successful or unsuccessful pursuit of

given ends." *The Golden Road to Modernity: Village Life in Contemporary Burma* (New York: Wiley, 1965), p. 318.

   Clifford Gertz also argues for an approach to studying nation-building that focuses on the individual; see his "The Integrative Revolution: Primordial Sentiments and Civil Politics in the New States" in C. Gertz (ed.), *Old Societies and New States* (New York: Free Press, 1963).

2. Readers familiar with the literature will recognize our approach as a synthesis of a number of well-known approaches to the study of organizations. In particular, the following works were most influential: Herbert A. Simon, *Administrative Behavior: A Study of Decision-Making Processes in Administrative Organization* (New York: Macmillan Co., 2nd Edit., 1961, orig. 1947); Chris Argyris, *Personality and Organization* (New York: Harper, 1957); —— *Understanding Organizational Behavior* (Homewood, Ill.: Dorsey Press, 1960); James G. March and Herbert A. Simon, *Organizations* (New York: John Wiley & Sons, 1964); Daniel Katz and Robert L. Kahn, *The Social Psychology of Organizations* (New York: John Wiley & Sons, 1966); and Michael Crozier, *The Bureaucratic Phenomenon* (Chicago: The Chicago U. Press, 1964).

3. The notion of purposive behavior forms a cornerstone of Simon's *Administrative Behavior*. See Chapter V of that work and the classic discussion of Edward C. Tolman, *Purposive Behavior in Animals and Men* (New York: Appleton-Century, 1932).

4. See Alex Inkeles and Daniel J. Levinson, "National Character: the Study of Modal Personality and Sociocultural Systems" in G. Lindzey (ed.), *Handbook of Social Psychology* (Cambridge, Mass.: Addison-Wesley, 2nd Edit., 1969), Vol. 8, pp. 418–506.

5. Our term "demand" is similar to "role demand" or "role." However, the literature uses these latter terms to mean (1) prescribed role, (2) subjectively perceived role, or (3) enacted role. See John W. Thibaut and Harold H. Kelley, *Social Psychology of Groups* (New York: Wiley, 1959). When we use the term "role" or "demand," we will mean prescribed behavior.

6. Amitai Etzioni uses "compliance" as a crucial concept for the comparative analysis of organizations. See his *A Comparative Analysis of Complex Organizations* (New York, Free Press, 1961).

7. Cf. Huntington, *Political Order,* p. 10, and Eisenstadt, "Institutionalization," pp. 235–37.

8. Authority is, of course, a central concern of political science; nonetheless, no single definition is commonly accepted by either political theorists or empirical researchers. The definition used here follows Simon, *Administrative Behavior,* Chapter VII, pp. 118–153. Also see H.A. Simon, D. Smithburg, and V. Thompson, *Public Administration* (N.Y.: Knopf, 1950), Chap. 8. Our definition deviates somewhat from Simon's in the sense that it emphasizes acceptance of a *demand from the organization.* In more general terms, the "demand" could come from anyone and authority could be exercised by a person of lower rank in an organization over one with higher

official status. For other conceptions and discussions of authority, see Carl J. Friedrich (ed.), *Authority* (Cambridge: Harvard University Press, 1958); Max Weber, *The Theory of Social and Economic Organization,* ed. A.M. Henderson and Talcott Parsons (New York: Oxford U. Press, 1947), p. 328, and particularly Parsons' introduction, pp. 56–77; Robert A. Dahl, *Who Governs?* (New Haven: Yale U. Press, 1961); Harold D. Lasswell and Abraham Kaplan, *Power and Society* (New Haven: Yale U. Press, 1950); David Easton, *A Systems Analysis of Political Life* (New York: Wiley & Sons, 1965); and the review in Robert L. Peabody, *Organizational Authority* (New York: Atherton Press, 1964), chaps. 2, 3.

9. Simon, *Administrative Behavior,* p. 133.

10. The apt term "rules of obedience" is used by Charles E. Lindblom, *The Policy-Making Process* (New York: Prentice-Hall, 1968). Simon refers to rules in the following passage, "The individual sets himself a general rule which permits the communicated decision of another to guide his own choices . . . without deliberation on his own part on the expediency of those premises." [Orig. passage in italics, underlining added above], *Administrative Behavior,* p. 125.

11. Some studies have dealt directly with "consonance." However, the review of Inkeles and Levinson, "National Character," pp. 474–77, notes the rarity of such works. Among the few that have empirically analyzed "consonance" (or as Inkeles and Levinson call it, "congruence") are Michael Crozier, *The Bureaucratic Phenomenon*; G.D. Spindler, "American Character Structure as revealed by the Military," *Psychiatry,* 11, pp. 275–281; Lucian W. Pye, *The Spirit of Chinese Politics* (Cambridge, Mass.: M.I.T. Press, 1966), Chap. 9; James C. Abegglen, *The Japanese Factory: Aspects of Its Social Organization* (Glencoe, Ill.: Free Press, 1958); and Robert E. Lane, *Political Ideology* (New York: The Free Press, 1962), Chap. 25.

12. Easton, p. 278.

13. See Easton, Chap. 18, 19 for a discussion of legitimacy.

14. March and Simon, p. 48. March and Simon, following Simon, *Administrative Behavior* and Chester A. Barnard, *Functions of the Executive* (Cambridge, Mass.: Harvard University Press, 1936), divide the analysis of organizational behavior into consideration of the decision to "produce" and the decision to "participate." We make an analogous distinction; in our context, the decision to participate involves, on the one hand, a decision to "accept membership," and, on the other hand, a decision to remain in the organization (which we call cohesion); the decision to produce involves compliance.

15. Peter M. Blau and W. Richard Scott, identify maintenance—which they call "latency"—as one of the four basic problems that an organization must solve. See *Formal Organizations* (San Francisco: Chandler Publishing Co., 1962), pp. 38–39. The four basic problems are those identified for any social system by Talcott Parsons, *Structure and Process in Modern Societies* (Glencoe, Ill.: Free Press, 1960).

16. Easton, Chap. 17.

17. The definition refers to staying in or leaving the organization, *not* the group.

The literature on group dynamics uses cohesion to refer to the strength of the ties to the group. See Dorwin Cartwright's definition of *group* cohesiveness: "group cohesiveness refers to the degree to which the members of a group desire to remain in the group." In "The Nature of Group Cohesiveness," *Group Dynamics*, ed. by Cartwright and Zander (New York: Harper & Row, 3rd Edit., 1968), p. 91. Whether or not group cohesiveness implies organizational cohesiveness is, we believe, an issue requiring empirical analysis.

18. For tentative comparisons between the PLAF and the PAVN, see my study *Cohesion and Defection in the Viet Cong* (Santa Monica, Calif.: The RAND Corp., Nov. 1967). Jeffrey Race presents a fine, systematic comparative analysis of the rewards and incentives offered to peasants by the NLF and the GNV; see his *War Comes to Long An*.

19. Race, p. 179++, deals with these issues for the province of Long An.

20. The *Chieu Hoi* program, started in April, 1963, was an "amnesty" program. This study will not treat, except incidentally, the various programs and activities of the GVN. For comments about the *Chieu Hoi* program, see Bernard B. Fall, *The Two Viet-Nams: A Political and Military Analysis* (2nd rev. edit.; New York: Praeger, 1967), p. 387. Since April 1967, there have been a number of changes in this program; see Douglas Pike, *War, Peace, and the Viet Cong* (Cambridge, Mass.: The M.I.T. Press, 1969), pp. 102–7.

21. The infiltration of these regroupees is of historical significance in explaining the development of the leadership corps of the Front. Since our concern rests elsewhere, we will not analyze these veteran soldiers separately from other soldiers except in those cases where a distinction is necessary. Regroupees served in both regular PLAF units and in units of ethnic Northerners. The later units, which operated in small numbers prior to massive PAVN involvement, will not be considered here nor will the regroupees assigned to them. For an analysis of the regroupees, see J.J. Zasloff, *Political Motivation of the Viet Cong: The Vietminh Regroupees* (Santa Monica, Calif.: The RAND Corp., RM-4703/2-ISA/ARPA, May 1968; original edition, August 1966).

22. For a discussion of the interview situation and of various sources of response bias for the RAND interviews, see Zasloff, pp. 17–22. The Zasloff discussion only describes a small number (71) of the RAND interviews, but his comments are pertinent for the entire set.

### Notes to Introduction to Part II

1. Three works that take a broad perspective without losing the reality of mobilization are John T. McAlister, Jr., *Viet Nam: The Origins of Revolution*; Jeffrey Race, *War Comes to Long An* (Berkeley, Calif.: Univ. of Calif. Press, 1972); and Frances Fitzgerald, *Fire in the Lake*.

2. Karl Keutsch, "Social Mobilization and Political Development," *The American Political Science Review* 55 (Sept. 1961), p. 493.

Notes to Chapter 3
Aspects of Vietnamese Peasant Characteristics

1.  For a fine review and analysis of the literature on modal personality, see
    Alex Inkeles and Daniel J. Levinson, "National Character: the Study of
    Modal Personality and Sociocultural Systems" in G. Lindzey (ed.), *Hand-
    book of Social Psychology,* (Cambridge, Mass.: Addison Wesley, 2nd Edit.,
    1969) Vol. 4, pp. 418–506. Their definition of "national character" is those
    "relatively enduring personality characteristics and patterns that are modal
    among the adult members of the society," p. 428.
2.  The phrase "little community" refers to Robert Redfield's classic distinc-
    tion; see *The Little Community and Peasant Society and Culture* (Chicago:
    U. of Chicago Press, Phoenix Paper Ed., 1960).
3.  Vietnam contains a variety of different subcultures. The predominant one
    represented in the PLAF during the time period under consideration was
    the rural-villager population, or, what we call the peasant culture. We thus
    do *not* investigate urban Westernized Vietnamese, peasants belonging to a
    variety of religious "minorities," and such subcultures as the Montagnards.
    See F.M. Le Bar et al., *Ethnic Groups of Mainland Southeast Asia* (New
    York: Taplinger, 1963); G.C. Hickey, *The Major Ethnic Groups of the
    South Vietnamese Highlands* (Santa Monica, Calif: RAND Corp., mimeo,
    1964); *Montagnard Tribal Groups* (Fort Bragg: U.S. Army Special Warfare
    School, 1965); George Condominas, "Aspects of a Minority Problem in
    Indochina," *Pacific Affairs,* 24 (March 1951); and John T. McAlister, Jr.,
    "Mountain Minorities and the Viet Minh: A Key to the Indochina War," in
    Peter Kunstadter (ed.), *Southeast Asian Tribes, Minorities and Nations*
    (Princeton: Princeton Univ. Press, 1967).
       Within the peasant culture treated in this study, the major sources of
    systematic differences appear to be region, perhaps religion, and "colonial"
    and war experience. See G.C. Hickey, "Problems of Social Change" *BSEI*
    33, 4, (1958), pp. 1–12. Few empirical studies exist that systematically
    analyze differences among Vietnamese. Three such studies based upon the
    same field investigations are Phillip Worschel et al., RF/PF Study (New
    York: Simulmatics Corp., August 1967); Joseph P. Jackson, *The Manage-
    ment of Projected Aggression by South Vietnamese,* Dept. of Psychology,
    The University of Texas, Ph.D. dissertation, 1968; and Samuel Popkin,
    *Organization and Stability in Rural Vietnam,* Dept. of Political Science,
    M.I.T., Ph.D. dissertation, 1969.
4.  See Fitzgerald, *Fire in the Lake,* p. 48. Hickey, *Village in Vietnam,* p. 82
    suggests a difference in village social structure between the South and the
    North which could have profound implications for enculturation—viz., that
    southern villages did not have as closely-knit, ordered society as northern
    villages.
5.  Hickey, p. 285.
6.  This list of psychocultural characteristics is similar to the "standardized" list
    for cross-cultural comparison suggested by Inkeles and Levinson, pp. 448–50.

7. Fitzgerald, *Fire in the Lake,* Ch. 1.
8. *Vietnam: Yesterday and Today* (New York: Holt, Rinehart and Winston, Inc., 1966), p. 28. For similar characterizations, see V. Thompson, *French Indochina* (London: George Allen & Unwin Ltd., 1937), pp. 43–4; P. Giran, *Psychologie du peuple Annamite* (Paris: Ernest Lerou, 1904), Chap. 2.
9. For histories of the cultural heritage of Vietnam, see J. Buttinger, *The Smaller Dragon* (New York: Praeger, 1958); Nguyen Dang Thuc, *Asian Culture and Vietnamese Humanism* (Saigon, 1965); Nguyen Khac Kham, *An Introduction to Vietnamese Culture* (Tokyo: The Centre for East Asian Cultural Studies, #10, 1967); and Nguyen Van Thai and Nguyen Van Mung, *A Short History of Viet Nam* (Saigon, Viet Nam: The Times Publishing Co., 1958). Confucianism and Taoism in Vietnam receive special attention in Nguyen Huu Chi, *Political Socialization and Political Change* (Dept. of Political Science, Ph.D. dissertation, Michigan State University, 1965), Chap. 2. For the Buddhist heritage, see Paul Mus, *The Buddhist Background to the Crisis in Vietnamese Politics* (New Haven: Yale U., mimeograph, 1958) and K.W. Morgan, "The Buddhists: The Problem and the Promise," *ASIA* 4 (1966). For general background on religion and culture, see K.W. Morgan (ed.), *The Path of the Buddha* (New York: Ronald Press, 1956); W.T. De Bary et al., *Sources of Chinese Tradition* (New York: Columbia U. Press, 1960); and E.O. Reischauer (ed.), *East Asia: The Great Tradition* (Boston: Houghton Mifflin, 1958). For religious practices and popular beliefs at the village level, see Gerald C. Hickey, *Village in Vietnam* (New Haven: Yale University Press, 1964), Chap. 3.
10. For example, F.R. Kluckhohm and F.L. Strodtbeck depict the fatalistic peasant in the following way:

> The typical Spanish-American sheepherder, in a time as recent as twenty-five years ago, believed firmly that there was little or nothing a man could do to save or protect either land or flocks when damaging storms descended upon them. He simply accepted the inevitable. In Spanish-American attitudes towards illness and death one finds the same fatalism. "If it is the Lord's will that I die, I shall die" is the way they express it, and many a Spanish-American has been known to refuse the services of a doctor because of the attitude.

> From *Variations in Value Orientations* (Evanston, Illinois: Row, Peterson & Co., 1961), p. 13.
11. Vietnamese folk proverbs deal so often with fatalistic themes that Huynh Dinh Te's analysis of them suggests "an attitude of acceptance towards life which amounts to a Stoicism. [The Vietnamese peasant] seems to be content with his fate no matter how humble it may be." Huynh Dinh Te, *Vietnamese Cultural Patterns and Values as Expressed in Proverbs* (Columbia U., Ph.D. dissertation, 1962), p. 167. In this study, a random sample of 1679 proverbs from a collection of 5,038 are analyzed for clues to cultural patterns and the results are compared to the "consensus" cultural description of writers on Vietnam. An example of a folk proverb expressing resignation is "If one's fate is poverty and misfortune, one must resign one-

self to it." (p. 167). However, Huynh Dinh Te also examined many proverbs
dealing with "individual will" and he, thus, concludes: "Fate does not preclude man's efforts and work. . . . Happiness or suffering, success or failure,
all result from one's own work, will, and endeavor." (p. 179). Huynh Dinh
Te found an approximately even split in proverbs depicting the "inexorability of fate versus the power of the individual's will." See his Appendix.
This suggests that both strains are present in the culture. By contending that
they are not psychologically incompatible, we do not intend to rule out
ambivalence or underlying tensions. We gratefully acknowledge the permission of Columbia University to reproduce material from Huynh Dinh Te's
dissertation.

12. Hickey, p. 56. Contrast this assessment to the Kluckhohm-Strodtbeck image
    in note 10 of this chapter.

13. This well-known saying is from Confucius, *The Book of History,* Book 5,
    Chap. 21, sec. 4, J. Legge (trans.): "You are the wind; the common people
    are the grass. For it is the nature of grass to bend when the wind blows." Cf.
    Hickey's comment: "Khanh Hau people are of a tradition in which one
    guards the old ways while adopting the new ways necessary to changed
    circumstances." (p. 285).

14. As Huynh Dinh Te notes, "The future appears to be shrouded in a veil of
    mystery. 'Man can only know for sure what happens to him today' [a folk
    proverb says] ; what tomorrow has in store for him is beyond the reach of
    his knowledge." (p. 166). Cf. Kluckhohm and Strodtbeck's discussion of
    temporal focus, *Variations,* Chap. 1.

15. We shall discuss subsequently the Vietnamese concern and drive for status
    in regards to which a number of commentators on Vietnamese cultures have
    observed the Vietnamese "overexaggerated emphasis on the act of maneu-
    vering," W.H. Slote, *Observations on Psychodynamic Structures in Viet-
    namese Personality,* p. 28.

16. That Vietnamese peasants (and, indeed, the peasantry of many other lands)
    deal in *concrete* associations and symbols as opposed to the more abstract
    notions of Western intellectual thought has been noted by many writers. See,
    for example, Fitzgerald, *Fire in the Lake,* p. 18. Concreteness, short time
    horizon for action, and emphasis on tactics in a given situation are all com-
    ponents of an integrated mode of cognitive functioning. Throughout this
    chapter, other components will be noted.

17. See Francis L.K. Hsu, *Americans and Chinese: Two Ways of Life* (New
    York: Henry Schuman, 1953), p. 10. Hsu uses the term "situation-centered"
    culture to connote the importance of the immediate interpersonal situa-
    tion (behaving in a manner appropriate to the situation, particularly in terms
    of status relationships) for the Chinese culture. As this chapter unfolds,
    similar concerns in the Vietnamese psychoculture will become apparent.

18. Paul Mus, "Cultural Backgrounds of Present Problems," *Asia* 4 (Winter
    1966), p. 19. For a subtle discussion of the Mandate of Heaven in Vietnam,
    see J.T. McAlister, Jr. and P. Mus, *The Vietnamese and Their Revolution*
    (New York: Harper & Row, 1970), Chapter 3 and Frances Fitzgerald, "The

Struggle and the War," *The Atlantic Monthly* 220 (Aug. 1967). The discussions of the Mandate of Heaven in political histories of China and Vietnam focus primarily on dynastic changes and the "legitimizing" role played the Mandate of Heaven in the acceptance by the population of new rulers. Since we focus on the microlevel of individual personality traits, we will characterize various elements of the Mandate of Heaven in terms of the orientation towards authority and the cognitive functioning of Vietnamese peasants. Paul Mus' work is extraordinarily perceptive on these subtle issues.

19. Cognitive theorists have not yet reached a consensus on the best way to describe cognitive structure and processes: therefore, we eclectically pick features of Vietnamese cognitive functioning that seem pertinent to understanding organizational behavior. The term "differentiation" is employed by M. Brewster Smith, Bruner, and White, *Opinions and Personality* (New York: John Wiley, Science Ed., 1964), p. 34. Also see J. Bieri et al., *Clinical and Social Judgment: The Discrimination of Behavioral Information* (New York: Wiley, 1966). Though peasants differentiate concrete experiences in a more detailed way than modernized Westerners, they deal with abstract concepts in a highly diffuse manner. Thus, Frances Fitzgerald observes that "the Vietnamese does not live within the segmented Western world of cause and effect, of conceptual analysis, of theoretical distinctions between form and substance." "The Struggle and the War," *The Atlantic Monthly* 220 (Aug. 1967), p. 74. Or as Mus has put it, "We think in terms of concepts. They think in terms of the complete man." From "Cultural Backgrounds," p. 12.

The tendency to judge choices as polarized and as being proper or improper, "correct" or "incorrect" is noted by Paul Mus, *Vietnam: Sociologie d'une Guerre* (Paris: Editions due Seuil, partial translation, Yale University) Chapter 2, "In the Confucian tradition which was still deeply rooted in the countryside there was no room for a compromise; either there was a close identification or antagonisms." This characteristic is associated with other cognitive characteristics described by W.H. Slote, *Observations on Psychodynamic Structures in Vietnamese Personality* (New York: The Simulmatics Corp., 1966); Vietnamese cognitions of "the world was stringently divided into good people and bad people, with absolutes attached to both and very few shadings between." p. 15. Cf. to note 48 of this chapter.

20. Hammer, p. 96. Cf. V. Thompson, "Death is a release and a repose which is accepted with indifference, where there is no escape, and with contempt because it is the supreme manifestation of force." p. 44.

21. Hickey, *Village in Vietnam,* p. 96. Ancestor worship is fundamental to Vietnamese life regardless of varieties of religious persuasions. As Nguyen Dinh Hoa, *Verbal and Non-Verbal Patterns of Respect Behavior*, New York University, Ph.D. dissertation, 1957, p. 185 puts it: "the survival of the ancestors, their presence amidst the family, is not an empty word, a way of speaking, a figure of speech: 'it is a profound reality, admitted by everyone.'" The quotation is from a standard French source Leopold Cadiere, *Croyances et Pratiques Religieuses des Annamates* (Hanoi: Société de Géographie, 1944.) Also see Nguyen Van Thuan, *Rites of Passage* (New York: American Friends of Vietnam, 1968).

22. A folk proverb states it simply: "It is better to die in honor than live in disgrace." As quoted by Huynh Dinh Te, p. 53.

23. For suggestive remarks on this topic in the Chinese context, see R.J. Lifton, *Revolutionary Immortality* (New York: Alfred Knopf, 1968).

24. There seems to be a reasonably wide consensus among a diverse body of scholars about the strong sense of Vietnamese identity vis-à-vis other "foreigners." For persuasive historical evidence, see Truong Buu Lam, *Patterns of Vietnamese Response to Foreign Intervention* (New Haven: Yale U. Southeast Asia Studies No. 11, 1967); David G. Marr, *Vietnamese Anticolonialism: 1885–1925* (Berkeley: Univ. of Calif., 1971); and Milton E. Osborne, "The Vietnamese perception of the identity of the State," *Australian Outlook* 23 (No. 1) pp. 7–17. See the next note for additional evidence. For convenience, we shall refer to this sense of Vietnameseness as "nationalism" even though it is less than completely accurate to do so.

25. Huynh Dinh Te found what we have called nationalism as a recurrent theme in proverbs: "Patriotic feelings are manifest in proverbs expressing his [the individual's] readiness to fight and give his life for the country and his contempt for traitors." Two such proverbs may give a flavor of this sentiment: "When pirates (aggressors) come to the house (invade the country) even women must take arms." "Dragons come from dragons' eggs; snakes' eggs give birth to snakes." (The dragon is the symbol of the Vietnamese race.) As quoted by Huynh Dinh Te, p. 148. Also see Nguyen Huu Chi's attempts to operationalize nationalism by psychological testing, to differentiate various forms of nationalism, and then to relate nationalism to measures of "authoritarianism" and "familism."

26. See W.H. Slote, *Vietnamese Ego Structure and Identity Patterns* (New York: The Simulmatics Corp., 1968), p. 26. Slote, a psychoanalytically trained psychologist, did a series of in-depth interviews with a variety of Vietnamese (and also did field work in villages). Since Western concepts are not easily transferred to Eastern personality, his findings must be treated cautiously. Nonetheless, his results are insightful and in accord with observations made by other researchers.

27. Hammer, p. 209. This point emerges clearly in Nguyen Dinh Hoa metalinguistic analysis of Vietnamese language, *Verbal and Non-Verbal Patterns of Respect Behavior in Vietnamese Society,* New York U., Ph.D. dissertation, 1957. See his discussion of "names," Chap. 7.

28. Slote suggests that "within the unconscious self-image of the Vietnamese . . . he is a component within a broader ego structure . . . One fits into the totality of a family or societal unit." *Vietnamese Ego Structure,* p. 4. Frances Fitzgerald makes a similar observation: "In the villages of Vietnam man is not an individual in the Western sense, for he has not quite distinguished himself from the community living and dead, natural and supernatural, to which he belongs. He behaves not as a man of absolute free will, but as a junior partner, the executor of community opinion." "The Struggle and the War," p. 78.

29. In addition to the Slote paper cited above, an earlier paper was helpful, *Observations on Psychodynamic Structures in Vietnamese Personality* (New

York: The Simulmatics Corp., 1966). The following works on the Chinese psychoculture were most useful: R.H. Solomon, *The Chinese Revolution and the Politics of Dependency*, Cambridge, Mass.: Dept. of Pol. Sci., Massachusetts Institute of Technology, Ph.D. dissertation, 1966, and Lucian W. Pye, *The Spirit of Chinese Politics* (Cambridge, Mass.: The M.I.T. Press, 1966).

30. See Hickey, p. 111.

31. See Frances L.K. Hsu's discussion in *American and Chinese*, p. 10 and see note 17 of this chapter.

32. "Every child is expected to learn certain forms of politeness, the foremost of which is respect for the aged, a reflection of the strong value placed on filial piety." Hickey, p. 111. The key notion in this quotation is that of filial piety. In traditional training, children studied the 24 acts of filial devotion from *Nhi Thop Tu Hien* adapted from Chinese Confucianism. See Hammer, p. 23, Nguyen Huu Chi, pp. 80 ff., and Nguyen Khac Kham, Chap. 3. For the purposes of this study, the important point is that, at least in the ideal, no personal sacrifice, including humiliation, should stand in the way of fulfilling filial duties. Southern contemporary villages may have been more lax in their filial training than Northern traditional villages.

33. See Slote, *Vietnamese Ego Structure*, pp. 21–23.

34. The "evidence" is projective tests (Rorschach and TATs) administered by Slote to which this author had access. The TATs seemed particularly revealing of deeply repressed hostilities that would not normally have surfaced. Further confirmatory evidence is supplied by TATs administered to Vietnamese villagers as part of Philip Worschel's study, Worschel et al., *RF/PF Study* (New York: The Simulmatics Corp., undated draft manuscript). For a discussion and review of projective techniques in cross-cultural research, see Gárdner Lindzey, *Projective Techniques and Cross-Cultural Research* (New York: Appleton-Century-Crofts, 1961).

35. McAlister and Mus, p. 96. Paul Mus' "informal" observations agree with the findings of Slote established by projective techniques. The following passage shows Mus' insight to the inner tensions and anxieties generated by the psychoculture: "The explosion set off by a scene between women in the street or a fit of defiance and anger in a young child—real tragedies acted out right on the sidewalk—give some idea of all that is smoldering under the conventions of civility and show why it is necessary. . . . Here is a society under tension; . . . The society must manage the reactions of individuals caught between general rules of conduct and the latent human intolerance toward any kind of rules." (McAlister and Mus, p. 96).

36. Slote, *Vietnamese Ego*, p. 21. Slote's analysis parallels Richard Solomon's interpretations of Chinese culture in a number of major ways. In particular, Solomon argues, in a detailed and convincing manner, that dependency is a primary dynamic in Chinese psychoculture. See Solomon, *The Chinese Revolution and the Politics of Dependency*, Cambridge, Mass.: Dept. of Political Science, M.I.T., Ph.D. dissertation, 1966.

37. Since the family is so fundamental to the peasant's self-identity, the fear that conflict in the family will lead to the family unit disintegrating is par-

ticularly threatening. Thus, Nguyen Huu Chi notes: "In Vietnam, it is widely believed that antagonisms between family members—e.g., between brothers, cousins, etc.—are signs of decadence in that family. The family is viewed as an epitome of the cosmos. If harmony is wanting in the cosmos, calamity will certainly occur. Family relationships must be kept as harmonious as possible." (*Political Socialization,* p. 83.). We gratefully acknowledge the permission of Nguyen Huu Chi to reproduce material from his dissertation.

38. On traditional village life, see Pierre Gourou, *The Peasants of the Tonkin Delta* (New Haven: Human Relations Area File, 1955); _____, *Land Utilization in French Indochina* (Institute of Pacific Relations, 1945); Nguyen Dang Thuc, *Democracy in Traditional Vietnamese Society* (Saigon: Ministry of Nat. Ed., #4); and Gabrielle M. Vassal, *On and Off Duty in Annam* (London: William Heineman, 1910). Among the French language sources are Giran, Cadiere, Vu Quoc Thuc, *L'Economie Communaliste du Viet Nam* (Hanoi: Presses Universiturs du Viet Nam, 1950); and Nguyen Xuan Dao, *Village Government in Viet Nam: A Survey of Historical Development* (Saigon: Michigan State U., Vietnam Advisory Group, 1958).

39. As we noted earlier, some writers argue that Southern villages did not have as highly an integrated village life as traditional Northern villages. For studies examining contemporary village life or changes that have taken place in village social life, see Paul Mus, "The Role of the Village in Vietnamese Politics," *Pacific Affairs* 22 (1949), pp. 265–72; _____, "Vietnam: A Nation off Balance," *Yale Review* 41 (1952), pp. 524–38; J.D. Donoghue *Cam An* (Saigon: Michigan State U. Vietnam Advisory Group, 1958); J.B. Hendry, *The Small World of Khanh Hau* (Chicago: Aldine, 1964); Truong Ngoc Giau, *The Delta Village of My Thuan* (Saigon: Michigan State U. Vietnam Advisory Group, 1964); L. Woodruff, *Local Administration in Vietnam* (Saigon: Michigan State U. Vietnam Advisory Group, 1961); S. Popkin, "Village Authority Patterns" (Mimeo, paper prepared for Peace Research Society meeting, June, 1968); Vu Quoc Thuc, "The Influence of Western Civilization on Economic Behavior of the Vietnamese," *Asian Culture* 1 (2); P.J. Honey, "Village Life in North Vietnam," *China News Quarterly* 486 (Sept. 20, 1963); Nguyen Dinh Hoa, "Country Life in Vietnam," *Vietnam Bulletin* 1.3 (March 1953); and G.C. Hickey, "Problems of Social Change in Vietnam," *BSEI* 33, 4 (1958).

40. Hickey, *Village in Vietnam,* p. 47.

41. Ibid., p. 282.

42. As Paul Mus observes, "Long acquaintance with Vietnamese reveals that they have abundant group spirit, not only in their family life, but also in their village communities, the touchstone of their traditional society ("Vietnam: A Nation Off Balance," *Yale Review* 41 (1952), p. 528.)

43. McAlister and Mus, p. 96.

44. Hu Hsien-Chin, "The Chinese concept of face," *American Anthropologist* 46 (1944), p. 46. Also see Nguyen Huu Chi, pp. 86–88. On the cultural contrasts between shame and guilt, see W. LaBarre, "Some observations on character structure in the Orient" *Psychiatry*, 8 and 9; and G. Pierz and

M.B. Singer, *Shame and Guilt: A Psychoanalytic and a Cultural Study* (Springfield: Thomas, 1953).

45. McAlister and Mus, p. 96.

46. Hu, p. 48, makes an analogous distinction, though these particular terms are not used.

47. Huynh Dinh Te found distrust revealed in proverbs: "If popular wisdom urges the Vietnamese to treat his fellow men with courtesy and kindness, it nevertheless warns him not to put much faith in others. People are often hard to please, stupid, selfish, [self-] interested, slanderous, ungrateful and treacherous. It is almost impossible to know other people's real feelings and intentions. Appearances are often deceiving. In social intercourse, one should be cautious." pp. 115–117. Pierre Gourou's comment on traditional village life is also revealing, "some [villagers] watch jealously the place which is due them, others speculate about the place which they will occupy later on." *The Peasants*, p. 280. Gerald Hickey found an absence of close relationships at the village level: "The lack at village level [as contrasted to kin or hamlet level] of communal personal association was manifest in the unsuccessful village cooperative. . . . The trust and cooperation needed to make a success of the organization clearly was lacking." *Village in Vietnam*, p. 280.

48. *Political Socialization*, pp. 59–60 *interalia*.

49. Huynh Dinh Te's analysis of proverbs shows that, "Proverbs contain many practical hints for the Vietnamese to conduct himself in society without causing friction and attracting animosity from others. Stress is laid on discretion, equity, leniency, and conformity." (p. 114). As we shall see subsequently, each one of these "defenses" enters into an appreciation of the operation of the PLAF.

50. Hammer, p. 217.

51. Nguyen Dinh Hoa, pp. 3 and 62. The situation-centered nature of this respect behavior is further discussed on the same pages by Nguyen Dinh Hoa: "The Vietnamese value personalized relationships over impersonal relationships and have a strong sense of social differences. . . . In this status-minded Vietnamese society, the position of each individual is clearly defined . . . in terms of interpersonal behavior." We gratefully acknowledge the permission of Nguyen Dinh Hoa to reproduce material from his dissertation.

52. As a proverb puts it, "Respect for one's superiors, kindness for one's inferiors." Huynh Dinh Te, p. 125.

53. Nguyen Dinh Hoa shows this "extension" of the family in the use of language status discriminations and, particularly, in the use of personal pronouns. See Chapter 4. The PLAF recruitment cadre addressed the people in terms of an "extension" of the family. See Fitzgerald, *Fire in the Lake*, pp. 157++.

54. *Observations on Psychodynamic Structures in Vietnamese Personality*, p. 20: ". . . camaraderie as a social form was well integrated [although] each informant stated that he never had what he would consider a best friend— one with whom there were no interpersonal restraints." Also see Solomon,

pp. 176–78. Huynh Dinh Te, p. 117, found: "Friendship is so important that proverbs advise one to be careful about friends and associates. . . . Loyalty between friends is stressed not only in proverbs but also in folk lyrics, folk tales, and classical poetry."

55. See McAlister and Mus, p. 96, and Samuel L. Popkin, "Village Authority Patterns in Vietnam" (Paper for Peace Research Society, June 1968, mimeo.), p. 9.

56. Hickey, p. 195: "When a difference remains unresolved, it usually comes to the attention of the five-family group head or the hamlet chief. Either can arbitrate, and should the decision prove unsatisfactory, it is taken to the Village Council." Nguyen Dinh Hoa, p. 230 suggests a similar general mechanism: "Among people with an almost pathological fear of losing face, face-saving devices cannot be lacking. . . . Indeed in any sort of dispute as long as the reputations of both parties are preserved and neither has been overly humiliated, the good offices of an intermediary or middleman are always welcomed and sometimes indirectly sought."

57. Frances Fitzgerald, "The Struggle and the War" *The Atlantic Monthly* 220 (Aug. 1967), p. 74, offers a similar summary of security and fitting-in, "If [the villager] imitates the correct procedures, if he behaves in conformity with established patterns, his reward is the approval of the community around him, and by extension, that of the spiritual community of ancestors and the transcendent heaven."

58. A "status" drive, as used here, can be viewed as a universal trait. It is a person's "social aspiration," his propensity to pursue goals valued and considered legitimate by the culture. (See Inkeles and Levinson, *National Character*, p. 473). Similar to our description of the need for security (another universal trait), the important task is to characterize the way the status drive is manifested in the Vietnamese peasant psychoculture. We use the term "status drive" rather than "social aspiration" because the major legitimate and valued social goals in Vietnamese culture relate to rising in the status hierarchy of the village.

59. Robert L. Merton discusses the balance, and lack of balance, between cultural goals and institutionalized means in his *Social Theory and Social Structure* (Glencoe: Free Press, 1957), pp. 132++.

60. Hammer, p. 217, observes: "Great care was taken to establish the rules of hierarchy, which varied from village to village and in some were reported to have included as many as twelve separate categories."

61. In the traditional Mandarin system, public offices were open to civil service competition. The examination required memorization of classics but could be passed after years of study. See Pierre Gourou, *The Peasants; The Vietnamese Peasant: His Value System* (United States Information Agency, R-138-65, Oct. 1965); Nguyen Khac Kham; and Nguyen Dinh Hoa, p. 210, who quotes Andre Dumarest, *La Formation de classes Sociales en Pays Annamite* (Lyon: U. of Lyon, 1935): "It is possible to say that the Annamese society did not know class differentiations of an economic order. Social position was determined by the literary knowledge and the intellectual value displayed by everyone. The elite was recruited among small

people. . . ." Finally, Hickey, p. 272, observed in the village of Khanh Hau
that: "upward mobility is good fortune and downward mobility is bad
fortune, and villagers are likely to attribute changes in status to destiny; but
this does not imply fatalism—one can still strive to improve one's lot or
make it possible for children to improve theirs."

62. The belief in the necessity for hard work and labor is revealed in Huynh
    Dinh Te's analysis of proverbs. Three concomitants of this belief are the
    attitudes that *hardships are expected*—e.g., a proverb says "Present hardships
    pave the way for future wealth and ease" (p. 130), that one should be *self-
    critical in order to improve oneself*—e.g., "Reproach yourself ten times
    when you reproach others once" (p. 64), and that *laziness is condemned* —
    e.g., "people who lie down under the fig tree and wait for the fig to fall into
    their mouth" are held in contempt (p. 130.) We shall see subsequently that
    these themes, like so many of the others discussed here, appear in Front life.

63. P. 227.

64. Hickey, p. 272.

65. For a fine discussion and analysis of landlord-tenant relations, see Robert L.
    Samson, *The Economics of Insurgency in the Mekong Delta of Vietnam*
    (Cambridge, Mass.: M.I.T. Press, 1970), pp. 28++. These landlord-tenant
    relations were similar to patron-clients ties often existing in peasant
    societies, see James C. Scott, "Patron-Client Politics and Political Change in
    Southeast Asia," *American Political Science Review* 66 (1972), pp. 91–113.

66. Hickey, p. 274.

67. Huynh Dinh Te notes: "the love for learning does not spring from purely
    disinterested motives. The lure of prestige and prospect of improved social
    status are among the strongest incentives to the pursuit of knowledge."
    (p. 146).

68. Huynh Dinh Te, p. 144. Again, both the notion of virtue and its specific
    qualities will be evident when we examine Front life.

69. See McAlister and Mus, pp. 57–59, and Popkin, Village Authority Patterns,"
    pp. 4–9.

## Notes to Chapter 4
## Recruitment and Acceptance

1. Pike, *Viet Cong,* p. 160.

2. See Pike, *War, Peace, and the Viet Cong* (Cambridge, Mass.: The M.I.T. Press,
   1969), p. 7; and W.P. Davison, *Some Observations on Viet Cong Operations
   in the Villages* (Santa Monica: The RAND Corp., RM-5267, May 1968),
   Section 2.

3. *Viet Cong,* p. 291.

4. Davison, p. 15.

5. *War Comes to Long An,* p. 164.

6. That the Front deliberately placed considerable operational responsibility
   on their local cadres is evident from reading excerpts from their training

manuals. (A large number of NLF documents have been captured.) See Race, pp. 161–163.

7. The importance of reliable implementation at the local level is particularly evident when one contrasts the performance of NLF recruitment cadre with the largely unproductive efforts of GVN local workers. See Race, pp. 193–208; Fitzgerald, *Fire in the Lake,* p. 162, and P. Worschel et al., *RF/PF Study* (New York: Simulmatics Corp., August 1962).

8. The use of ideology in the Chinese Communist context for both motivational and "rational ideas" is nicely developed by Franz Schurmann, *Ideology and Organization in Communist China* (Berkeley: Univ. of California Press, 1966), p. 34.

9. The literature on organizations seldom deals with the control of low-level members who have considerable operational antonomy and whose activities cannot be easily monitored. The importance of commonly held norms and values for obtaining behavior in accord with the general interests of the organization in this "decentralized" situation is dealt with in H. Kaufman, *The Forest Ranger* (Baltimore: Johns Hopkins Press, 1960).

10. Race, p. 140.

11. Fitzgerald, *Fire in the Lake,* p. 157.

12. It is beyond the scope of this study to deal with the hows and whys of village control or to treat in detail the nature of the "liberated" village. For relevant studies see D.W.P. Elliott and W.A. Stewart, *Pacification and the Viet Cong System in Dinh Thuong: 1966–1967* (Santa Monica: The RAND Corp., RM-5788, January 1969), R.H. Betts, *Viet Cong Village Control: Some Observations on the Origin and Dynamics of Modern Revolutionary Warfare* (Cambridge, Mass.: M.I.T. Center for International Studies, August, 1964); Michael Charles Conley, *The Communist Insurgent Infrastructure in South Vietnam: A Study of Organization and Strategy* (Washington: Center for Research in Social Systems, American University, Dept. of the Army Pamphlet 550-106, 1967); Race, *War Comes to Long An;* and Pike, *Viet Cong,* Chapter 4.

13. "Control" was a word much used by those who tried to judge how the war was "going," and, like so many other of the war "indicators," it was poorly conceived and even more poorly measured. See B.B. Fall, *The Two Viet-Nams* (2nd ed.; New York: Praeger, 1967), pp. 369, and his citation of *The Komer Report.*

14. See D.W.P. Elliott and W.A. Stewart, *Pacification and the Viet Cong System in Dinh Tuong: 1966–1967* (Santa Monica: The RAND Corp., RM-5788, January 1969), p. 31.

15. Gabriel A. Almond and Sidney Verba, *The Civic Culture* (Boston: Little, Brown & Co., 1965), p. 17.

16. Fitzgerald, *Fire in the Lake,* p. 161. Nathan Leites sensitively discusses the way cadre treated villagers and the way villagers perceived this treatment; see his *Viet Cong Style of Politics* (Santa Monica, Calif.: The RAND Corp., RM-5487, May 1969), p. 108++.

17. Chapters 7 and 8 of this study will examine the effect of these ideological themes on the socialization of PLAF members. However, we will not study

their effects on villagers. For an insightful discussion of how sensitively these Front propaganda themes employed refrains from the traditional culture, see McAlister and Mus, *The Vietnamese*, "Marxism and Traditionalism in Viet Nam," Chapter 7. Also see Frances Fitzgerald, *Fire in the Lake*, pp. 212–226.

18. Leites discusses the symbolic importance of volunteering. See *Viet Cong Style of Politics*, pp. 87–89.

19. For a description of the activities of NLF agit-prop teams, see Pike, *Viet Cong*, pp. 126–28.

20. For the purposes of this study, the taxonomy offered above seems the most appropriate. However, as noted, this categorization is an abstraction from more concrete reasons. Other ways of categorizing these reasons could be constructed. For two examples, see Ithiel de Sola Pool, "Political Alternatives to the Viet Cong," *Asian Survey* 7 (Aug. 1967), pp. 555–66, and W.P. Davison, *Some Observations on Viet Cong Operations in the Villages*, pp. 16–17.

21. Elliott and Stewart, *Pacification and the Viet Cong System* make the following argument: "Inevitably, each zone of control generates different problems for the VC, which are met by varying policies. In the liberated zone, Viet Cong programs are executed in a blunt and uncompromising manner. 'Liberated' people are assumed to be more 'enlightened' than their counterparts in areas of lesser VC control; hence, recalcitrance and resistance to Viet Cong programs is a greater sin. When control is not absolute, more delicate 'political' measures are employed. Persuasion rather than compulsion is considered the correct strategy for areas of weak control." (p. 31). The data of table 4.3 do show that peasants were less likely to volunteer from Front controlled villages. The percentage coerced for Front controlled villages reflects drafting (without other inducements or positive appeals cited) as well as more overt force.

22. "Political Alternatives to the Viet Cong," p. 59.

23. See Pike, *Viet Cong*, p. 94. We will discuss (in Chapter 7) the role of hate—and the stimulation of hate—in developing commitment on the part of PLAF soldiers. The interview data do not provide evidence of sufficient quality or quantity to attempt serious analysis of the role of hate *in recruitment* per se. However, since the last chapter argued that feelings of hostility against authority were both generated and deeply repressed in Vietnamese personality, the channeling of hate against an "outside" authority could have been highly effective. In terms of recruitment (rather than general village mobilization), the generation of hate appears to have been more effective in initial access than in the final acceptance of membership. Compare Pike's discussion of the role of hate in village control with Fitzgerald's analysis as indicated by her assessment, "Hatred was the beginning of the revolution, for hatred meant a clean break in all the circuits of dependency that had bound the Vietnamese to the Westerners, the landlords, and the old notables." (*Fire in the Lake*, p. 169).

24. Pool, p. 558.

25. See Leites, *Viet Cong Style of Politics*, 41–87 and 197–202. Leites discussion of these points is both subtle and appropriate.
26. *Viet Cong*, p. 376.


## Notes to Introduction to Part II

1. Franz Schurmann, *Ideology and Organization in Communist China* (Berkeley: University of California Press, 1966).


## Notes to Chapter 5
## Organizational Ideology

1. These suggestive terms are used in John W. Lewis, *Leadership in Communist China* (Ithaca: Cornell U. Press, 1963), p. 36. Though this study makes no attempt at comparative analysis, the Vietnamese Communists are similar in many ways to the Chinese Communists. Thus, we have been able to draw upon a number of excellent studies of the Chinese Communist system. Our indebtedness to these studies will become apparent in the notes.
2. Commitment, as defined in the text, is thus a special pattern of compliance. The committed automatically accepts the decisional premises posed by the organization—i.e., the organization defines the situation, evokes the action, and prescribes the "correct" alternative. Moreover, as Daniel Katz and Robert L. Kahn, *The Social Psychology of Organizations* (New York: John Wiley, 1966) observe, "satisfactions accrue to the [committed] person from the expression of attitudes and behavior reflecting his cherished beliefs and self-image. The reward [of complying] is not so much a matter of social recognition or monetary advantage as of establishing his self-identity, confirming his notion of the sort of person he sees himself to be, and expressing the values appropriate to this self-concept." (p. 346).
3. Franz Schurmann distinguishes between class ideology, individual ideology, and organizational ideology. He defines organizational ideology as "a systematic set of ideas with action consequences serving the purposes of creating and using organization." (*Ideology and Organization in Communist China*, p. 18). We adopt his definition of organizational ideology. To avoid semantic confusion, we use the term "beliefs" (rather than ideology) to denote the set of ideas, cognitions, and values characteristic of an individual. Thus, in our usage, the referent of ideology will be the organization; the referent of beliefs will be the individual. See Robert E. Lane, *Political Ideology* (New York: The Free Press, 1962), pp. 14–16 and Milton Rokeach, *The Open and Closed Mind* (New York: Basic Books, 1960), p. 35. Of course, the important point is that the set of ideas constituting organizational ideology imply expectations, norms, values (what we generically call formal demands) that the organization prescribes for the individual. One

could distinguish between those demands that are primarily political (and thus defined by many as ideological) and those not political; however, to do so in this organization where politics was pervasive might be excessively artificial.

4. As quoted by Alexander L. George, *The Chinese Communist Army in Action,* p. 25, from Mao Tse-tung, *On Guerrilla Warfare* (New York: Praeger, 1961). The full Mao quote used by George is:

> A revolutionary army must have discipline that is established on a limited democratic basis. In all armies, obedience of the subordinates to their superiors must be expected. This is true in the case of guerrilla discipline, but the basis for guerrilla discipline must be individual awareness. With guerrillas, a discipline of compulsion is ineffective . . . [It] must be self-imposed, because only when it is, is the soldier able to understand completely why he fights and how he must obey.

This study owes a great deal to the George work both in terms of specific hypotheses and general approach. The NLF, as well as the PAVN and the government of the Democratic Republic of Vietnam (North Vietnam), had a great deal in common with the Chinese Communist regime and army in terms of organizational principles, doctrine, and structure. The NLF was modeled after the Viet Minh which was modeled after the Chinese Communist experience. It is not our purpose here to investigate these connections.

5. Putting "theory into practice" is a major concern in Communist systems. Schurmann's *Ideology and Organization in Communist China,* pp. 24–33, provides an excellent analysis of this problem in China. A number of Ho Chi Minh's internal communique's deal with this problem; see, for example, *On Revolution,* ed. by B.B. Fall (New York: Praeger, 1967), p. 319.

6. Our approach emphasizes what Rokeach calls the "formal content" of the ideology as opposed to its "specific content." That is, we do not analyze the substance of the Front's ideology but rather focus on those beliefs incorporated by an individual in the formation of his self-identity. See *The Open and Closed Mind,* p. 40.

7. This is Robert J. Lifton's suggestive phrase from his study of Chinese Communist indoctrination techniques, *Thought Reform and the Psychology of Totalism: A Study of "Brainwashing" in China* (New York: W.W. Norton, 1961).

8. Pike, *Viet Cong,* p. 232.

9. Ch'en Yun, "How to be a Communist Party member," in B. Compton, ed., *Mao's China: Party Reform Documents 1942-1944* (Seattle: Univ. of Washington Press, 1952), p. 101. This quotation is from a well-known document that states the required characteristics of the ideal Chinese Communist Party member. Hans Toch analyzes Ch'en Yun's statement in terms of a demand for the sacrifice of the individual's autonomy. See Toch, *The Social Psychology of Social Movements* (New York: Bobbs-Merrill, 1965), p. 134.

10. Gabriel A. Almond, *The Appeals of Communism* (Princeton: Princeton Univ. Press, 1954), p. 52. The works describing the ideal Communist Party member are numerous ranging from the social scientific treatment, e.g.,

Almond, *The Appeals of Communism,* to the autobiographical analysis, e.g., Frank S. Meyer, *The Moulding of Communists* (New York: Harcourt, Brace and Company, 1961), to the novel, e.g., Arthur Koestler, *Darkness at Noon.*

11. As quoted by Pike, *Viet Cong,* p. 232.
12. *On Revolution,* p. 251. For similar comments by the North Vietnamese military commander, Vo Nguyen Giap, see his *People's War, People's Army,* pp. 123–124.
13. *On Revolution,* p. 249.
14. See Truong Chinh, *The Resistance Will Win,* p. 162. Also see Mao's statement quoted in note 4 of this chapter and compare to the following analysis by Raymond A. Bauer, *The New Man in Soviet Psychology* (Cambridge: Harvard University Press, 1952) of the "principle of conscious understanding" in Bolshevik didactics: "The Bolshevik insists on man's responsibility for his behavior and on his ability to make his own destiny. He follows the Party line because the Party is 'right' and because he presumably understands why it is right . . ." (p. 178).
15. The language of ideological totalism is, in Lifton's words, an "all-encompassing jargon, prematurely abstract, highly categorized, relentlessly judging." *Thought Reform and the Psychology of Totalism,* p. 459.

## Notes to Chapter 6
## The Formal Organizational Structure,
## Processes, and Environment

1. See note 5, Chap. 5.
2. Pike, *Viet Cong,* p. 232.
3. For details of the formal structure of the NLF and the formal structure of the PLAF as well as the relationship between the two, see Pike, *Viet Cong,* Chapters 12 and 13 respectively. Material in the interviews used for this study supports Pike's descriptions.
4. The NLF's organizational structure, as well as its principles and doctrines, closely follows that of the Chinese Communists. For an excellent description of the political organization in the Chinese Communist army at the time of the Korean War, see A.L. George, *The Chinese Communist Army in Action: The Korean War and Its Aftermath* (New York: Columbia University Press, 1967), pp. 43–55. For a discussion of the Party in Chinese organizations, see F. Schurmann, "Organizational Principles of the Chinese Communists," *The China Quarterly,* No. 2 (April–June, 1960) and Schurmann, *Ideology and Organization in Communist China,* Chapter 2.
5. For details of the PRP's organizational structure and principles, see Pike, *Viet Cong,* pp. 145–153 and pp. 413–420.
6. Prospective Party membership (also often called, by the soldiers, the Group or Labor Youth Group) had organizational functions similar to the PRP's civilian Youth League (see Pike, *Viet Cong,* pp. 150–153 for a description of the Youth League). It served the purpose of initial selection of soldiers

for possible advancement to the Party. During the probationary period—of
from four to six months on the average—Party rules had to be learned and
the individual's potential commitment was assessed.

7. For the meaning and computation of the gamma statistic, see Goodman and
Kruskal, "Measures of association for cross-classification," *Journal of the
American Statistical Association* 49 (1954), 732–64.

8. Primary group is sometimes defined as "a group characterized by a high
degree of solidarity, informality in the code of rules which regulates the
behavior of its members, and autonomy in the creation of these rules,"
E.A. Shils, "The Study of the Primary Group" in D. Lerner and H. Lasswell
(eds.), *The Policy Sciences* (Stanford: Stanford U. Press, 1951), p. 44. However, we use the designation in a more neutral way merely indicating that
small, face-to-face social group which the soldier is assigned to and in which
he spends most of his time. Whether solidarity, informality, and autonomy
characterize this group are taken to be empirical questions.

9. See Morris Janowitz and Roger Little, *Sociology and the Military Establishment* (New York: Russell Sage Foundation, 1965), Chapter 4.

10. Pike, *Viet Cong,* p. 229.

11. For reviews of empirical research on leadership, see D. Katz and R. Kahn,
*The Social Psychology of Organizations* (New York: Wiley, 1966), Chap. 6;
B. Bass, *Leadership, Psychology, and Organizational Behavior* (New York:
Harper, 1960); and R. Likert, "An emerging theory of organization, leader-
ship, and management," in L. Petrullo and B. Bass (eds.), *Leadership and
Interpersonal Behavior* (New York: Holt, Rinehart, and Winston, 1961). For
research on military leadership, see M. Janowitz, *The Professional Soldier*
(New York: Free Press, 1960); Kurt Lang, "Military Organizations," *Hand-
book of Organizations,* ed. J.G. March (Chicago: Rand McNally, 1965),
Chap. 4; H. Selvin, *The Effects of Leadership* (New York: Free Press, 1966);
R.W. Little, *A study of the relationship between collective solidarity and
combat performance,* doctoral dissertation, Michigan State University, 1955;
and George, *The Chinese Communist Army in Action,* Chap. 4.

12. See R.F. Bales, "Task roles and social roles in problem-solving groups,"
*Readings in Social Psychology,* eds. E.E. Maccoby, T.M. Newcomb, and E.L.
Hartley, (3rd Edit.; New York: Holt, 1958) and J.W. Thibaut and H.H.
Kelley, *The Social Psychology of Groups* (New York: Wiley, 1959).

13. *The Chinese Communist Army in Action,* p. 38.

14. See Edgar H. Schein et al., *Coercive Persuasion* (New York: W.W. Norton
& Co., 1961). The series of studies dealing with brainwashing, or thought
reform, of Chinese Communist prisoners synthesized by Schein are relevant
for examining indoctrination in the PLAF. However, as George, *The Chinese
Communist Army in Action,* p. 87 notes, these indoctrination methods
were "a form of group therapy in contrast to the individual psychotherapy"
described in the brainwashing studies.

15. "Instructions Given at the Meeting for Ideological Remolding of General
and Field Officers, May 16, 1957" in *On Revolution,* p. 314.

16. Lifton, *Thought Reform and the Psychology of Totalism,* p. 420. The
thoroughness of milieu control, both outer and "inner" communication,

exercised over the Chinese Communist prisoners interviewed by Lifton was not matched in the NLF. Nonetheless, its importance should not be underestimated.

17. For a discussion of study methods employed in China, see A. Doak Barnett, *Communist China: The Early Years, 1949-55* (New York: Praeger, 1964), Chap. 8. The Chinese techniques appear to have been more thorough. Of course, the circumstances were quite different.

18. For a description of the agit-prop team in the NLF, see Pike, *Viet Cong,* pp. 120-124.

19. *The Appeals of Communism,* Chap. 2.

20. Ibid., Chap. 3.

21. As quoted by Pike, *Viet Cong,* p. 411.


## Notes to Chapter 7
## The Development of Commitment

1. Commitment has been written about extensively in several diverse bodies of literature. Literary works—e.g., Camus' *The Rebel* or Malraux's *The Human Condition*—often capture the sense of commitment better than scientific studies. In the scientific vein, one body of literature deals with revolutionary personality either in terms of leaders—e.g., E. Victor Wolfenstein, *The Revolutionary Personality: Lenin, Trotsky, Gandhi* (Princeton: Princeton Univ. Press, 1967) or followers of mass movements—e.g., see Eric Hoffer, *The True Believer* (New York: Harper & Brothers, 1951) and Hans Toch, *The Social Psychology of Social Movements* (New York: Bobbs-Merrill, 1965). The social psychological literature on attitude change and on group dynamics offers many hypotheses and insights relevant to why particular Front socialization mechanisms may have been effective and we will draw upon various findings eclectically. Since commitment in the Front involved personality development (not just attitude change), the developmental psychology literature is relevant, the most pertinent work being Erik Erikson's analysis of identity-formation (specific studies will be cited in the text). Unfortunately, little of the literature treats non-Western psychological processes or even broader socialization processes; hence, transferring Western concepts to the Vietnamese context needs to be done selectively and with care. Of the writings on Vietnam, numerous journalistic accounts discuss commitment; however, aside from insightful sections in Fitzgerald's *Fire in the Lake,* pp. 197-211 and in Leites, *Viet Cong Style of Politics,* systematic examination is lacking. The small number of intensive studies on Chinese "thought reform"—particularly Lifton, *Thought Reform and the Psychology of Totalism* and Edgar A. Schein et al. *Coercive Persuasion* (New York: Norton, 1961)—deal directly with relevant processes in a culture similar to the Vietnamese psychoculture; however, the intensive nature of "brainwashing" discussed in these studies was not matched in the NLF.

2. Webster defines consonance as "harmony or agreement among components." This definition is perhaps as useful as any other in the literature. Aside from

psychological theories of attitude change (for a review see C.A. Kiesler, B.E. Collins, and N. Miller, *Attitude Change* [New York: Wiley, 1969]), the notion of consonance or congruence arises in works analyzing the fit, or lack of fit, between society and modal personality. For a review, see Inkeles and Levinson, "National Character," pp. 479–89. Some studies have specifically dealt with the relationship between institutional change and modal personality. Perhaps the best examples are studies of the Soviet Union; however, these studies focus on noncongruence (or dissonance). For example, see H.V. Dicks, "Observations on contemporary Russian Behavior," *Human Relations* 5 (1952), pp. 111–175 and A. Inkeles, E. Haufmann, and H. Beier, "Modal personality and adjustment to the Soviet socio-political system," *Human Rights* 11 (1958), pp. 3–22. Studies on the traditional Chinese system stress congruence—e.g., F.L.K. Hsu, ed., *Psychological Anthropology* (Homewood, Ill.: Dorsey, 1954), pp. 400–457. For a study that highlights the consonance between Chinese Communism and traditional Chinese characteristics, see Lucian W. Pye, *The Spirit of Chinese Politics* (Cambridge, Mass.: M.I.T. Press, 1966). In political science, the theoretical conceptualizations of Lane and of Eckstein greatly influenced the present discussion. See Robert E. Lane, *Political Ideology* (New York: The Free Press, 1962), Chap. 25, and Harry Eckstein, *A Theory of Stable Democracy* (Princeton, N.J.: Princeton U., Center for International Studies, #10, 1961).

3.  Milton Rokeach, *The Open and Closed Mind* (New York: Basic Books, 1960), p. 35. For the sake of clarity, a distinction will be drawn between "idea" and "belief"; the former implies a concept (e.g., words, symbols, behaviors, norms, values, sentiments, etc.) presented to the individual whereas the latter denotes an "internalized concept." Any attempt to discuss the meaning of these terms beyond the arbitrary definitions suggested above, would take this study far afield. This distinction is consistent with our early definition of ideology.

4.  *Viet Cong,* p. 287.

5.  *Young Man Luther* (New York: W.W. Norton, 1958), p. 134.

6.  Erikson, *Childhood and Society* (New York: W.W. Norton, 2nd Edit., 1963), pp. 261–3. See also his "The Problem of Ego-Identity," *Journal of the American Psychoanalytic Association* 4 (January 1956).

7.  McAlister and Mus, p. 161.

8.  Pye, *Guerrilla Communism in Malaya,* p. 348. The search for identity and its efficacy in explaining the potential support for People's Liberation Communism is a central thesis of Lucian W. Pye's excellent study.

9.  Gerald Hickey, *Village in Vietnam* observed this "turning inward" in the contemporary village he studied:

[T]he political events of the past several decades have greatly disrupted village life. Whereas war may have the effect of generating solidarity among a people, the guerrilla type of hostilities characteristic of the Indochina War bred only conflict and suspicion. Pro-Viet Minh and pro-French factions existed in the village, and although most villagers did not take sides actively, accusations of being on one side or the other was rampant. This pattern continued as the Viet Cong movement against the national government reached Khanh Hau, and the effect has been to turn many villagers inward. They now are primarily concerned with survival for themselves and their families (p. 279).

10. In the literature on group dynamics and organizations, one finds integration, cohesiveness, and solidarity employed in ambiguous and overlapping ways. See Dorwin Cartwright, "The Nature of Group Cohesiveness," *Group Dynamics,* eds. Cartwright and A. Zander, Chapter 7; and Robert T. Golembiewski, "Small Groups and Large Organizations," *Handbook of Organizations,* Chap. 3. In our use, cohesion refers to the individual decision to stay or leave the organization; integration to the individual's participation in group activities; solidarity to an individual's sentiments of trust, likeability, love, identification with the group and its members. These terms can be applied to the individual or, with proper modification, to the large units. Group solidarity is one source of organizational cohesion and one basis for group integration.

11. S. Schacter, *The Psychology of Affiliation* (Stanford: Stanford University Press, 1959), p. 123.

12. "Group Identification Under Conditions of External Danger," Cartwright and Zander, *Group Dynamics* (3rd Edit.), p. 82. See also R. Hamblin, "Group integration during crisis," *Human Relations,* 1958, 11, 67–76.

13. G. Homans has hypothesized the mutual reinforcing nature of "activity," "interaction," and "affective sentiments." See *The Human Group* (New York: Harpers, 1950), Chap. 5. In the Vietnamese, affective sentiments take the form of solidarity.

14. Ho Chi Minh, *On Revolution,* p. 251.

15. See S. Scheidlinger, *Psychoanalysis and Group Behavior* (New York: Norton, 1952).

16. S. Freud, *Group Psychology and the Analysis of the Ego* (New York: Bantam Books, 7th Edit., 1965), p. 61.

17. Ibid., p. 68.

18. S. Schacter, Ellertson et al., "An Experimental Study of Cohesiveness and Productivity," Cartwright and Zander, *Group Dynamics* (2nd Edit.), p. 92.

19. *Thought Reform and the Psychology of Totalism,* p. 361. Lifton's analysis is an excellent treatment of Confucianism and communism.

20. The emphasis placed upon "sincerity" in both Communist (Vietnamese as well as Chinese) and Confucian writings suggests that sincerity was a problem. We shall return to this point in Chapter 8. See Lifton, p. 391, for a discussion of sincerity.

21. Ibid., p. 379.

22. W.H. Slote, *Vietnamese Ego Structure and Identity Patterns.*

23. F. Schurmann's observation about the Chinese Communists seems appropriate to the NLF, "By correct thought, the Chinese Communists do not mean simply a certain manner of thinking, but a manner of behaving. One can only know that an individual has attained correct thought through seeing his actual behavior." *Organization and Ideology,* p. 45. Cf. our observation on cognitive dissonance, Chap. 8.

24. Lifton, p. 425. Lifton's analysis of the "cult of confession" in totalistic

ideology is excellent and served as our primary source of insight into this critical area. Also see Nathan Leites and Elsa Bernant, *Ritual of Liquidation* (Glencoe, Ill.: The Free Press, 1954).

25.  Lifton, p. 426.

26.  In the context of the criticism sessions the "mutual" aspect of mutual criticism of self-criticism implied a continuing evaluation of sincerity. The punishment, particularly in the sense of shame from his comrades and cadre, could then be direct and immediate. Similarly, as "progress" towards sincerity was detected, rewards—in terms of praise, encouragement, self-esteem, increased acceptance from the group—were also direct and immediate. As Edgar Schein et al. observe, "It is a well-known principle of learning that the efficacy of reward and punishment [increases] as the time lag between the response and the administration of reward or punishment [decreases]." *Coercive Persuasion*, p. 182.

27.  This phrase is a Goffmanism. Although we will not use Erving Goffman's terminology, we have been greatly influenced by the cognitive aspects of his approach to identity. See his "On the characteristics of total institutions," *Proceedings of the Symposium on Preventive and Social Psychiatry* (Washington, D.C.: Walter Reed Army Institute of Research, 1957) and *Presentation of Self in Everyday Life,* (Garden City, N.Y.: Doubleday Anchor Books, 1959).

28.  See Schurmann, *Ideology and Organization in Communist China,* pp. 45–53 and especially his reference on page 46 to David E. Apter, *Ideology and Discontent.*

29.  M.B. Smith, J.S. Bruner, and R.W. White, *Opinions and Personality* (New York: Wiley, 1956), p. 41.

30.  Such consonance is a major proposition of Paul Mus' writings. Also see H.J. Benda, "Reflections on Asian Communism," *The Yale Review* 56 (Oct. 1966), 1–16.

31.  *Opinions and Personality,* p. 41.

32.  *Guerrilla Communism in Malaya,* p. 303.

33.  As Mus observed: "To understand the impact of Communism on East Asia it is necessary to grasp the fundamental yet antithetic analogy between animist cosmology and Marxist cosmology." McAlister and Mus, *The Vietnamese and Their Revolution,* p. 119.

34.  See Mus, "Cultural Backgrounds of Present Problems," *Asia,* No. 4 (Winter, 1966), pp. 10–22 and McAlister and Mus, pp. 65–69.

35.  Schein *Coercive Persuasion,* p. 262. Schein's discussion, which we have drawn from heavily, calls this process "ritualization of beliefs" and uses the term "ritualistic beliefs" for the concept we have called ideologized beliefs. We will use ritualization in a different sense in Chapter 8.

36.  See Pike, *The Viet Cong,* p. 284.

37.  Fitzgerald, *Fire in the Lake,* p. 169.

38.  "Political Alternatives to the Viet Cong," p. 561.

Notes to Chapter 8
Realities of Life in the Front: Adaptation
and Integration

1. Cf. Schein, *Coercive Persuasion,* Chapter 10.
2. It could be argued that the very act of repeated behavior, and repeated confession, induced by forced compliance could cause a change in belief
   consistent with the behavior even though the confession was not initially
   believed. Cognitive dissonance theory postulates such a process of change.
   This theory hypothesizes that when a person is forced to behave in a
   manner that is "inconsistent" with his cognitions and evaluations, he will
   tend to alter his cognitions and/or evaluations so that they become consistent with his behavior. In terms of the *kiem thao* sessions, the soldier was
   forced to criticize himself even though he did not believe the ideological
   suppositions upon which the criticism had to be based; cognitive dissonance
   theory predicts that, under this condition of forced compliance, he will
   come to believe.
      The validity of cognitive dissonance for Western cultures is a matter of
   dispute; even were it valid for Western cultures, it is of questionable validity
   for the Vietnamese culture. Paul Hiniker offers relevant empirical evidence
   on this point. Using experimental procedures similar to those performed in
   American cognitive dissonance experiments, Hiniker's experiments with
   Chinese subjects disconfirmed the forced compliance hypothesis. Hiniker
   observes that cognitive dissonance rests on an implicit assumption that
   anxiety results when one does not believe what he says. As we noted, this
   assumption need not hold in Vietnamese culture—concern with the situation
   and with proper behavior in the situational group permit dissimulation
   between words and thoughts. Hiniker's conclusion seems to hold for Vietnamese: "Overt compliance by no means implies private acceptance, nor
   does it appear to engender it." *Chinese Attitudinal Reactions to Forced Compliance* (Cambridge, Mass.: M.I.T. Center for International Studies, c/65-18,
   1965), p. 59. See also Roger Brown, *Social Psychology* (New York: The
   Free Press, 1965), pp. 584-684. For a review of the debate over cognitive
   dissonance and related attitudinal change theories, see J.W. Brehm and A.R.
   Cohen, *Explorations in Cognitive Dissonance* (New York: Wiley, 1962);
   R.P. Abelson and M.J. Rosenberg, "Symbolic psychologic: a model of
   attitudinal cognition," *Behavioral Science,* 1958, 3, 1-13; N.P. Chapanis
   and A. Chapanis, "Cognitive Dissonance: Five Years Later," *Psychological
   Bulletin,* 61, (1964), 1-22, W.J. McGuire, "The Current Status of Cognitive
   Consistency Theories," *Attitude Theory and Measurement,* ed. M. Fishbein
   (New York: Wiley, 1967); and C.A. Kiesler, B.E. Collins, and N. Miller,
   *Attitude Change* (New York: Wiley, 1969), especially chaps. 5, 7.
3. R.K. Merton, "The unanticipated consequences of purposive social action,"
   *American Sociological Review,* 1936, 1, pp. 894-904; and _____, "Bureau-

cratic Structure and Personality," *Social Forces,* 1940, 18, pp. 560–68.

4. There is considerable literature on group defenses to organizational demands. See Chris Argyris, *Interpersonal Competence and Organizational Effectiveness* (Homewood, Illinois: The Dorsey Press, 1962).

5. See Harry H. Harman, *Modern Factor Analysis* (Chicago: University of Chicago Press, 1960), Chapter 9, for a discussion of the Principal Components method used in this analysis. The computation program was *The Data-Text System: A Computer Language for Social Science Research* (Cambridge, Mass.: Harvard U., 1967 version). For a review that indicates the assumptions and particularly the weaknesses inherent in our type of approach, see R.B. Cattell, "The Meaning and Strategic Use of Factor Analysis," *Handbook of Multivariable Experimental Psychology,* ed. Raymond Cattell (Chicago Rand McNally, 1966), pp. 174–243. Other clustering methods that do not presume the linear structure necessary for factor analysis were used in preliminary analysis; they substantially discriminated similar dimensions.

6. See Harman, Chap. 14.

7. Etzioni, *A Comparative Analysis of Complex Organizations,* pp. 91, following Parsons, uses these terms.

8. *Guerrilla Communism in Malaya,* p. 259. Also see George's comments on this problem, *Chinese Communist Army in Action,* pp. 108–10.

9. Katz and Kahn see the leader's principal task to be "the successful integrator of primary and secondary relationships" where primary relationships refer to the bonds of solidarity developed in the primary group and secondary relationships refer to the role requirements of the organization. Katz and Kahn, p. 325.

10. E.A. Shils, "Primary Groups in the American Army" in R.K. Merton and P.F. Lazarsfeld (eds.), *Continuities in Social Research* (Glencoe, Illinois: The Free Press, 1950), p. 22. Also see, Shils' comments in "The Study of the Primary Group" in D. Lerner and H. Lasswell, *The Policy Sciences* (Stanford: Stanford University Press, 1951), pp. 44–69; M. Janowitz, *Sociology and the Military Establishment* (New York: Russell Sage Foundation, 1959), Chapter 3; and J. Dollard, *Fear in Battle* (Institute of Human Relations, Yale University, 1943), p. 56.

11. *Guerrilla Communism in Malaya,* p. 249.

12. For a discussion of NLF terrorism see Douglas Pike, *The Viet Cong Strategy of Terror* (Saigon: United States Mission, Viet-Nam, 1970). The interview material tended to confirm the following view offered by Pike: "The public rationale for use of terror employed by the communists is that the enemy has permitted no alternative. Such justification . . . never has been an easy matter among the rank and file. The natural abhorrence of Vietnamese for systematic assassination was and is a major and continuous doctrinal problem to the cadres." p. 8. The relatively high loading of dissatisfaction with Village Policy on the demoralization factor is partly due to this difficulty. (See table 8.3) In light of this problem, the ideological nature of answers denying dissatisfaction with such policy becomes clearer. To balance Pike's

views about the use of terrorism, see N. Leites, *Viet Cong Style of Politics,* pp. 44–49.

13. See R.P. Abelson and J.W. Tukey, "Efficient utilization of non-numerical information in quantitative analysis," *Annals of Mathematical Statistics* 34 (1963), pp. 1347–69. Making an interval scale from a measurement that is ordinal is a question of making a statistical bet, one that appears worthwhile in the present context.

14. The general issue has been treated by a wide variety of authors and studies. For an abstract formulation, see H.C. Kelman, "Compliance, Identification, and Internalization: Three Processes of Attitude Change," *Journal of Conflict Resolution* 2 (1958), pp. 51–60.

   In addition to the issue of the "depth" of commitment, another not unrelated question might be raised: Were the committed "fanatics?" The answer depends upon one's meaning of fanatic. If fanatic means cultural deviants or psychopaths, then a simple answer can be given: no, the committed as a group were not psychopaths. However, differences in personality undoubtedly played an important role in *who* became committed. I speculate that peasants whose needs for identification were greatest were more likely to become committed. Chapter 7 suggested three possible causes for higher than average needs for identification (disruption of village life, youth, and uncertainty); moreover, other factors (e.g., severe personal experiences with the ARVN or French) probably contributed. In any event, though the needs and susceptibilities of those who became committed might have been more exaggerated compared to the general peasant population, they were on one side of a distribution of traits held in common and not a different mode of personality.

15. See Leites, *Viet Cong Style of Politics,* pp. 48–54. Pye's comment about the Chinese penchant to gain self-esteem by exaggerating hardships seems appropriate to the Vietnamese: "The child develops a strong need to appear praiseworthy in the eyes of others, but when this is not possible he can still gain self-esteem by finding satisfaction in suffering at the hand of an unjust world." *The Spirit of Chinese Politics,* p. 99. Also see R.H. Solomon, *The Chinese Revolution and the Politics of Dependency,* Chapter 4, and particularly his discussion of the symbolic importance of food.

16. Alexander George, p. 191, describes a similar situation in the Chinese Communist Army: "The morale doctrine . . . recognized no limits to what a communist could accomplish if his political ideology was strong enough. The result was a pronounced tendency to demand of the individual, and especially of the communist cadre, more than seems humanly possible. Related to this was the communist definition of morale in political terms and the practice of accounting for shortcomings in an individual's performance in terms of his political deficiencies."

17. The negative loading may result from two situations: (a) soldiers who could not identify with their primary group for one reason or another were subject to demoralization and alienation and (b) demoralization led to demands that "exacerbated the problems of maintaining group solidarity" as George,

p. 191, observes about the Chinese Army. Both of these cases do exist in the sample; however, the quantitative importance is slight.

18. George suggests that in the primary groups of the Chinese Communist Army an in-group phenomenon developed wherein some soldiers were isolated. A similar condition seemed to have held in the PLAF. See *Chinese Communist Army in Action,* Chapter 7.

19. Rough estimates were made by stratifying the sample according to critical structural variables, particularly rank and party membership, and weighing the strata according to their distribution in the PLAF as gleaned from captured documents. Though such a procedure was used in preliminary analysis, the potential errors involved are significant enough that the following estimates must be employed in a highly tentative way.

   The bulk of the peasants adapted by conforming. This estimate must be qualified in two ways. First of all, we exclude from consideration those peasants who were not under Front control long enough to have accepted membership; there were, depending upon the year and phase of the war, a large absolute and relative number of such peasants. Secondly, we include in this assessment soldiers who essentially adapted by conforming and then—because of external and internal stress—became dissatisfied, demoralized, discontent, etc. This inclusion renders the estimate as one which assumes a minimal stressful environment. We believe this approach justified since, in addition to technical problems in making reasonable estimates, we are, at this juncture of the study, concerned with assessing the maximum potential of the PLAF for compliance; we shall deal with the effects of stress in Part III.

   A minority, but a sizable minority, of soldiers were committed. This estimate must be further qualified beyond the conditions discussed for conformity. Commitment represents both a qualitative and quantitative concept. Our measurement procedure assigns each soldier a degree of commitment. But to offer a meaningful statement of how many soldiers were committed, we had to assume a specific threshold level that establishes the boundary between commitment and non-commitment; the estimate of the number of committed is especially sensitive to the level chosen. As a corollary of the somewhat quantitative nature of commitment, it is clear that some of the soldiers assigned as conformers were to some degree committed. To offer a more exact statement than the "committed formed a minority" is hazardous; nonetheless, we speculate that the percentage committed was more than the "tiny elite" of committed found by John Lewis in his analysis of the Chinese Communist Party and substantially less than a majority. See his *Leadership in Communist China* (Ithaca: Cornell University Press, 1963), p. 37.

   The proportion of nonintegrated soldiers was not relatively large, though even a small number could have acute effects on organizational operation.

20. Of course, cadres were responsible for the dissemination and execution of orders from the hierarchy. In doing so, they had minimum latitude except for high level commanders who appeared to have reasonable tactical flexibility within political-military strategic plans. Other functions that might be served by a leader in innovative organizations (see for an example of a fine

analytical discussion of leadership in the organization literature, Katz and Kahn, Chapter 11) were not performed in the PLAF at the low-level of command. That is, cadres, at this level of command, neither initiated nor altered policy of an external or internal nature. That they did not may imply a rigidity in the organization that could have led to organizational ineffectiveness. For a discussion of these issues in the Chinese Communist context, see Schurman, *Organization and Ideology* and Lewis, *Leadership in Communist China*. In cases where difficulties arose, there was a tendency to pass the problems up to a higher level of authority. The general literature on leadership is cited by note 11, Chapter 6 of this book.

21. More cross-cultural research needs to be done here. Both Schein, p. 180, and Hiniker, p. 58, assume the validity of personal identification with a concrete model in their Chinese subjects. Insofar as identification requires imitation, I suspect—considering the Vietnamese predisposition towards imitative behavior—that this mechanism may be more efficacious than in non-Oriental cultures.

22. George, *The Chinese Communist Army in Action*, p. 102. The sense of mobilization used here is stimulating high morale and a willingness to fight.

23. Estimates of reliability are a complicated issue for this type of analysis. Due to the coding restrictions, a number of interviews were eliminated (on the order of 20 percent). Since the sample is not assumed representative, such exclusion does not automatically bias the results. However, about 3/4 of the eliminated were omitted due to a lack of sufficient depth or coverage in the interview and this circumstance was more likely for apathetic, non-accepting peasants; thus, this group is underestimated in this analysis. The RAND content analysis coded a similar satisfaction theme and its overall inter-coder reliability was on the order of 65 percent–80 percent; the coding scheme reported here modified and revised that coding with a consequent increase in reliability to 70 percent–85 percent. The main improvement resulted from a greater agreement in the boundaries of the categorized themes. These rough reliability figures were calculated by independently recoding a random sub-selection of the sample and calculating the percentage of agreement. The primary source of inter-coder disagreement arose from divergent classifications of highly correlated categories. Considering the quantitative purpose to which the results were applied—viz., factor analysis—the reliability was adequate. See H. Guetzkow, "Unitizing and categorizing problems in coding qualitative data," *Journal of Abnormal Social Psychology*, 1950, 45, pp. 682–90.

24. F. Mosteller and J.W. Tukey, "Data Analysis, Including Statistics," in G. Lindzey and E. Aronson, *Handbook of Social Psychology* (Reading, Mass.: Addison-Wesley, Rev. Edit., 1968), p. 101.

## Notes to Introduction to Part III

1. *Politics, Personality and Nation-Building* (New Haven: Yale University Press, 1962), p. 51. Also see Samuel P. Huntington, *Political Order in Changing Societies* (New Haven: Yale University Press, 1968), pp. 12–32.

Notes to Chapter 9
Cohesion, Discrimination, and
Maintenance

1. *Intervention Theory and Methods* (Reading, Mass.: Addison-Wesley, 1970)
   p. 77. Also see his "Organizational Effectiveness Under Stress," *Harvard
   Business Review* 38 (May–June 1960), pp. 137–46.
2. Cf. March and Simon, *Organizations,* Chapter 4.
3. For example, E.A. Shils and M. Janowitz offer the following classification
   on "the modes of social disintegration found in any modern army": desertion, active surrender, passive surrender, routine resistance, and last-ditch
   resistance. "Cohesion and Disintegration in Wehrmacht in World War II,"
   *Public Opinion Quarterly* 12 (1948–49), p. 282.
4. I. Janis, "Group Identification under Conditions of External Dangers,"
   *British Journal of Medical Psychology,* 1963, 36.
5. Many factors, particularly of a direct nature, can not be considered here.
   For a discussion of such factors, see Stouffer et al., *The American Soldier,*
   Vol. II, chapters 1, 2, 9, and J.W. Appel and G.W. Bebe, "Preventive
   Psychiatry," *Journal of the American Medical Association* 131 (1946).
6. Using standard mathematical symbols, the basic model is:

$$Y = \Sigma \beta_i X_i + u$$

   where Y is the regressor, $\beta_i$'s are the coefficients to be estimated, $X_i$'s are the
   independent variables, and $u$ is the statistical error term. For reasons outlined in this section, the model employed in the text involved a rank
   dummy variable:

$$Y = \Sigma \beta_i r_i + \Sigma \beta_j r_j X_j + u$$

   where $r_i$'s represent different levels of rank. See J. Johnston, *Econometric
   Methods* (New York: McGraw-Hill, 1963) for dummy variable notation.
      Preliminary analyses explored an extensive variety of alternative models:
   some involved variables other than those used in the text; some involved
   different specifications (e.g., non-linear terms and interactive terms), and
   some involved simultaneous equations. Such explorations were both
   necessary and valuable for deciding what the data validly revealed given its
   limitations as well as the author's lack of a powerful theory. The model
   selected for presentation has the advantage of simplicity and ease of interpretation and does not require the extraordinary assumptions about the
   nature of statistical errors that would be necessary for more complex
   specifications. For the sake of limiting this presentation to a reasonable
   length, the results of these preliminary analyses are not included in the text.
   In addition to using a variety of models, several alternative estimation
   procedures were used in preliminary work; for a brief discussion, see note 7
   of this chapter.

7. See Guy H. Orcutt et al., *Microanalysis of Socioeconomic Systems* (Harper & Row, 1961) and J. Johnston, *Econometric Methods,* Chapter 8. A major difficulty with using least squares when the dependent variable is dichotomous is the violation of the assumption of homoscedastic disturbances. A.S. Goldberger, *Econometric Theory* (New York: Wiley, 1964) suggests the use of probit analysis in this case and Henri Thiel, *Principles of Econometrics* (New York: Wiley, 1971), suggests the use of logit analysis. Preliminary trials with probit analysis agreed with the main findings to be presented, though specific estimates differed. The principal effect of the probit analysis was in the reduction of the standard error of the estimates; in the case of low-level cadres (where the degrees of freedom were relatively small) these reductions had an effect on significance. The substantive discussion in subsequent sections of the impact and significance of the independent variables draws upon these findings to complement the regression findings. However, since the cost of doing a full-scale probit analyses for the various preliminary models was prohibitive and since the interpretation of probit results are not as easily explained as regression, we shall not burden the reader with reference to probit findings.

   Another serious estimation problem involves the measurement errors in the explanatory variables. These errors could lead to biased and inconsistent estimates. Though the order, the sign, and the significance of the estimates are crucial to the analysis rather than their exact values, nonetheless the order, the sign, and the significance could all be wrong. To help evaluate these problems, we relied on complementary qualitative analysis. A serious candidate for a least squares bias due to a simultaneity problem arises from the possible dependent relationship between combat experience and other explanatory variables. Preliminary analysis using simultaneous equations and a variety of instrumental variables did not prove fruitful in sorting out potential bias.

8. I. Sarnoff and P.G. Zimbardo have made, following Freud, an important distinction between fear and anxiety and their separable effects on solidarity. This distinction may be relevant in the Vietnamese context, but we were unable to explore it. See their "Anxiety, Fear, and Social Affiliation," *Journal of Abnormal and Social Psychology* 62 (1961), 356–63.

9. Chapter 4 discusses the coding of Potential Defecting Prisoners. If the coding of Potential Defecting Prisoners were valid, the main difference between these prisoners and defectors would be their different assessments of the costs of leaving.

10. Shils and Janowitz, p. 303.

11. This finding is similar to Pye's comment about the Malayan (Chinese) guerrillas: [When the Malayan guerrillas realized they were fighting for a losing cause] "it is . . . amazing how fast they sought to disengage themselves from the party. They were not people who could appreciate the romantic sentiment of heroically and honorably fighting on for a losing cause. They had joined the party because they had perceived Communism as a strong and stable force, and when they saw it as weak they were quick to feel that they had made a great mistake." *Guerrilla Communism in Malaya,* p. 334.

12. McAlister and Mus, p. 114.

13. According to Pike, *The Viet Cong Strategy of Terror,* p. 29–31, captured NLF documents list among their fifteen categories of targets of assassination the following two: "Defectors who have given information to the enemy, who have taken with them automatic weapons or important documents, or who are suspected of having done same; or who were cadres or officers" and "Deserters or AWOL's who have returned to the Revolution but without clear explanation (i.e., who may be government penetration agents)."

14. See Katz and Kahn, *The Social Psychology of Organizations,* p. 184.

15. Pye presents an excellent analysis of this "dilemma of promotion" for the Chinese guerrillas in *Guerrilla Communism in Malaya,* p. 323.

16. Pye reaches a similar conclusion for the Malayan (Chinese) Guerrillas in his *Guerrilla Communism in Malaya,* p. 336.

17. The symbolic concern with food and bodily safety is shown in the study of common proverbs by Huynh Dinh Te, *Vietnamese Cultural Patterns and Values as Expressed in Proverbs,* Columbia University: Ph.D. dissertation, 1966. Richard Solomon analyzes the symbolic import of references to food in Chinese culture. See his *The Chinese Revolution and the Politics of Dependency,* Chapter 6.

18. Joseph Zasloff discusses the "iron framework" provided by regroupees in his *Political Motivation of the Viet Cong,* Chapter 4.

## Notes to Chapter 10
## Micro-Conditions of Institutional Development

1. For a useful assessment of relevant literature, see Samuel P. Huntington, "The Change to Change: Modernization, Development, and Politics," *Comparative Politics* 3 (April 1971), pp. 283–322.

2. In some sense people always act in their self-interests. The phrase "narrowly defined" is intended to exclude from the definition of self-interest other motivations such as pure emotion, altruism, habit, etc. Narrowly defined is not meant to exclude situations in which the "self" encompasses more than the individual, e.g., the family. See the concept of amoral familism in Edward C. Banfield, *The Moral Basis of a Backward Society* (Glencoe, Ill., Free Press, 1958).

3. For a review of studies and evidence relating these motives to revolutionary participation and violence, see Ted Robert Gurr, *Why Men Rebel* (Princeton, New Jersey: Princeton University Press, 1970), pp. 193–209.

4. An increasing number of analysts of peasant societies have begun to formulate "rational" models to explain peasant behavior. A pioneering effort involves exchange theory to explain patron-client ties. See James C. Scott, "Patron-Client Politics and Political Change in Southeast Asia," *American Political Science Review* 66 (1972), pp. 91–113. Though it is beyond the

scope of this study to formulate a rational model of peasant choice, some potential ingredients of such a model can be proposed.

In weighing a decision to change behavior, the peasant evaluates his alternatives in terms of a variety of personal interests. For Vietnamese, we grouped personal interests into two attributes—security needs and status drives. As discussed previously, "security" denotes a complex configuration of needs and beliefs, and though the substance and structure of the Vietnamese security configuration differs from that of peasants in other settings, security needs may be a dominant concern in many cultures. "Status drives" denotes a complex configuration of motivations, values and beliefs that taken together constitute goal-seeking behavior oriented towards social advancement; though the substance and structure of such a "status drive" undoubtedly differs across cultures, the existence of positive drives towards social advancement may be a common concern in many peasant cultures. In short, we suggest that a model of peasant behavior should include both types of human motivation, which for convenience we denote as security needs and status drives.

Peasants must somehow combine security and status concerns to arrive at an integrated evaluation of their alternatives. We hypothesize that peasants employ (unconsciously, of course) a "lexiographic order" in that they *first* satisfy their security requirement and *then* evaluate the alternatives in terms of social advancement. In other words, security is the dominant concern followed by status.

Though security is presumed to be evaluated first, we do not propose that the peasant necessarily chooses the alternative having the highest level of security. Instead, we postulate a *minimum level of security* such that an alternative is not acceptable unless the peasant feels it will assure him a level of security at least as high as his threshold values. The level of the threshold for any particular individual, the existence of a modal level for a culture, and the cross-cultural comparability of modal levels are all questions for empirical research.

If the peasant perceives both his traditional behavior and a new opportunity to be above his minimum acceptable level, then he considers social advancement and prefers that alternative offering the highest opportunity to achieve. If the peasant perceives a new opportunity as failing to meet his security requirement whereas he perceives his traditional activities as remaining above the threshold, then the peasant would continue his old behavior; for the reverse situation (viz., new opportunity acceptable, traditional patterns not), the peasant would choose the new option. To deal with the remaining possibility—both alternatives unacceptable—we call upon the inertia hypothesis.

Based upon the Vietnamese situation, we postulate that inertia affects the peasant's choices in the following way: if the peasant believes that all his alternatives—including, of course, that of continuing his traditional behavior —would *not* provide a minimum level of security, then he would continue his traditional behavior, would not initiate a search for other alternatives, and would adopt an attitude of "wait and see."

Insofar as the above feeling of the decline of traditional ways coupled with an insecurity about new alternatives were widespread among peasants, one would expect an interregnum—a transitory period in which traditional behavior continues but peasants are susceptible to more secure arrangements. (The terms "wait and see" and "interregnum" are borrowed from McAlister and Mus, *The Vietnamese and Their Revolution,* p. 114, who use them with much the same connotation.)

5. The relationship of consonance to legitimacy described above is similar to the formulation of Harry Eckstein, *A Theory of Stable Democracy* (Princeton, N.J.: Center of International Studies, Princeton University, No. 10, April 10, 1961). Some cross-cultural empirical research on legitimacy has been conducted, but research on illegitimacy is rare. See Gurr, *Why Men Rebel,* Chapter 6, and Richard Rose, "Dynamic Tendencies in The Authority of Regimes," *World Politics* 21 (July 1969), pp. 602–628.

6. This finding is consistent with a well-documented conclusion of the literature. Namely, whereas ideology per se motivates high-level leaders, it usually has not been effective appeal for the masses. However, the literature also suggests that ideology—in the form of slogans and simple ideas—can mobilize people in either of two situations: when individuals are "intensely discontent" or when strong nationalistic sentiments are aroused by war. Since neither focused discontent nor nationalism were widely spread or intensely felt in the Second Indochina War, ideology was not an important independent appeal. See Gurr, *Why Men Rebel,* pp. 194–200, for a review of the literature on the role of ideology in revolutions and violence.

7. For an insightful discussion of these problems of institution-building, see Lucian W. Pye, *Politics, Personality and Nation Building* (New Haven: Yale University Press, 1962), pp. 38–42.

8. For a conceptualization of the development of legitimacy in terms of a learning process, see Richard M. Merelman, "Learning and Legitimacy," *American Political Science Review* 60 (September 1966), pp. 548–61.

9. Unless the realities of institutional patterns within the organization and within the culture are empirically described and compared, the extent of consonance has no meaning and its relationship to institutionalization remains idle, perhaps obvious, speculation. However, we believe these basic notions can be researched by microlevel approaches. Two goals of such research might be (a) to conceptualize the meaning and operationalize the measurement of consonance and (b) to identify the dimensions that are crucial for the comparison of consonance. See Inkeles and Levinson, "National Character," pp. 479–89, for other operational suggestions.

10. Huntington, *Political Order in Changing Societies,* p. 30.

# Index

Acceptance of membership, 6, 29; and coercion, 66–72; conclusions for PLAF, 76–77; and illegitimacy, 67, 199; and nonintegration, 140; and opportunities, 64–65, 74–75, 76, 198; and participation in mobilizing organizations, 198–200; and persuasion, 54–58, 61; quantitative patterns of, 65–75; and reasons for joining, 67, 72–75; and volunteering, 57, 58, 60; *see also* Decision to participate; Legitimacy and recruitment

Adaptation: empirical patterns of, 22–42; pattern of defined, 11

Agit-prop teams, 61–62, 63, 97

Almond, Gabriel, 54, 84, 97

An Xuyen Province, 62

Ancestor worship, 22, 36, 37, 218

Annamese society, 223–24

Anti-Americanism, 133, 135

Ap Bac, Battle of, 210

Argyris, Chris, 163

ARVN, 18, 24n, 53, 75, 180, 190

Assassination, 73, 236, 242

Astrology, 35

Authority: acceptance of, 13–14, 64, 130, 204, 213; area of acceptance of, 13–15, 131, 203–5; and avoidance of conflict, harmony, 41–44, 130–31; and centrality, 102; and commitment, 82–84, 108, 110, 117, 203; and conformity, 122, 131–32, 201–3; defined, 12, 212–13; and institutionalization, 2–5, 7–8, 9; and legitimacy, 14, 130, 204, 205; orientation towards, 14, 82–84, 203–5; perception of in joining, 52–65; and revolution, 2, 5; in village life, 41–44

Barnard, Chester A., 13

Bauer, Raymond A., 229

Betts, Ardie, 26n

Betts, Russell H., 26n

Bias: response, 23–27; sampling, 20–21, 144, 154n

Binh-Luong Province, 52

Buddhists, 22, 35

Ca Mau peninsula, 3

Cadre, 19, 20, 22, 69, 81, 84, 153, 242; character, 85, 107, 119, 128, 139, 140, 149–52, 238–39; commitment, 144, 182–84, 187; discipline, 96, 97; indoctrination, 94–95, 98; low-level, 50–51, 91, 142, 144, 148, 149–51, 183–87, 191, 206; middle-level, 91–93, 142, 148, 157, 187–91; and stress, 173; training, 77, 142, 224–25

Cao Daists, 22

Cartwright, Dorwin, 214

Catholics, 22

Cell members, 93–94, 98, 106, 179–80, 203

Centrality, 101–3

*Chieu Hoi* program, 20, 23, 25, 180, 190, 214

Child-rearing effects, 33, 38–39

China: Army, 95, 230, 237, 238; culture, 109, 220, 237, 242; Revolution, 1–2; and Vietnamese, 34, 38, 79, 227

*Chinh Dao,* 42

Coders, 25, 26n, 65, 91, 122–28, 133–36, 155–59, 165, 239

Coercion, 7, 13, 26; and defection, 69–72; and recruitment, 50, 58–61, 66–72, 76

Cognitive dissonance, 235

Cohesion: analysis, 164–79; and cadre, 183–91, 192; concept of, 17, 161, 205n, 213–14, 233; and stress, 168, 187, 202

Combat experience: effects of, 173–75, 183–84, 187, 193–94; measurement of, 167–71; and PLAF's response to, 178–82; *see also* Stress

Commitment, 7, 79; and cadres, 144, 182–83, 184, 187; and contingent gratification, 117; defined, 81, 227; development of, 101–17; distribution of, 142–49, 238; failure of, 120–22; and filialism, 108–10; and institutional development, 202–3, 206–7; in the literature, 231; measurement of, 132–37, 237; and milieu control, 112–13; the PLAF's ideal of, 81–88; and stress, 181–83, 191–92; and susceptibility, 103–6; *see also* Authority and; Cadres and; Legitimacy and; Structural integration and; True believer

245

## About the Author

Paul Berman is Assistant Professor of Political Science and a member of the Governing Board of the Institution for Social and Policy Studies at Yale University. He has worked in systems analysis and operations research and is a frequent consultant to the Rand Corporation. Dr. Berman received the B.S. in mathematics from the City College of New York and the Ph.D. in political science from the Massachusetts Institute of Technology. His current research concerns institutionalization and organizational adaptation in various settings.